33

D0903293

"PECOS BILL"

"PECOS BILL"

A Military Biography of William R. Shafter

★

PAUL H. CARLSON

Texas A&M University Press
College Station

Frontispiece
GEN. WILLIAM R. SHAFTER
Courtesy U.S. Signal Corps, National Archives

The paper used in this book meets the minimum requirements
of the American National Standard for Permanence
of Paper for Printed Library Materials, Z39.48-1984.
Binding materials have been chosen for durability.

LIBRARY OF CONGRESS CATALOGING-IN-PUBLICATION DATA

Carlson, Paul Howard.
  "Pecos Bill", a military biography of William R.
Shafter / Paul H. Carlson. — 1st ed.
      p.   cm.
  Bibliography: p.
  Includes index.
  ISBN 0-89096-348-7 (alk. paper)
    1. Shafter, William Rufus, 1835–1906.
2. Generals—United States—Biography.
3. United States. Army—Biography.   4. United
States. Army—History—19th century.   I. Title.
U53.S53C37   1989
355'.0092'4—dc19
  [B]   88-36465
                                                 CIP

With appreciation to
ELLEN
and our children
DIANE, STEVE, AND KEVIN

Contents

Illustrations

Preface

WILLIAM RUFUS SHAFTER was no gallant hero. He drank heartily, gambled earnestly, ate plentifully, and cursed incessantly. He suffered from gout, varicose veins, and obesity. A victim of persistent and malicious gossip, he was constantly surrounded by controversy. Because he became associated in the public mind with American military blunders in Cuba during the Spanish-American War, people often pictured him as a fat, incompetent buffoon of a field commander.

But it is easy to make too much of these petty faults. Clearly the United States Army judged Shafter a responsible, if coarse and abrasive, officer with considerable good sense. Moreover, the flaws did not seriously disturb Shafter or his happiness and peace of mind. He was a bulky, lumbering, disheveled man, with distinctive features and blue eyes that peered out from shaggy brows. He talked quickly and cockily, his language concise, pungent, and often sarcastically profane. Underneath the hard-boiled pose, however, was a surprisingly quick sensitivity to human moods and relationships. Energetic, ambitious, and determined, to a great extent he epitomized the American frontier type so eloquently described by Frederick Jackson Turner, Theodore Roosevelt, and others. Once he understood what had to be done, he wasted little time in formalities but assumed responsibility, gave orders, and took action. His drive was intense, earning him on an 1875 campaign to reach the Pecos River the nickname he carried for years—Pecos Bill.

Shafter's official record abundantly reveals courage, zeal, and intelligence. He received the Congressional Medal of Honor for distinguished action in the Civil War. He led Negro troops during the war, and afterward, while assigned to the Texas frontier, he trained and commanded one of the army's first all-black regiments. The first to explore systematically the treacherous southern plains of West Texas while searching for water and recording topographical data, his 1875 expedition was a major factor in opening the region for the westward-moving pioneers. He led several daring punitive expeditions into Mexico to stop dangerous Indian and Mexican desperado raids upon settlements north of the Rio Grande. He helped restore peace at Pine Ridge, South Dakota, following the Wounded Knee massacre in 1890. During the American Railway Union strike in 1894, he protected the mails and maintained peace in Los Angeles. He commanded several military posts in Texas, California, Arizona, and Dakota before directing American troops to victory in Cuba in 1898, where the record shows he improvised and carried out one of the swiftest and most successful military campaigns in the history of American warfare.

During the nearly fifteen years he served on the Texas frontier, Shafter was a civil war unto himself. He was accused of trying to start a war with Mexico and became deeply embroiled in a sordid embezzlement case with ugly racial overtones. He got into fights with his men and looked down disdainfully from his huge frame upon the Spanish-speaking people among whom he lived and with whom he dealt. Some people believed that he regularly took licentious liberties with young women while on military leave in San Antonio. His partnership in a Big Bend silver mine cost him the friendship of one of his closest military companions and professional confidants. So hard did he push his black troops that on two occasions they initiated court-martial proceedings against him. He fought back with every legal and other weapon available. Through it all Shafter ruled his command with verve and daring as one of the most colorful soldiers on the Texas frontier. Yet Shafter, whose long military career was interesting, varied, and significant for both Texas and the United States, remains today one of history's enduring enigmas. Considering his long career on the western frontier and his important role in the Spanish-American War, it is surprising that so little has been written about him.

My purpose is to provide a biography of William R. Shafter with emphasis on his years as a regimental officer in Texas. I have tried to present an account of a United States Army field commander of the late nineteenth century who represents an exception to other officers in two ways: his long-term duty with black troops, and his command of a major United States overseas expeditionary force. An important theme is that although he had difficulty getting along with subordinates and enlisted men, his superiors believed that he was a reliable officer who got results.

This book owes much of whatever merit it may possess to the late

Horn Professor Emeritus Ernest Wallace of Texas Tech University. He read the manuscript in its early stages, made valuable suggestions, and contributed many of the basic ideas. His encouragement lightened the years spent in gathering material, and his expert criticism gave the work whatever literary qualities and scholarly accuracy it may have. Professor Wallace was both a guide and an inspiration.

Many others generously contributed much toward the book. Earl H. Elam of Sul Ross State University, through assistance on a related project, enabled me to review records in the National Archives. James V. Reese, William R. Johnson, and the late David M. Vigness read early versions of the manuscript and offered helpful criticism. Prof. William W. White, a stimulating colleague, read the manuscript in its late stages, and his comments on style helped smooth out a few of the wrinkles.

I am grateful to officials of the many libraries and archives where I have gathered material. My debt first to R. Sylvan Dunn, later to David J. Murrah, and to their staffs at Texas Tech University's fine Southwest Collection is especially great, for it was there that most of my sources were found. The officials of the Texas Lutheran College library, the University of Texas at Austin library, the Barker History Center at the University of Texas, the Western Michigan University library, the University of Michigan library, the Stanford University library, the Texas State Archives, and the National Archives contributed much toward completion of this work.

I owe a debt of gratitude to Alwyn Barr, Don Abbe, and James Harper of Texas Tech University, Kenneth D. Yeilding of Odessa College, Preston Reeves of Texas Lutheran College, Wayne Daniel of the Fort Concho Museum, John Sutton of the Fort Davis Natural Historic Site, James I. Fenton, John Ingebritson, and my typist, Joan Weldon. Thanks also goes to Jay A. Matthews, who allowed me to use material in chapters 5, 6, and 7 that was published in different form in *Military History of Texas and the Southwest*. Portions of some chapters also have appeared in *Red River Valley Historical Review* and *Journal of Big Bend Studies*. For whatever errors exist, I accept responsibility.

Finally, I am grateful to my wife, Ellen, who was patient and understanding throughout the entire process.

"PECOS BILL"

CHAPTER ONE

The Early Years

AT DUSK on August 14, 1875, just when all seemed lost, a small group of tired and trail-weary black soldiers rode their horses into the Pecos River near present-day Carlsbad, New Mexico, and rolled off their mounts into the refreshing water of the stream. Behind them, stretching back for over ten miles, came additional small groups of black troops with their white officers, over two hundred men in all. For more than two days through steaming summer heat they had been without water. Thirsty, weak, and clinging to their saddles, they had struggled across the barren tableland of West Texas and eastern New Mexico. Their tongues swollen, most men, unable to swallow, had not eaten supper. Some had been tied in their saddles and forced at gunpoint to continue. Many of the soldiers, suspecting they would never reach the Pecos, had written letters to be sent home by anyone fortunate enough to survive. Several continued only because their tired horses wearily followed the dusty trail.

But group after weary group struggled to the river. After refreshing themselves, the advance troops sent back word that the Pecos had at last been reached and set about preparing a camp for the others. They pitched tents, built fires, watered horses, and aided the late arrivals as they rode in after dark. Shortly after midnight all men had arrived safely. Reaching the desperately sought goal without a single loss was due largely to the persistent and aggressive determination of the commanding officer, Lt. Col. William R. Shafter, Twenty-fourth United States Infantry Regiment, one of the frontier army's most remarkable field officers.[1]

---

[1] William R. Shafter to J. H. Taylor, Ass't. Adj. Gen., Dept. of Texas, Aug. 5, 1875, and Shafter to Taylor, Jan. 4, 1876, in United States, William R. Shafter, Letters Re-

William Rufus Shafter was born October 16, 1835, near Galesburg, Michigan. He came from a family of robust and hardy pioneer farmers whose ancestors had arrived in America from Wales early in the eighteenth century. The original family name was Shaugter or Slaugter, but "from some cause or means unknown" both names became Shafter.[2] Initially colonizing in New England, the family grubbed out an existence in the rocky hills of Massachusetts and Connecticut. During the decade preceding the American Revolution, some members of the family, in search of a better life, moved to Vermont. Among these, Shafter's grandparents, William Rufus and Mary Lovell Shafter, settled near Townshend in Windham County where they produced fair crops of grain and reared several sons. Two sons, James McMillian and Oscar Lovell, migrated to California where, according to a family letter, James became a state attorney and rancher and Oscar served for several years as a member of the state supreme court.[3] A third son, Hugh Morris, pioneered in Michigan. Shafter's maternal grandparents, Mathias and Sarah Berry Sumner, also from New England, were related to Charles Sumner, the powerful abolitionist senator from Massachusetts.

Hugh Morris Shafter was a typical frontiersman. Optimistic, sociable, and vigorous, he came with his cousin, George Lovell, to the Michigan wilderness as a bachelor in May, 1833. Laying claim for himself and his father to some two hundred acres of prairie land in northeast Comstock Township, Kalamazoo County, he built with the help of friendly Indians a log cabin among "oak openings."[4] Oak openings, which at the time covered approximately two-thirds of Kalamazoo County, were areas having scattered oaks and very little undergrowth

---

ceived, Appointments, Commission, and Personal Branch, Adjutant General's Office, Record Group 94, National Archives (hereafter ACP File, AGO, RG94, NA); Shafter to Taylor, Sept. 29, 1875, William R. Shafter Papers, Stanford University Library, Stanford, Calif., photocopies in Southwest Collection, Texas Tech University, Lubbock (hereafter Shafter Papers); William H. Leckie, *The Buffalo Soldiers: A Narrative of the Negro Cavalry in the West*, pp. 143–47; L. F. Sheffy, ed., "Letters and Reminiscences of General Theodore A. Baldwin: Scouting after Indians on the Plains of West Texas," *Panhandle-Plains Historical Review* 11 (1938): 7–30.

[2] William Rufus Shafter (grandfather) to Shafter, Aug. 10, 1863, Shafter Papers; William W. Potter, address delivered at the dedication of the Gen. W. R. Shafter Monument at Galesburg, Mich., *Michigan History Magazine* 4 (Spring, 1920): 485.

[3] Sovis [?] S. Lovell, Tonia, Mich., to Zachariah Chandler, U.S. Senate, March 31, 1866, Shafter Papers.

[4] Samuel W. Durant, *History of Kalamazoo County, Michigan*, pp. 354, 364–65; Charles D. Rhodes, "William Rufus Shafter," *Michigan History Magazine* 16 (Fall, 1932): 375–76.

or other trees. Much of the land Hugh purchased was identified as "burr oak openings," distinguished from other openings by the presence of burr oaks, which grew only at very wide intervals as a regularly planted orchard, and by considerable grass as the only undergrowth. Believing that burr oaks grew in soil of the very best quality, he concluded that his was excellent land.[5]

Hugh Shafter kept active. Besides building the log house during the spring and summer, with Lovell's help he plowed and cultivated some ground for corn and wheat. That fall he enjoyed small but profitable crops. During the winter the young settler took steps to improve the attractiveness of his neighborhood. Among other things, in January, 1834, he transplanted with meticulous care an apple tree, a rarity in the region, from near the Kalamazoo River to a spot aside the busy Territorial Road near the farm. While the ground lay frozen, Hugh removed the tree, which was six inches in diameter, without loosening the icy earth within four feet of its trunk and hauled it on a sleigh to its new location. As a result, the tree suffered no shock. Indeed, it produced an excellent crop of fruit that year and continued to do so for the next fifty years, becoming a well-known landmark in Comstock Township.[6]

In the spring Hugh returned briefly to his ancestral New England home to wed Eliza Sumner. After the marriage and with little delay the young couple headed west to Michigan by way of the Erie Canal and a lake steamer. From Detroit they traveled by wagon along the Territorial Road, arriving in late spring at their pioneer farm. From the first they prospered. Livestock that Hugh bought grew fat, and the rich loam produced abundant crops. Furthermore, Hugh earned supplementary income as a surveyor.[7]

Surveyors in western Michigan easily found work, for a veritable flood of settlers had created a major land boom in the area. Several factors precipitated the sudden migration, including the completion of the Erie Canal and the introduction of steamboats on Lake Erie, which lowered transportation costs. In the 1830's a settler was able to secure comfortable deck passage from Massachusetts to Michigan for less than ten dollars. Even more modest freight rates enabled immi-

[5]Bernard C. Peters. "No Trees on the Prairie: Persistence of Error in Landscape Terminology," *Michigan History* 54 (Spring, 1970): 22–23; Douglas H. Gordon and George S. May, eds., "Michigan Journal, 1836, John M. Gordon," *Michigan History* 43 (March, 1959): 263–64, 271; 43 (Sept., 1959): 277, 280.

[6]Durant, *History of Kalamazoo County*, pp. 364–65.

[7]Rhodes, "William Rufus Shafter," p. 371; Gordon and May, "Michigan Journal," p. 281.

grants to bring with them all their belongings.[8] The Kalamazoo River also promoted settlement, for during high water ships ascended it from Lake Michigan with merchandise and carried away produce from the adjoining farms. The level land, the fertile soil, and the Territorial Road also encouraged pioneers. The region also attracted land speculators and town promoters, who founded Battle Creek, Albion, and Augusta in 1836 and Galesburg in 1837 to complement the existing towns of Kalamazoo, Comstock, and Jackson.[9] To plat the villages and lay out the town lots, the pioneers needed surveyors.

Hugh Shafter consequently found plenty of work. Because he wanted to farm, however, surveying remained a part-time, secondary enterprise that he enjoyed when he was not busy clearing land, constructing a barn and some sheds, planting and harvesting crops, or adding an extra room and a porch to his little log cabin. Hugh also took an active part in the social and political affairs of Comstock Township. Diligent in attendance at township meetings, he was outspoken and persistent in his political sentiments and convictions. Serving for several years in various township offices, he did what he believed to be his duty, regardless of what others might think. He became a strong and active abolitionist. Many runaway slaves may have used his cabin as a station on the underground railroad on their way to Canada.[10]

Amid this active pioneer environment, the Shafters reared their family of three boys and one girl. The couple's first child, William, born in 1835, was named for his grandfather. A gregarious little fellow, the boy became a lively and sizable youngster. Anne, James, and John followed William at intervals of about two years. As they grew the boys worked hard in the fields beside their father, learning to fell trees and handle a plow, tasks James later remembered as often accompanied by aching backs and bleeding fingers. They escaped the drudgery periodically to hunt deer and small game, including the massasauga, a rattlesnake. Rainy days also brought relief from farm chores. Congregationalist in religious faith, the family members were in many ways Puritan moralists, but otherwise the church seemed to have exerted little influence on them.[11]

---

[8]Morris C. Taber, "New England Influence in South Central Michigan," *Michigan History* 45 (Dec., 1961): 307.

[9]F. Clever Bald, *Michigan in Four Centuries*, p. 170; George Newman Fuller, *Economic and Social Beginnings of Michigan*, pp. 306, 347–51.

[10]Durant, *History of Kalamazoo County*, p. 357; *Detroit Journal*, Nov. 14, 1906, clipping, Daniel D. Brockway Papers, Michigan Historical Collections, University of Michigan. Ann Arbor (hereafter Brockway Papers).

[11]Rhodes, "William Rufus Shafter," pp. 375–76.

Young William Shafter, aggressive and self-assured, matured rapidly. Alert mentally, stocky in build, and endowed with a powerful phy-
sique, he was a leader among boys, excelling in nearly all impromptu
athletic sports. He became the neighborhood wrestling champion, allowing his opponents the preference of either what he called the "side
hold" or the "square hold."[12] Known as "Bull" Shafter, he was defeated
in a wrestling match only once, when Peter Grant, a huge woods-
man from Barry County, not only threw Shafter, but rolled him into
a millpond.[13]

A spirited youth, Shafter was a mischief-maker. In one of his unfriendly pranks he stole girls' dolls, hanged them on trees near his home,
and used them as targets when he practiced shooting. Another he pulled
on an old stagecoach driver. Shafter and several other boys of Galesburg, knowing that the driver's team was nervous and prone to run
away when excited, hid and pelted the ponies with stones. The incident gave rise to a story, told around Galesburg for many years, that
the angry and embarrassed driver applied brakes with little success
while going up hill.[14]

Concerning his years at school before the Civil War the record is
scant. Shafter was an enthusiastic student. Although his learning would
be accounted superficial today, he was widely read in adventure and
romantic literature. He was recognized, in addition, as one of the best
spellers in the Galesburg district. On several occasions he won the
popular frontier spelling bees.[15]

With his classmates, however, Shafter proved troublesome. Mrs. Ezra
Beckwith, one of his teachers, sometimes detained him twenty or thirty
minutes at the close of the school day so the other students might
escape the "licking" he would otherwise give them. During recess
Shafter often directed army games, marching the other pupils up and
down the school yard and in the winter leading them in organized
snowball fights, but on occasion the entertainment took the form of
intimidation of other youngsters, harassment that required and received sharp punishment from the teacher. As he grew older, how-

[12]Charles A. Weissert, Dedicatory Address, MS, ca. 1939, Charles A. Weissert Collection, Michigan Historical Collections, University of Michigan, Ann Arbor (hereafter Weissert Collection).

[13]Recounted by Elizabeth Cousins, "Unsung Hero of Galesburg: William Rufus
Shafter, 1835–1906," MS, William R. Shafter Collection, University Archives and Re-
gional History Collections, Western Michigan University, Kalamazoo (hereafter
Shafter Collection, WMU).

[14]Rhodes, "William Rufus Shafter," pp. 382–83.

[15]Cousins, "Unsung Hero of Galesburg," Shafter Collection, WMU.

ever, few teachers disciplined William Shafter, because those who tried, he roughly handled.[16]

Although he was a good student, Shafter's reputation as a pugnacious youth caused embarrassment. During his courting days, some girls were simply not allowed to date him, and one father, a Baptist deacon in Galesburg, told his pretty daughter to give up her first beau. Nevertheless, as a gregarious young leader in the community, Shafter made friends easily. He may have been a bully, but unlike most he was never ostracized. When he was in town, others sought his companionship.[17]

In the winter of 1856, with only the common school education, Shafter became at age twenty-one a country school teacher, first at Galesburg and afterward at Mendon. Because of his tough reputation, the big, insubordinate students who made life miserable for other pioneer community instructors gave Shafter no trouble. For that and other reasons, the young schoolmaster had little difficulty imparting the rudiments of reading, writing, and arithmetic to his students, all of whom sat on the hard, uncomfortable benches characteristic of frontier schools. Rather strict as a pedagogue, Shafter demanded quality work from his pupils and meted out to those who misbehaved stern but equitable punishment.[18]

In the fall of 1860, Shafter determined to apply for a higher salaried teaching post. He set out for Athens, Michigan, to present his credentials to the local school officials. A short distance north of the town, he met a man who had stopped to repair a broken harness. In the buggy sat a young lady who attracted his attention. Although his offer of assistance was rejected, Shafter nonetheless tarried to help. Later, at the village, he obtained the job he sought and upon inquiry learned that the pretty girl he had seen in the buggy was twenty-year-old Harriett Grimes, the stepdaughter of Dr. J. W. Lee, a physician at Athens. To Shafter's delight, when he reported for duty to teach the winter term of 1860–61, Miss Grimes was one of his pupils.[19] Although the history of the courtship was not recorded, two years later pupil and teacher married.

Ambitious to receive further education, Shafter enrolled for the 1861 spring term at Prairie Seminary in nearby Richland. The school offered work approximately equivalent to the first two years of study at

[16]Ibid.; Weissert, Dedicatory Address, Weissert Collection.

[17]Cousins, "Unsung Hero of Galesburg," Shafter Collection, WMU.

[18]*Detroit Journal*, Nov. 14, 1906, clipping, Brockway Papers; Rhodes, "William Rufus Shafter," pp. 375–76.

[19]Rhodes, "William Rufus Shafter," pp. 375–76.

the University of Michigan. The curriculum emphasized classical languages and mathematics and left the students little if any choice in the selection of courses. Not only were the classes prescribed, but the faculty controlled how a student, whether preparatory and mature, spent most of his time out of class. Literary society debates and readings offered the most exciting extracurricular activities, frequently promoting some intellectual stimulation. Although the records are no longer extant, William Shafter probably participated in the activities.[20]

While Shafter attended school at Richland, the Civil War erupted. Shocked, like millions of other Americans, by the Southern action at Fort Sumter, Shafter decided to enlist in the Union Army. Early in June, shortly after the close of the spring term, he enrolled at Galesburg as a private with the Seventh Michigan Volunteer Infantry. His father, disappointed by his son's decision, unsuccessfully tried to prevent the enlistment, warning Shafter that he would be shot in the "ass."[21]

William Shafter's early enlistment surprised few people. Despite his father's attitude, family tradition played a role in Shafter's action. His great-grandfather, James Shafter, and a great-grand-uncle had participated in the American Revolution. Other kinfolk had fought in the War of 1812.[22] Because some of his friends and neighbors had already joined or had decided to join the service, social and patriotic pressures to enroll were strong. Moreover, teaching failed to satisfy his restless energy, his bold adventuresome spirit, and his glowing ambition; enlistment was a logical reaction.

Shortly after he joined the Seventh Michigan, Shafter received orders from Ira B. Grosvenor, regimental colonel, to report about June 19 to an instruction camp at Fort Wayne, Michigan. While in Detroit, en route to camp, Shafter was named first lieutenant of Company I, although he did not receive his commission until June 28. The position came about in an unexpected manner. Company I captain, Bezalel W. Lovell, instructed Shafter and Elhanan Phetteplace of Tuscola to decide between themselves the first lieutenant and the second lieutenant appointments.

"Phetteplace," suggested Shafter, "you have been in service, you go as First and I as Second."

"No!" Phetteplace replied. "You must be first."

---

[20]William C. Ringenberg, "College Life in Frontier Michigan," *Michigan History* 54 (Summer, 1970): 19–32.

[21]Wayne C. Mann, Director, University Archives and Regional History Collections, Western Michigan University, Kalamazoo, to author, March 24, 1972.

[22]James McMillian Shafter, Calif. State Att., to L. A. Grant, Asst. Secy. of War, Dec. 9, 1891, ACP File, AGO, RG94, NA.

Shafter offered to toss up a half dollar for the position, but Phette-place objected, as it was gambling. To solve the friendly dilemma, the two men approached Colonel Grosvenor, who decided that Shafter should have the higher rank.[23]

The officers and enlisted men had been under instruction eight hours a day for a month when news of the disastrous Union defeat at the first battle of Bull Run, which occurred on July 21, 1861, arrived at Fort Wayne. Upon receipt of the news, officers of each of the ten companies of the Seventh Michigan returned home on recruiting duty to fill out the companies and regiment. Back home, it took Shafter only two or three days to recruit his quota for Company I. Then, after two weeks of drill around Galesburg "to stir up enthusiasm," including a classy parade at double time down main street with his troops marching five abreast, Shafter returned to Fort Wayne with the new recruits.[24]

As he arrived with his men at the training camp, Shafter, a sensible and steady twenty-five-year-old junior officer, prepared to begin military service. An adaptable young man, he was ready enough to make the best of things as he found them, and with all the energy of his ardent nature he threw himself into the new life opening out before him. The modest success he had already won seemed to justify his ambitions and to urge him on to bolder action.

[23]William R. Shafter, "Remarks of General Shafter before the Thomas Post, G.A.R.," MS, March. 18, 1902, William R. Shafter Collection, Michigan Historical Collection, University of Michigan, Ann Arbor.

[24]Ibid.; Joseph A. Tivy, *Souvenir of the Seventh, Containing a Brief History of It*, p. 29.

CHAPTER TWO

The Civil War Years

Wᴵʟʟɪᴀᴍ R. Sʜᴀꜰᴛᴇʀ was an ardent patriot who, like all partisans, could not view the issues of the day with the unbiased eyes of history. Shafter shared the fervent enthusiasm of those whose ambitions for the Union cause ran highest, and he championed immediate and heroic confrontation with the Confederate rebels to rout the enemy in a quick series of gallant and daring battles.

Although he soon discarded romantic notions of warfare, Shafter remained a partisan soldier who yearned for action. At first he was disappointed, for his Seventh Michigan Infantry Regiment bogged down at the training camp in a seemingly endless parade of drills and fatigue duty assignments. When marching orders finally arrived, the monotony ended and Shafter's infantry, 884 officers and enlisted men, marched out of Fort Wayne. After a brief layover at Monroe, the regiment on September 5, 1861, boarded two trains and left for the East. Four days later, in Washington, it became part of the Union Army of the Potomac, commanded by Gen. George B. McClellan.[1]

Shafter's brief stay in Washington was memorable. He used part of his off-duty time to see the United States Capitol building, climb into its lofty dome, and observe the rotunda with its beautiful gallery. Afterward, he walked about the city streets, passing before the mansion occupied by President Abraham Lincoln and visiting other sites. He took in a play and stopped for a while at a fancy tavern before returning to camp.[2]

---

[1] Joseph A. Tivy, *Souvenir of the Seventh, Containing a Brief History of It*, p. 29.
[2] William R. Shafter, "Remarks of General Shafter before the Thomas Post, G.A.R.," MS, March 18, 1902, William R. Shafter Collection, Michigan Historical Collections, University of Michigan, Ann Arbor (hereafter Shafter Collection).

Within a week the Seventh marched toward winter quarters at Poolesville, Maryland, about forty miles above the capital and near Edward's Ferry on the Potomac River. On its second day out the Seventh received startling reports that the fearsome Black Horse Cavalry, which formed part of the Confederate Army of the Potomac, had crossed the famous river and was in the vicinity. Late that evening the Michigan recruits mistakenly presumed that they heard the long, awesome Black Horse roll call. Unfamiliar with the sound, they prepared for an immediate attack. Shafter was thoroughly frightened. He rushed into battle array clad only in his undershirt and drawers and with a little five-shot colt in one hand and his sword in the other. After a few minutes of silence, someone uttered a muffled prayer for safety and mercy. Just as the frightened trooper finished his plea, the regimental adjutant informed Shafter and the Seventh Michigan that the noise had been a false alarm.[3]

At Poolesville the Seventh found itself part of the Second Brigade in Brig. Gen. Charles P. Stone's Sixth Division of the Army of the Potomac. The Second Brigade, commanded by Brig. Gen. Frederick W. Lander, had orders to protect the ferries and fords of the Potomac River and to prevent the Confederates from crossing. Stationed among people unfriendly to the Union cause, the Federal troops maintained a heavy guard.

While serving as officer of the guard one evening some three to four weeks later, Shafter committed a breach of military discipline. Investigating a noise in the tent of one of the company captains, he found three gray-headed captains and his own Captain Lovell nearly drunk on whiskey. Although thinking it a very ludicrous scene, he joined the four men, who were discussing who should kill General Lander for insulting the Seventh Michigan. Lander, referring to the fact that eleven men of the Seventh had died from measles in ten days, was reputed to have said, "It was no wonder they were all dying, they were so damned dirty!"[4]

After consuming a generous tin cup full of whiskey, Shafter likewise got drunk. Returning to his guard tent, he fell unconscious on his bed. Shortly afterward, the general field officer of the day, Col. Edward Hinks, appeared and ordered the guard to turn out. Shafter failed to make his appearance in the inspection line. Because it was raining lightly, however, Hinks did not get off his horse to investigate and so

[3]Shafter, "Remarks of General Shafter," Shafter Collection.
[4]Ibid.

spared Shafter from exposure, possible court-martial, and certain disgrace.[5]

Meanwhile, the Seventh Michigan suffered a problem with their arms, 72-caliber Belgian muskets, inferior weapons that seldom worked well. Shafter complained that "the [United States] government had unloaded them on us." Having owned and tinkered with guns since early boyhood, he discovered that the problem stemmed from the "green" lumber used in the stocks, which in damp weather caused the guns' locks to bind. Even when they could be fired, the weapons were not always accurate. He solved the binding problem by having the locks cleaned and some wood cut away.[6]

While Shafter restored the weapons, another false alarm occurred. It began when the brigade commander Lander rode rapidly up to Colonel Grosvenor's tent with information that Confederate troops had crossed the Potomac at a ferry about one and one-half miles away and ordered him to send Company I as soon as possible to check the enemy advance. The absurdity of only one company's performing the task apparently did not occur to Shafter, who had his troops supplied with extra ammunition and ready to march at once. A boy on Shafter's left, his weapon not yet put in order, shivered in fear.

"Lieutenant," the young trooper complained to Shafter, "my gun won't shoot!"

"I can't help it," snapped Shafter.

The young man took another look at his gun, and then with tears streaming down his cheeks pleaded with Shafter: "Lieutenant, have I got to go down to the ferry with this old gun and die like a damned dog?"

"Yes!" came Shafter's blunt and only answer.[7]

After covering a quarter-mile, the troops halted. Here, the regimental adjutant informed them that the enemy had retired and that they could return to their post. When they arrived back at camp, General Lander reported that the exercise had been a speed test and that he was well pleased with the results.

[5]Tivy, *Souvenir of the Seventh*, p. 34; Shafter, "Remarks of General Shafter," Shafter Collection.

[6]Ibid.; Brig. Gen. Willis A. Gorman, U.S. Army, "Report of Operations Opposite Edward's Ferry, Maryland," Oct. 26, 1861, *The War of the Rebellion: A Compilation of the Official Records of the Union and Confederate Armies* (hereafter *Official Records*), ser. 1, 5:333; Shafter, "Remarks of General Shafter," Shafter Collection; Tivy, *Souvenir of the Seventh*, p. 26.

[7]Shafter, "Remarks of General Shafter," Shafter Collection.

Shafter was piqued. The scare figured as the second false alarm since he had left Washington less than six weeks before. False alarms, the young officer reasoned, were dangerous and unwise; they reminded him of the story of the boy who cried wolf until, when the wolf finally did approach, no help appeared. In his later frontier commands, Shafter always informed his subalterns beforehand when similar practices were planned.[8]

During the months after the battle of Bull Run, the Union and Confederate armies faced each other along the Potomac, sparring for tactical advantage while at the same time protecting their respective capitals, Washington and Richmond. One of these tactical maneuvers occurred toward the end of October, 1861, when General McClellan ordered Brig. Gen. George A. McCall, commanding the Fourth Division, on the upper Potomac to ford the river, crossing to Dranesville, Virginia. McClellan also telegraphed General Stone, farther up the river at Poolesville, to keep a sharp watch on Leesburg, Virginia, and advised him that, should McCall encounter difficulty in driving the Confederates away, "perhaps a slight demonstration on your part would have the effect to move them."[9] Stone's maneuver to aid McCall resulted in the disastrous battle of Ball's Bluff.

Shortly after sending McCall across the Potomac, McClellan ordered him back to the Maryland side but neglected to inform General Stone. Unaware of the new plans, Stone assumed that he was to assist McCall in a southward advance. Splitting his force, the Sixth Division, Stone maneuvered with most of his troops toward Ball's Bluff, a wooded hill on the south bank of the Potomac opposite Harrison's Island about forty miles above Washington. At the same time he sent a full brigade, of which the Seventh Michigan was a part, over the river at Edward's Ferry five or six miles below Ball's Bluff. After crossing the rain-swollen river, the brigade moved forward about a mile, where a picket line went up. At dawn on October 21, the line fell back closer to the river.

Later that day the fighting started. In a massive assault Southern forces attacked Stone at Ball's Bluff, and a spirited detachment struck the Federal pickets at Edward's Ferry. Although Union artillery at the ferry played havoc in the advancing Confederate ranks, the Southern charge, aimed at keeping Northern troops from helping at Ball's Bluff, worked. The Federal army dug in at Edward's Ferry.[10]

[8]Ibid.

[9]George B. McClellan, *Report of the Organization and Campaigns of the Army of the Potomac*, pp. 76–78; Joseph D. Patch, *The Battle of Ball's Bluff*, p. 13.

[10]Brig. Gen. Charles P. Stone, U.S. Army, "Report of the Battle of Ball's Bluff," Oct. 29, 1861, *Official Records*, ser. 1, 5:293; Tivy, *Souvenir of the Seventh*, p. 35.

At Ball's Bluff the Confederates routed the Union army. By 6:00 P.M. they had forced the Federal troops back to the river, causing panic and disaster. In the last desperate fighting, many Northern soldiers died; others, pleading for mercy, threw their arms into the river or fled in terror across the Potomac. Scores of men drowned trying to escape to the Maryland shore. At 8:00 P.M., with the rout complete, what was left of the Union force surrendered. The North suffered substantial losses. Some 1,300 troops were killed, wounded, or drowned; another 750 were taken prisoner and marched off to Leesburg.[11]

When news of heavy action at Ball's Bluff reached them, Northern officers at Edward's Ferry feared a similar barrage. They put Shafter's Seventh Michigan to work. Because of its poor weapons, the Seventh exchanged guns for tools to start rifle pits and other entrenchments. Expecting a heavy attack at any moment, it worked feverishly for several hours. After completing the necessary defense works, it took a position near the ferry on the crest of a hill some 450 yards from the river. Here it rested on its arms, waiting nervously for the onslaught. None came.[12]

The next morning Union troops at Edward's Ferry anxiously held the position, but Confederate troops did not renew the battle. On the twenty-third, General McClellan, hoping to avoid another disaster as at Ball's Bluff, ordered a quiet return to the Maryland shore. General Stone, who supervised the withdrawal, detailed the Seventh Michigan to man the boats and guard the landing, a wise decision given the Seventh's unreliable muskets. In contrast to the panic at Ball's Bluff forty-eight hours earlier, the brigade at Edward's Ferry retreated with what was described as great "propriety and coolness."[13] The next morning, after all the troops had reached the Maryland side, Shafter and the Seventh made their way back to Poolesville.

The whole affair had little military significance, but Congress made it a spectacular issue. Disturbed that Col. Edward Baker, until recently a member of the Senate, was among those killed at Ball's Bluff, Congress set up the notorious Joint Committee on the Conduct of the War to look into operations and tactics of the Union generals. The com-

[11] Stone, "Report of Operations Opposite Edward's Ferry, Maryland," Nov. 2, 1861, *Official Records,* ser. I, 5:330–32.

[12] Gorman, "Report of Operations Opposite Edward's Ferry, Maryland," Oct. 26, 1861, *Official Records,* ser. I, 5:333; Brig. Gen. John J. Abercrombie, U.S. Army, "Report of Operations Opposite Edward's Ferry, Maryland," Nov. 2, 1861, *Official Records,* ser. I, 5:336–38.

[13] Abercrombie, "Report of Operations Opposite Edward's Ferry, Maryland," Nov. 2, 1861, *Official Records,* ser. I, 5:336–38.

mittee raised a lot of fuss throughout the war, particularly regarding generals who had a rough time against the Confederates.[14]

As winter approached, the Seventh found camp life wanting. Their Sibley tents were cold, unpleasant, and inconvenient, and the food was inadequate. Shafter and some other skillful woodsmen in the regiment, deciding to end the dreary situation, cut lumber and built some of the finest winter quarters in the army. The Seventh's camp attracted such attention that an artist sketched it, and later in Baltimore a widely circulated lithograph of the camp appeared.[15] Although the quarters improved, the food did not, and nearly all the men of the Seventh stole chickens, pigs, potatoes, and many kinds of fruit and vegetables. Moreover, the routine of endless drills, parades, instruction, and fatigue duty was wearysome. To vary the monotony the troops turned to alcohol and heavy drinking, resulting in several arrests for public drunkenness and disorderly conduct. Afterward, as the soldiers learned about summary military discipline, the public drunkenness and disorderly conduct decreased. The propensity to steal chickens, as well as other food, however, continued and even increased as the winter passed.[16]

For Shafter, the winter of 1861-62 passed slowly. In the East, McClellan, a perfectionist, drilled and trained his army, while the western forces, also under his general command, seemed to accomplish little. President Lincoln grew impatient for action and with the Union military commanders planned a major offensive campaign against the Confederate capital. The success of such a campaign, Lincoln and his aides believed, called for control of the lower Shenandoah Valley, which would keep Southern troops from encircling Washington while the bulk of the Northern troops in the East stormed Richmond. New orders followed.

Two of the new orders affected Shafter. One transferred the Seventh Michigan to the reorganized First Brigade, Sixth Division. Commanded by Brig. Gen. Napoleon J. T. Dana, a veteran of the war with Mexico, the brigade also included the Nineteenth and Twentieth Massachusetts and the Forty-second New York Volunteers. Another called upon the First Brigade, early in March, to ascend the Potomac by canal boats to Harper's Ferry, where it joined a larger force commanded by Maj. Gen. Nathaniel P. Banks. When the reinforcements arrived at Harper's

[14]Bruce Catton, *This Hallowed Ground: The Story of the Union Side of the Civil War,* pp. 81-82.
[15]Tivy, *Souvenir of the Seventh,* p. 34.
[16]Ibid., pp. 34-39.

Ferry, Banks dispatched two brigades, including Dana's First, overland up the Shenandoah. In an effort to outflank enemy troops led by Gen. Joseph E. Johnston, the detachment hurried thirty-three miles to Barryville, Virginia, but found that the confederates had escaped. The Union troops thereupon pulled back to Charlestown near the site of John Brown's trial and execution.[17]

As the Northern command started its return, Shafter went to capture a senior division Confederate quartermaster. According to a friend, at daylight on March 14, taking Sgt. Andrew McFarlin and a private, Shafter started in pursuit of the Southern officer, a major, reported to be at his home, a splendid Southern mansion about four miles away. Shafter found the family at home and inquired of the officer. When told that the major was not there, Shafter politely replied that he considered it his duty to search the house. In the garret Shafter found a large amount of solid silver tableware. By assuring the family in a friendly manner that the Union soldiers were not robbers, he put everyone at ease. Indeed, on hearing the searcher's cordial tone of voice, the Confederate officer came from his hiding place, showed Shafter his commmission papers, and asked the intruders to breakfast, which was served on the silver plates. After finishing the meal Shafter proceeded with his prisoner to Charlestown to rejoin his regiment.[18]

Two days later, March 16, the Seventh Michigan returned to Harper's Ferry. Instructed to hold the famous river crossing and expecting an extended stay, the regiment prepared semipermanent quarters. Here also the men finally exchanged their nearly worthless Belgian muskets for some new, splendid Springfield rifles with recently patented combustible cartridge wrappers.[19]

Meanwhile, on March 13, Lincoln and the military commanders had concluded their plans. Rather than advance toward the Confederate capital directly south through Manassas Junction, they had decided to strike Richmond with McClellan's large and powerful Army of the Potomac via the peninsula formed by the York and James rivers. Selecting Fort Monroe, Virginia, on the extreme tip of the peninsula as his base of operations, McClellan shifted the bulk of his army. A week later thousands of additional support troops, including the Seventh

[17]Ibid.; Samuel C. Hodgman, Adj., Company I, Seventh Michigan, to his mother, Climax Prairie, Mich., Feb. 23, 1862, and March 16, 1862, Samuel Chase Hodgman Letters, University Archives and Regional History Collections, Western Michigan University, Kalamazoo (hereafter Hodgman Letters).

[18]Hodgman to his brother, Frank, Chicago, Ill., March 20, 1862, Hodgman Letters.

[19]Hodgman to his mother, March 16, 1862, Hodgman Letters; Tivy, *Souvenir of the Seventh*, p. 40.

Michigan, proceeded to Alexandria on the coast, where they boarded steamers for transportation to the fort.

Reaching Fort Monroe about March 30, the support troops disembarked to await further directions. The new orders placed the Seventh Michigan in the Third Brigade, Second Division, Second Corps, commanded by Maj. Gen. Edwin V. Sumner of Massachusetts, a veteran of the war with Mexico. Upon receiving its instructions, Shafter's regiment tramped some three or four miles inland to a site where wood and water were readily available. Here it encamped under sunny skies in warm weather and amid brightly blooming peach trees. With the regimental band on parade each evening, the scene hardly presented the picture of an army about to launch a major military campaign.[20]

The tableau changed quickly. On April 3, the Second Division, commanded by Brig. Gen. John Sedgwick, received marching orders. The next morning it filed up the peninsula toward Yorktown, a heavily fortified Confederate city. The bloody Peninsular Campaign had begun.[21]

Shafter's regiment played several key roles. It scouted the Warwick River, observing enemy troops entrenched on its right bank. When he heard the news, General McClellan determined not to cross the Warwick and strike for Richmond, but instead to lay siege to Yorktown.[22] A month later, as the Confederates abandoned the city, the Seventh Michigan joined a detachment of infantry that followed Union cavalry in pursuit. The Confederates fought a brisk delaying action at Williamsburg, Virginia's colonial capital, but retreated and did not make a firm stand until they had reached Richmond. Near the end of May, as he pushed slowly toward the Southern capital, McClellan ordered two corps of troops, including Shafter's regiment, across the Chickahominy River. A violent rainstorm on May 30 isolated the Union detachment south of the flooded river and placed it in a perilous position. The enemy outnumbered it, the river could be recrossed only at a few bridges, and roads in the vicinity were almost impassable.[23]

Gen. Joseph E. Johnston, the astute Southern commander, took advantage of the situation. Late the next afternoon at a rustic stop on

[20]Tivy, *Souvenir of the Seventh*, pp. 40–41.

[21]McClellan, *Army of the Potomac*, p. 164; Tivy, *Souvenir of the Seventh*, pp. 40–44; Catton, *This Hallowed Ground*, pp. 129–30.

[22]Thomas G. Rhett, Asst. Adj. Gen., Dept. of Northern Virginia, to Maj. Gen. D. H. Hill, Commanding Left Wing, Yorktown, May 1, 1862, *Official Records*, ser. I, 5 (pt. 3): 487.

[23]Brig. Gen. William F. Barry, Chief of Artillery, Army of the Potomac, "Report of Siege of Yorktown," May 5, 1862, *Official Records*, ser. I, II (pt. I): 338–49; Tivy, *Souvenir of the Seventh*, pp. 40–44; McClellan, *Army of the Potomac*, p. 186.

the little Richmond and York Railroad seven miles east of Richmond, his troops stormed the Federals in the battle of Fair Oaks Station, one of the bloodiest engagements of the war.

Shafter with a special company of pioneers, about forty-five soldiers, was repairing and improving approaches to a bridge across the Chickahominy. When the fighting started, he did not hesitate. Leaving half his group at the muddy crossing, with the remainder he ran quickly to join troops of the Third Brigade under Dana's command on the battlefield. Moments later, caught at short range in a withering volley, Shafter's pioneer force fell to five or six men. Sending the survivors into their respective regiments, Shafter reported to Maj. James Anderson, commanding the Seventh Michigan, who directed him to take the place of the disabled regimental adjutant.[24]

Heavy action followed. The Federals held steady throughout and even succeeded in compelling the Confederates to take cover in timber about 150 yards to the rear. Then forming a skirmish line, Dana's brigade advanced against the enemy. Within about 50 yards of the woods, the Union force met a storm of gunshot. Quickly changing its front to face the Southern rally, the Union brigade opened with well-executed volleys. After a few exchanges the gray-clad troops withdrew.[25]

On the following morning, June 1, the Confederates renewed the attack. They hoped to pierce the enemy lines, but the Union army held. At the end of a long day of fighting the Southern troops withdrew, having lost some 6,150 killed and wounded; the Northern casualties amounted to 5,000. Some of the wounded lay on the field unattended for over fifty-six hours. Both sides were severely shaken and immobilized.[26]

During the fighting Shafter received a flesh wound much like a four-inch cut in the side above the hip joint, and his horse was killed. When the bullet struck him, he reputedly turned to his men with a startled expression on his face and said, "Right where Papy [*sic*] said I'd get it!" Shafter remained on duty for twenty-four hours afterwards,

[24]Brig. Gen. N. J. T. Dana, Commanding the Third Brigade, "Report of Operations at Fair Oaks Station, Virginia," June 3, 1862, William R. Shafter Collection, University Archives and Regional History Collections, Western Michigan University, Kalamazoo; Dana to Col. F. C. Ainsworth, Chief, Records and Pension Office, War Dept., May 9, 1895, United States, William R. Shafter, Letters Received, Appointments, Commission, and Personal Branch, Adjutant General's Office, Record Group 94, National Archives (hereafter ACP File, AGO, RG94, NA).

[25]Michigan, Adj. Gen. Office, *Michigan in the War*, rev. ed., comp. Jno. Robertson (Lansing, Mich.: W. S. George Co., 1888), p. 271.

[26]Allan Nevins, *The War for the Union*, 2:120–23, 130.

refusing to go to the field hospital until after the second day's battle. The neglect proved costly. When he returned from the hospital, Shafter was compelled to perform his duties as adjutant while lying down, and even four weeks later surgeons advised him that he should not ride on horseback. The wound took nearly two months to heal.[27]

After the battle of Fair Oaks, General Dana praised Shafter's performance. He reported that Shafter "furnished beautiful exhibitions of gallant conduct and intelligent activity." A few days later he asked Shafter to serve on his staff as commissary of subsistence with the rank of captain. Hoping to attain soon a higher command of fighting men, the ambitious young lieutenant declined the offer. Years later, on June 12, 1895, Shafter received the Congressional Medal of Honor for his gallant and meritorious service.[28]

The day after fighting ended a large detail of the Seventh Michigan established a picket line about one mile in advance of the army. The line, only six miles from the long-sought Confederate capital at Richmond, was fortified and maintained until the end of the month, when the Army of the Potomac withdrew toward Harrison's Landing on the James River where McClellan planned to establish a new base of operations.[29]

The retreat marked the beginning of a new battle, the disastrous Seven Days affair. As the Federals withdrew from Fair Oaks, the Confederates followed in hot pursuit. Overtaking the Union force on June 29 at Peach Orchard and Savage Station, the Confederates drove McClellan's army before them with heavy casualties. During the following day the Seventh Michigan participated in a skirmish at White Oak Swamp and a disastrous battle at Frayser's Farm (Glendale). On July 1 the Federals abandoned Malvern Hill and retreated to Harrison's Landing. By this time McClellan's Army of the Potomac was badly shattered, but the Confederates, unable to continue the offensive, withdrew to Richmond.[30]

The Army of the Potomac remained in camp at Harrison's Landing through July, 1862. At the beginning of August, when it became ob-

[27]Wayne C. Mann, Director, University Archives and Regional History Collections, Western Michigan University, Kalamazoo to author, March 24, 1972; Dana to Joseph B. Doe, War Dept. June 5, 1895, ACP File, AGO, RG94, NA.

[28]Dana, "Report of Operations at Fair Oaks Station, Virginia," June 3, 1862, *Official Records*, ser. I, II (pt. 1): 807–808; Dana to Ainsworth, May 9, 1895, ACP File, AGO, RG94, NA. Many soldiers, like Shafter, were awarded the Congressional Medal of Honor several years after the Civil War.

[29]Tivy, *Souvenir of the Seventh*, pp. 44–46.

[30]Ibid.

vious that McClellan could not take Richmond, President Lincoln called the army back to the Union capital and replaced McClellan with Gen. John Pope, who had achieved fame for his success in the western theater under Gen. Henry W. Halleck. Pope, with an even larger command, decided to strike Richmond from Washington by an overland route through Manassas Junction and Fredericksburg. The maneuver failed. Pope had no more success than McClellan.[31]

Shafter, when he arrived back in Washington, obtained a leave of absence to visit his family, Miss Grimes, and other friends. As he rode the slow train to Michigan, he could look back with satisfaction upon a year in which he clearly had proved his ability. His Company I had been well trained and disciplined and his camp had been orderly and thoroughly policed. In repairing the inferior muskets and in building comfortable winter quarters, he had demonstrated his skill and resourcefulness. No one had ever doubted his courage. He had changed from a new recruit to an experienced, battle-scarred veteran, recognized by his superior officers as an exceptional junior officer who got results as he waited impatiently for a chance to command.

[31]Ibid.

CHAPTER THREE

Emergence as a Commander of Black Troops

As HE RETURNED by train to Michigan, William R. Shafter considered his future. He was twenty-six years old, unmarried, without a profession or trade, but zealous for an army career and anxious for a wife. His education, his recent military travel, and the awakening in him of a national consciousness had stirred his dreams of command. His extended absence from home and Harriett Grimes's friendly letters had encouraged thoughts of matrimony.

After he arrived home in mid-August, Shafter renewed his courtship with Harriett, or Hattie, as he called her. During the previous year they had corresponded, and Shafter's furlough was obtained primarily to be with her. Shortly after his return the young lovers decided to wed. Plans were rapidly concluded, and on the morning of September 11, 1862, in the home of the bride's parents at Athens, the two were married.[1] Whatever the depth of his feeling for Hattie, and it would be surprising if it were not deep, it did not save Shafter from the dangers and delights of falling under other spells. But the flirtations came later, when he found himself stationed on the lonely and isolated frontier.

Meanwhile, Shafter initiated action that led to a command. Early in August he resigned his position with the Seventh Michigan to accept an appointment as major of the newly organized Nineteenth Michigan Volunteer Infantry Regiment. Shafter went into camp with his new outfit, commanded by Col. Henry C. Gilbert, at Dowagiac, Michigan, some forty miles southwest of Kalamazoo, where on September 5, only six days before his marriage, he received his commission.

[1] Charles A. Weissert, Dedicatory Address, MS, ca. 1939, Charles A. Weissert Collection, Michigan Historical Collections, University of Michigan, Ann Arbor.

Nine days later, the Nineteenth Michigan started for the western theater, arriving on the fifteenth at Cincinnati, Ohio. On the following afternoon, having found in the city a temporary home for his bride, Shafter left with the command by railroad for Gravel Hill Station some eighteen miles west of Cincinnati. Officers ordered a picket line up the Ohio toward Cincinnati and another downriver to the extreme southwest corner of the state. Since the river was very low and could be forded without difficulty, they maintained a tight guard, hoping to lessen any danger that the Confederates might attack Cincinnati and Louisville.[2]

Except for a rumor that John Hunt Morgan, the famous Confederate raider, was nearby, life at camp until Sunday, September 28, was routine. During the Sunday morning inspection, Shafter, already a stern disciplinarian, objected to the sloppy appearance of some of the men who, still unaccustomed to military discipline, balked at the strict regulations. Shafter succeeded in restoring order only after a tussle with a few of the insubordinates.[3]

Two weeks later the Nineteenth Michigan moved. After crossing the Ohio River on a pontoon bridge, it joined in Kentucky some battle-weary regiments retreating from Cumberland Gap. The two contingents organized into the Second Brigade, Army of Kentucky, commanded by Maj. Gen. Gordon Granger. The new brigade marched southward to Lexington where it remained for sixteen days.

In mid-November, the Nineteenth Michigan moved again, first to Nicholasville, where it encamped for a cold, dreary month before marching to Danville, Kentucky. At Danville, it transferred to the First Brigade, commanded by Col. John Coburn of the Thirty-third Indiana Volunteer Infantry, and joined the Third Division, commanded by Brig. Gen. Absalom Baird of General Granger's army. On Christmas Day Colonel Gilbert treated the regiment with an oyster dinner and beer, one keg for each company.[4]

At the end of January, 1863, having been ordered to Nashville, the Nineteenth again struck camp. Moving with the entire Third Division of some eight thousand men, the regiment marched to Louisville

---

[2]Francis B. Heitman, *Historical Register and Dictionary of the United States Army* 1:876; Weissert, Dedicatory Address; Franklin G. Rice, *Diary of the Nineteenth Michigan Volunteer Infantry during Their Three Years Service in the War of Rebellion*, pp. 2–3.

[3]Rice, *Diary of the Nineteenth Michigan*, p. 2. See also Bruce Catton, *This Hallowed Ground: The Story of the Union Side of the Civil War*, pp. 267–69.

[4]Cecil K. Byrd, ed., "Journal of Israel Cogshall, 1862–1863," *Indiana Magazine of History* 42 (1946): 72.

where it boarded steamboats, descended the Ohio River to the Cumberland, and then ascended the latter stream to Nashville. Disembarking on February 9, it encamped about two miles below the city.

Here Shafter twice caused problems. The first, a minor difficulty over gambling, affected only the Nineteenth Michigan. To pass the time, Shafter and a few fellow officers gambled at cards. To relieve their boredom, many enlisted men also played cards for money. Colonel Gilbert, concerned with camp discipline, prevailed upon Chaplain Israel Cogshall to urge the men to stop, but the chaplain complained that since the officers openly gambled every day, there was little he could do. The colonel thereupon ordered Shafter to discontinue the demoralizing practice, and subsequently the problem subsided.

The second incident affected the entire First Brigade. Late in the evening of February 26, because of an alarm south of camp, Shafter took a company of troops to investigate. Finding nothing, he returned to camp. As he approached in the dark, the reckless major allowed his dangling sword to rattle noisily. The outpost guards, suspecting the approach of enemy cavalry, signalled an alarm that spread through the whole brigade before Shafter's identity was discovered.[5]

Four days later the enforced idleness with its attendant problems came to an end. Colonel Coburn's First Brigade marched eighteen miles south of Nashville to Franklin, Tennessee, to reinforce the command of Gen. Charles C. Gilbert, who expected a Confederate attack. On March 6, the brigade, supported by six hundred cavalry, pushed southward toward Spring Hill with eighty wagons on a reconnoitering and foraging expedition.[6]

The maneuver resulted in a disastrous battle at Thompson's Station. After advancing only four miles, Coburn's force of 2,837 officers and enlisted men encountered Confederate troops. Only slight skirmishes took place, however, and the enemy retired. Three hours later the Federal force tramped an additional two miles and went into camp near Thompson's Station. Expecting a Confederate attack that night, most of the troops slept on their arms. Colonel Coburn, hoping to protect the wagons, wired General Gilbert for permission to fall back, but Gilbert ordered an advance instead. The following day, March 7, Co-

[5]These incidents are described in Rice, *Diary of the Nineteenth Michigan*, p. 5; and Byrd, "Journal of Israel Cogshall," pp. 72–74.

[6]Col. John Coburn, Thirty-third Indians Infantry, Commanding First Brigade, "Report of Operations at Thompson's Station," Aug. 1, 1863, *The War of the Rebellion: A Compilation of the Official Records of the Union and Confederate Armies* (hereafter *Official Records*), ser. 1, 23 (pt. 1): 85–91; John R. McBride, *History of the Thirty-Third Indiana Veteran Infantry*, pp. 74–78.

burn drove his troops southward. After proceeding two or three miles, a small force of the Federal cavalry sighted enemy troops and opened fire.[7]

The battle began in earnest. Three Federal infantry regiments hurried forward to assault a larger Confederate force on the right but just as quickly retreated. The Nineteenth, with Shafter out in front, charged to fight, taking a position on the left behind a stone wall. Holding the point only momentarily, the regiment, caught in range by an enemy battery, scurried to a nearby hill. Heavy Confederate firing again forced most of the Union command to fall back. Perhaps foolhardy but unwilling to quit, the Nineteenth under Shafter held its ground, taking some prisoners and capturing a Confederate flag. But when the Union cavalry galloped away, Coburn's entire brigade retreated, and the Southern troops closed on their enemy. Surrounded, his ammunition almost exhausted, and his cavalry fled, Colonel Coburn surrendered what was left of his command—about 1,050 troops, including the Nineteenth's Col. Henry Gilbert and Major Shafter.[8]

Two regiments of infantry and nearly all the mounted troops had fled. If the cavalry had held, the brigade might have escaped, but without the cavalry the brigade was easily surrounded. In his report of the battle the Third Division's General Baird indicated that with a few exceptions the troops fought with gallantry, determination, and good judgment. The Confederates permitted Coburn, Gilbert, Shafter, and other officers to retain their horses and side arms.[9]

The Confederates hustled their prisoners southward, and on March 8 the captured troops arrived at Shelbyville. The next morning, while camped on the courthouse yard, they traded pocket knives, wallets, gold pens, and whatever else they could spare for food or for money to buy food. Two days later they walked into Tullahoma, where they were confined to a muddy spot of ground once used as a mule pen.[10]

Nothing to sit or sleep on was provided in the old mule pen, only green oak logs were available for building fires, and for the enlisted

[7]Coburn, "Report of Operations," *Official Records*, 23:85–91; McBride, *History of the Thirty-Third Indiana*, pp. 74–78.

[8]McBride, *History of the Thirty-Third Indiana*, pp. 74–78. Also see Rice, *Diary of the Nineteenth Michigan*, p. 6; Byrd, ed., "Journal of Israel Cogshall," p. 76.

[9]Brig. Gen. Absalom Baird, Commanding Third Division, Army of Kentucky, "Report of Operations South of Franklin, Tennessee," March 11, 1863, *Official Records*, ser. 1, 23 (pt. 1): 83–85; Brig. Gen. Charles C. Gilbert, Commanding the forces at Franklin, "Report of Operations South of Franklin, Tennessee," March 13, 1863, *Official Records*, ser. 1, 23 (pt. 1): 75.

[10]Coburn "Report of Operations at Thompson's Station," Aug. 1, 1863, *Official Records*, ser. 1, 23 (pt. 1): 91–93.

men there was no protection from a pelting rain that night. Assigned to a crude old building, Shafter and the other officers kept dry during the storm but shivered from the cold. Rations of corn meal and bacon did little to relieve suffering during the gloomy night, one Shafter long remembered.

In the morning conditions worsened. All overcoats, leggings, knapsacks, and extra clothing were confiscated. Shivering, half-starved, and with little sleep or rest, the enlisted men squeezed into open cattle cars, some of which were still covered with wet manure. When the officers had crowded into two worn-out passenger cars, the train with its occupants started for Richmond, Virginia. Some men, too weak to go farther, were left at Knoxville a few days later. From Knoxville the captives passed through Lynchburg, Virginia, where a heavy snowfall delayed the trains. The prisoners had to wait out the storm without adequate clothing or rations. Finally reaching Richmond on March 22, the men entered Libby Prison, an old tobacco warehouse, where they crowded into rooms without fires or lights.[11]

Libby was a beastly prison. It was cold, with no glass in the windows. The captives received wretched blankets that Colonel Coburn reported "were lousy, filthy, fetid." The prison swarmed with vermin, and the Confederates provided no opportunity to wash the bedding or clothes. Rations were scanty, half a pound a day of bread and putrid meat, "totally unfit for use," according to Coburn. He noted that the men suffered "scurvy, itch, inflammatory sore throat, rheumatism, fever, lockjaw, delirium, and death in its most horrid forms."[12]

Time passed slowly at Libby. The captives broke the monotony by sawing, filing, and whittling beef bones into crochet needles, Odd Fellow or Masonic emblems, finger rings, and other items. Some men played games, some tried to study, some debated and wrangled, some sang songs, and at times some marched in double file around the rooms. Jefferson E. Brant, who was at Libby Prison with Shafter, reported that the prison was a "veritable University. To graduate there entitled one to rank high in the school of *versatility of suffering*."[13] Shafter played at cards and like the others sometimes marched about the building.

Within ten days of their confinement at Libby, some of the men left in exchange for Confederate prisoners. The officers, however, including Shafter, remained for more than two months. On May 5, they rode by train to City Point, Virginia, where they boarded a Confeder-

[11]Ibid.
[12]Ibid.
[13]Jefferson E. Brant, *History of the Eighty-fifth Indiana Volunteer Infantry*, p. 26.

ate steamer. On board, reported Colonel Coburn, the men were "fed, like dogs in a kennel, with bread and meat cut up and cast into two large boxes."[14] Arriving at Annapolis, Maryland, on May 8, they were exchanged for Southern officers.

Ordered to report to his regiment, which was reorganizing at Camp Chase, Ohio, near Columbus, Shafter boarded a westbound passenger train at Baltimore. At Columbus two days later, he found Hattie, whom he had not seen in eight months, waiting for him.

But Shafter had little time for pleasantries. There was the usual routine of camp duties, and he remained busy training and drilling his men, both the enlisted men who had escaped imprisonment and fresh recruits. On June 5, the same day the regiment reentered the service, Shafter received promotion to lieutenant colonel. Three days later the regiment headed for the Confederate Army of Tennessee.[15]

In the summer of 1863 two large armies faced each other in Tennessee. The Confederate Army of Tennessee, commanded by Gen. Braxton Bragg, was in the vicinity of Tullahoma. Facing it at Murfreesboro was the Federal Army of the Cumberland under Maj. Gen. William S. Rosecrans. Since late December and early January, when they had fought a desperate, inconclusive battle on the desolate frozen field at Stones River, the armies had been reorganizing and preparing for a second encounter. The clash came at the end of June when Rosecrans endeavored to drive the Confederates from Tullahoma.

Shafter and the Nineteenth Michigan joined Rosecrans in time for the offensive action. The regiment saw little fighting, however, for it marched to Guy's Gap about ten miles south of Murfreesboro to guard a railroad. Rosecrans was successful. On July 2, the rebels evacuated Tullahoma, and two days later Union troops occupied the city. In mid-July the Nineteenth left Guy's Gap to return to Murfreesboro, where it remained until the end of October.[16]

At Murfreesboro Shafter got his long-awaited chance to command. Late in August, 1863, when Col. Henry Gilbert left camp on a fifteen-day furlough, Shafter assumed leadership of the regiment. Making the most of his new authority, on September 7 he ordered his camp shifted to a position opposite the railroad depot at the edge of Murfreesboro. He took special care to see that companies tented together, that police

[14]Coburn, "Report of Operations at Thompson's Station," Aug. 1, 1863, *Official Records*, ser. 1, 23 (pt. 1): 93.

[15]George S. Bradley, *The Star Corps; or, Notes of an Army Chaplain, during Sherman's Famous "March to the Sea,"* p. 32.

[16]Catton, *This Hallowed Ground*, pp. 272–74; Stanley Horn, *The Army of Tennessee*, pp. 231–38.

detail improved, and that camp life remained orderly and well disciplined. Evidently he made an exemplary impression upon his superiors, for less than sixty days later he received instructions to recruit and organize the Seventeenth United States (Colored) Infantry.[17]

Before he left the Nineteenth, however, Shafter and his brother, John, a lieutenant in the outfit, caused trouble. In late October the regiment marched to McMinnville, about thirty miles southeast of Murfreesboro. Shortly afterward, John was arrested for stealing chickens (a charge of which he was later cleared). When his accomplices refused to stand by him, John tore out and destroyed some leaves of a private memorandum book on which Samuel M. Hubbard, captain of Company B, had written the testimony of other men involved in the matter.[18] A few weeks later, after emotionally charged investigations into the theft, Colonel Gilbert was arrested for involvement in the episode.

William Shafter and Maj. Eli Griffin, by struggling for control of the regiment, complicated the affair. Griffin had joined the Nineteenth in mid-November at the height of the chicken-stealing difficulties. Convinced that Griffin, who had been shot just above the left breast in a battle the previous May, could not stand the rigorous duties associated with his rank, Shafter told the mustering officer that Griffin was unfit for the service.[19] That officer, despite contrary testimony by all other officers of the regiment, thereupon refused to muster Griffin.[20]

When Austin Blair, governor of Michigan, named Griffin acting regimental commander, Shafter, although organizing his regiment of black troops, refused to recognize Griffin's authority. He planned to assume control of the Nineteenth himself and thereby help to secure the release of John and Colonel Gilbert. Griffin complained to Governor Blair and to Secretary of War Edwin M. Stanton about the regimental problems and his treatment by Shafter. Stanton sensibly asked for a surgeon's certificate of Griffin's good health, but Blair replied that Shafter could not defy the governor in matters of commissioning officers. Despite Governor Blair's support of Griffin, Shafter refused to ac-

[17]U.S. Dept. of War, Returns from United States Military Posts, Nashville, Tenn., April–May, 1864, Roll 832, Microcopy No. 617, National Archives (hereafter Post Returns, MC617, NA).
[18]Phinchas A. Hager to his wife, Nov. 19, 1863, Hager Family Collection, Michigan Historical Collections, University of Michigan, Ann Arbor.
[19]Ibid.
[20]Eli Griffin to his father, Dec. 13, 1863, Eli Griffin Collection, Michigan Historical Collections, University of Michigan, Ann Arbor (hereafter Griffin Collection).

cept the major's directives, the difficulties continued, and regimental morale deteriorated.[21]

Shafter's personality and temperament did not help. Only a few of the enlisted men and fellow officers liked Shafter. Some believed his attention to detail and discipline too severe; others, cowed by his harassment, were bitter and resentful. Griffin wrote to his wife that "Lieutenant Colonel Shafter is a gambler and a mean skunk so the officers and men say." Later he said Shafter was a "man without principles."[22] Although Griffin wrote in anger about the lieutenant colonel, Shafter during his stay in McMinnville did demonstrate a belligerent, even roguish, streak in his character.

Despite the problems at McMinnville, Shafter remained an excellent officer. Although he made no effort to be popular with his men, he was active, alert, and intelligent, and he faithfully discharged his military duties. Brigade commander Coburn reported years later that "there was not a better officer of any rank in the brigade." He stated that Shafter was always conspicuously gallant under fire, and that "he was an honor to the Volunteer service."[23]

Meanwhile, Shafter set about recruiting and organizing his command of black troops. From December, 1863, through March, 1864, when his regiment moved to Nashville, he remained busy near McMinnville. By December 20, he had already recruited some 680 blacks, but recruiting slowed and by the end of March, 1864, he had added less than another 160 officers and enlisted men.[24] Most of the enlisted men came from the vicinity of Murfreesboro, but Shafter got perhaps a hundred troops from Ohio and another three hundred with the help of black agents who had accompanied cavalry expeditions into northern Alabama.[25] As recruitment efforts proceeded, Shafter received his commission as colonel of the Seventeenth Infantry on April 19, 1864.[26]

Although Shafter welcomed his chance to serve with the Seven-

---

[21] Ibid.

[22] Griffin to his wife, Nov. 14, 1863, and Griffin to his father, Dec. 13, 1863, Griffin Collection.

[23] John Coburn to [?], Dec. 31, 1889, William R. Shafter Papers, Stanford University Library, Stanford, Calif., photocopy in Southwest Collection, Texas Tech University, Lubbock (hereafter Shafter Papers).

[24] Griffin to his father, Dec. 20, 1863, Griffin Collection; Post Returns, MC617, NA.

[25] L. Thomas, Adj. Gen., U.S. Army, to Edwin M. Stanton, Secy. of War, June 15, 1864, *Official Records*, ser. 3, 4:437; Reuben D. Mussey, Col., 100th U.S. Colored Infantry, Report of the Commissioner for Organization. U.S. Colored Troops, Oct. 10, 1864, *Official Records*, ser. 3, 4:768, 772.

[26] Heitman, *Historical Register*, 1:806.

teenth, not all white officers felt his way. Stout opposition developed, and many officers vowed never to serve with black units. Nelson Miles, later commanding general of the United States Army, did all he could to avoid service with blacks, and George A. Custer, the famous frontier commander, refused outright to join a Negro regiment. Gen. Ulysses S. Grant found it necessary to direct his subordinates to exert themselves not only in organizing and training black regiments, "but also in removing prejudice against them."[27]

White enlisted men also resisted service alongside black regiments. They did not want to be brigaded with blacks. In one division to which Negro regiments were assigned, whites threatened to stack their arms and return home. Although the threat was not carried out, discrimination persisted until the end of the war. Throughout the conflict black soldiers received wages of ten dollars per month, while their white counterparts got thirteen dollars. There was also a difference in bonuses.[28]

Commanding black troops provided Shafter many pleasant experiences. Nearly always illiterate ex-slaves, most recruits had never before handled a gun or fixed a bayonet or repaired a rifle. Some of the first drills and parades with the weapons, therefore, were undisciplined affairs in which soldiers tended to march off in any but the correct direction or to fumble inexpertly with the guns. With much satisfaction Shafter watched the transformation of his troops into an effective command.

Shafter's command of the regiment was thorough and systematic, requiring patience, vigilance, intelligence, and skill. An excellent organizer, Shafter made the outfit into one of the finest in the army. Colonel Coburn, who witnessed his leadership, reported years later that Shafter made "the regiment one of the very best I ever saw."[29]

Shafter maintained rigid policing policies. The Seventeenth's camp remained in top condition. The arms and equipment were also kept

[27]George W. Williams, *A History of the Negro Troops in the War of the Rebellion, 1861–65,* p. 108; Arlen L. Fowler, *The Black Infantry in the West, 1869–1891,* pp. 12, 19, 115–17.

[28]William H. Leckie, *The Buffalo Soldiers: A Narrative of the Negro Cavalry in the West,* pp. 4–5; Dudley T. Cornish, *The Sable Arm: Negro Troops in the Union Army, 1861–1865,* pp. 173–74; James G. Randall, *The Civil War and Reconstruction,* pp. 506–507.

[29]Coburn to [?], Dec. 31, 1899, Shafter Papers; Unsigned, undated letter to Mrs. Mary McKittrick (Shafter's daughter), William R. Shafter Collection, Michigan Historical Collections, University of Michigan, Ann Arbor (hereafter Shafter Collection).

in good, clean working order. W. C. Thorpe, inspector of the Post of Nashville, reported that Shafter and his black regiment deserved particular notice for the orderly camp, the soldierly bearing of the troops, and the fine care of the guns. Cleaned and burnished under Shafter's eye, the old, inferior weapons looked like new.[30]

Two of Shafter's relatives joined the Seventeenth. Sometime during the summer, Shafter, who had accompanied his pregnant wife home to Michigan, recruited his brother-in-law, Job S. Aldrich, as captain of Company E. Early in October, he appointed John Shafter first lieutenant of Company G and on October 24, 1864, promoted him to captain. Since few whites wanted to serve with Negro regiments, Shafter had difficulty acquiring and keeping qualified officers, at least two of whom he dismissed for habitual drinking. He knew that his kinsmen would improve the quality of the regiment.[31]

Decisions made in Georgia, late in October, 1864, affected Shafter's Seventeenth Infantry. After sparring at long range over Atlanta, Generals John B. Hood and William T. Sherman turned around and set off in opposite directions to carry out new objectives. While Sherman looked eastward toward the sea, Hood settled on a bold, desperate gamble to capture Nashville. By mid-November, the Confederate general was moving northwestward, striking for one of the best-fortified places in the country.

At Nashville, Gen. George H. Thomas, the "Rock of Chickamauga," had assembled an army of more than fifty thousand troops. As Hood approached, Thomas sent out cavalry divisions to harass his movement. Although he lost six thousand men, Hood succeeded in putting his troops in camp on high ground a few miles south of Nashville. Realizing that Hood's army now was too small to storm the city and too weak to lay siege to it, Thomas took the offensive. On December 15 and 16 he struck hard at Hood's command in the battle of Nashville.[32]

Shafter's Seventeenth Infantry found itself in the thick of the fight. Stationed on the left flank, southeast of Nashville along the road to Murfreesboro, the Seventeenth was brigaded with four other regiments of black troops under the command of Col. Thomas J. Morgan. On the evening of December 14, Morgan received orders to move at day-

[30]Post Returns, Nashville, Oct., 1864, Roll 832, MC617, NA.
[31]Ibid.
[32]Horn, *Army of Tennessee*, pp. 404–18; Richard M. Murry, *John Bell Hood and the War for Southern Independence*, pp. 169–82; Catton, *This Hallowed Ground*, pp. 362–69.

break, make a demonstration, menace the Confederate right, and prevent it from helping to resist the advance of the Union right flank, where the main attack was to be made.

At dawn Morgan moved his brigade, and about seven the Seventeenth joined him. As the Federal artillery opened fire, Shafter's regiment handsomely took some Confederate rifle pits, killing, wounding, capturing, or driving away the enemy. Instead of halting, Shafter pushed his regiment southward about three-fourths of a mile, where it met heavy fire from the Confederates and fell back in disorder. Once out of range of the enemy's artillery, however, Shafter reformed his command, moved around to the right of the Confederate earthworks, and took a new position. Here his men maintained a sharp skirmish until the Southern troops withdrew at nightfall.[33]

The following day Morgan's brigade, with the Seventeenth forming an echelon to the rear, pushed southward. Driving the enemy before it, the command advanced, skirmishing with the retreating Confederate troops as far as Overton Hill about five miles south of Nashville. Hood's army took a final stand there but after two or three frontal assaults retired southward in disorder. During the next three weeks Morgan's brigade moved through Murfreesboro and Decatur toward Tuscumbia, Alabama, before pulling back to Nashville.[34]

The battle of Nashville was of major importance. Called by one authority the most decisive battle of the Civil War, it represented one of the few times a Confederate army had been totally routed. The Union victory touched and modified plans of the commanders of both armies, it represented a great achievement for the black troops who played a conspicuous and creditable part, and it hastened the close of the war. After the battle of Nashville, it was clear to everyone that the South was defeated. All that remained of the Confederacy east of the Mississippi were the eastern portions of Virginia and North Carolina.[35]

In Nashville Colonel Shafter reviewed the fighting and prepared his reports. Because eighty-five of his officers and enlisted men had been killed during the battle, he reorganized the Seventeenth. Among the dead officers was brother-in-law Job Aldrich, and Shafter assumed the responsibility of caring for his widowed sister, Anne, completing ar-

[33]Col. W. R. Shafter, Seventeenth U.S. Colored Troops, "Report of Operations for Dec. 15-16, 1864," Jan. 30, 1865, *Official Records*, ser. 1, 46:538-39.

[34]Col. Thomas J. Morgan, Fourteenth U.S. Colored Troops, Commanding First Colored Brigade, "Report of Operations for Nov. 29, 1864-Jan. 12, 1865," Jan. 16, 1865, *Official Records*, ser. 1, 46 (pt. 1): 534-38.

[35]Stanley F. Horn, *The Decisive Battle of Nashville*, pp. v–xi. See also Jacob D. Cox, *The March to the Sea, Franklin and Nashville*, pp. 98-127.

rangements that made him Anne's guardian.[36] Upon fulfilling his immediate regimental responsibilities, Shafter took a leave of absence and went home.

As the fighting wound down in middle Tennessee, Shafter could look back upon a successful military record in the Civil War. He had served the Seventh Michigan Volunteers faithfully and well, and with the Nineteenth Michigan he had performed relentlessly and consistently. Of his work with the Seventeenth Infantry, Maj. Gen. George H. Thomas stated that "Colonel Shafter is one of the most successful officers who has ever [served] in the Colored regiments. He has given his whole attention to the subject of their improvement; and his command has attained a degree of discipline and soldierly bearing which is not only creditable but very remarkable." On March 13, 1865, Shafter received promotion to brevet brigadier general of volunteers for "gallant and meritorious service during the war."[37] Shafter had acquired military experience that would serve him well for training black troops on the Texas frontier.

[36]William R. Shafter to his wife, n.d. (probably March, 1865), Shafter Papers.

[37]Maj. Gen. George H. Thomas to George W. Howard, Asst. Adj. Gen., U.S. Army, Feb. 18, 1866, Shafter Collection; Adjutant General's Office, "Summary of the Military Service of William R. Shafter, Colonel, First U.S. Infantry," Oct. 22, 1894, Shafter Collection; Heitman, *Historical Register*, 1:876.

CHAPTER FOUR

From the Civil War to the Texas Frontier

THE UNITED STATES ARMY faced several awkward tasks after the Civil War. It had to garrison the recently defeated southern states; as rapidly as possible, it had to demobilize the huge volunteer armies; and it had to defend the frontier settlements against Indian depredations. Because of the presence of French troops in Mexico, the army also had to deal with international difficulties along the Lower Rio Grande Valley in Texas.

Garrisoning the South during Reconstruction proved largely peaceful. Although several clashes between Federal troops and private citizens were reported, especially when the regulars were Negroes, few major disorders occurred. For Col. William R. Shafter and the soldiers at Nashville, Tennessee, army life remained quiet and unexciting. Some regiments left the city, and Shafter's Seventeenth Infantry dwindled to nine companies totaling 721 officers and enlisted men. Many of the men took long-awaited furloughs; other troops performed little more than the usual routine of drills, parades, and fatigue duty. For the officers, only garrison and general court-martial duty relieved the monotony.

With the fighting over, volunteer soldiers left the service as the citizen armies demobilized. Discharge of a volunteer regiment depended largely on when the soldiers' terms of enlistment expired, and since most blacks in 1865 had another year remaining in their tour of duty, the army often retained them for service in the South. Perhaps, too, the army kept black soldiers as a means to provide them with a job and prepare them for a new kind of life. During 1865 and early the following year, however, records show an ever-decreasing number of Negro troops, and in April, 1866, the army discharged the Seventeenth Infantry.[1]

[1]Marvin Fletcher, "The Negro Volunteer in Reconstruction," *Military Affairs* 32

Col. William R. Shafter, apparently taken about the close of the Civil War.
Courtesy Library of Congress

Meanwhile, at a time when many good officers were being demoted, Shafter received several promotions. Two months after he became brevet brigadier general of volunteers, he assumed command at the

(Dec., 1968): 125–27; U.S. Dept. of War, Returns from United States Military Posts, 1800–1916, Nashville, Sept., 1865, Roll 832, Microcopy No. 617, National Archives (hereafter Post Returns, MC617, NA).

Post of Nashville. Then, in September, 1865, he took charge of the District of Middle Tennessee, a huge area in the center of the state occupied by five regiments of infantry, some 3,800 troops altogether.[2] He performed his duties well. Shafter so impressed the leading citizens of Nashville that they asked him, even while he commanded the District of Middle Tennessee, to serve as chief police commissioner for the city. A report recommending him for appointment stated that "his fine administrative qualities eminently fit him for the position."[3] Declining the offer, Shafter explained that he had enough work in the army. After completing his military obligations at Nashville, Shafter rode to Memphis to serve as president of a general court-martial. When the court-martial adjourned at the end of October, 1866, he awaited further orders of the War Department.[4]

Shafter did not have to wait long. On November 2, mustered out of the volunteer service, he returned to Michigan, where his wife more than a year earlier had given birth to their only child, a daughter they named Mary. Forced to find work, Shafter taught a class of girls for a week at nearby Prairie Seminary while one of the regular instructors took a vacation. Schoolteaching, however, no longer appealed to the restless soldier. "I'd rather go through the hardest battle I ever fought than try to teach [again]," he confessed. When his substitute teaching job ended, he hauled lumber and cord wood and worked on his father's farm.[5]

But the army had become Shafter's life. Indeed, it was a natural career for the rugged frontiersman. Since his youth Shafter had been a leader and adept with guns. He enjoyed being a soldier, and, moreover, he had been a fine officer. When he applied for a commission to the regular army, he encountered no difficulty in obtaining excellent recommendations from high-ranking military officers. Bvt. Maj. Gen.

[2]Post Returns, MC617, NA.

[3]Cited in Samuel W. Durant, *History of Kalamazoo County, Michigan*, p. 394.

[4]Shafter to Bvt. Brig. Gen. E. D. Townsend, Oct. 26, 1866, United States, William R. Shafter, Letters Received, Appointments, Commission, and Personal Branch, Adjutant General's Office, Record Group 94, National Archives (hereafter ACP File, AGO, RG94, NA).

[5]Cited in Elizabeth Cousins, "Unsung Hero of Galesburg, William Rufus Shafter, 1835–1906," William R. Shafter Collection, University Archives and Regional History Collections, Western Michigan University, Kalamazoo (hereafter Shafter Collection, WMU). See also James Parker, *The Old Army: Memories, 1872–1918*, p. 101. There is a story of doubtful validity that Shafter brought two buffalo back to Michigan with him at the close of the Civil War. Reputedly, the buffalo broke loose from the Shafter farm and caused considerable trouble in Galesburg. Cousins, "Unsung Hero of Galesburg."

James L. Donaldson wrote, "I can safely say that he is a most excellent officer; prompt, willing and intelligent; and his appointment would be a valuable acquisition to the service." Bvt. Maj. Gen. Clinton B. Fish of the United States Volunteers stated that "the country had had but few as brave, gallant and efficient officers as Colonel Shafter." And Maj. Gen. George H. Thomas described Shafter as "an officer of discretion and good judgment" whose conduct "has been gallant and his ability and zeal most commendable."[6]

To Shafter's good fortune, Congress, in response to various problems confronting the War Department, needed to increase the size of the regular army in mid-1866. Included in the expansion measure was a provision for the creation of six Negro regiments, four of infantry and two of cavalry. Late in January, 1867, the army offered Shafter the lieutenant colonelcy of the Forty-first United States Infantry, one of the new black regiments.

To be offered such a high rank came as a surprise. Because commissions in the regular army were in heavy demand, many distinguished regular, as well as volunteer, officers had to accept low rank. Although Shafter hoped to obtain a majority rank, he had been informed by his congressman that only a slim possibility existed. Shafter had decided that he would be passed over entirely. At the end of January, 1867, he rode into Galesburg perched high on a load of cord wood he had cut. As he passed the post office, the postmaster ran out and handed him a long envelope that contained his commission, subject to a satisfactory physical examination. When another officer had declined the command, Shafter received the position.

Although many white officers refused to serve with black soldiers, Shafter accepted without hesitation. He had thought "considerable" of his black troops in the Seventeenth Volunteer Infantry. He knew that blacks, properly trained and fairly treated, made excellent troops, in every respect comparable to whites, and he believed that promotion would be more rapid for officers of the black regiments.[7]

Upon receiving the news of his tentative appointment, Shafter completed all his business obligations and with Hattie and his daughter

[6]Bvt. Maj. Gen. J. L. Donaldson to Adj. Gen., U.S. Army, Jan. 1, 1866; Bvt. Maj. Gen. Clinton B. Fish to Adj. Gen., U.S. Army, Jan. 1, 1866; Maj. Gen. George H. Thomas to George W. Howard, Asst. Adj. Gen., U.S. Army, Feb. 18, 1866, William R. Shafter Collection, Michigan Historical Collections, University of Michigan, Ann Arbor (hereafter Shafter Collection).

[7]Hodgman to his father, Galesburg, Mich., Feb. 4, 1864, Samuel Chase Hodgman Letters, University Archives and Regional History Collections, Western Michigan University, Kalamazoo; Parker, The Old Army, p. 101.

left Galesburg for Louisville, Kentucky, where on February 2 he appeared before an army officer examining board. When the board reported favorably, Lt. Col. William R. Shafter took a train to Baton Rouge, Louisiana, to join the Forty-first Infantry.[8]

In Louisiana, Shafter's major responsibilities were to recruit, organize, and train soldiers for the regiment. Because a colonel of the Forty-first had not yet been appointed, Shafter found himself in command of both the regiment and the post at Baton Rouge. His earlier experiences at Nashville served him well, and he had little difficulty organizing and training the new command.

Nor did recruiting cause problems. Over 178,000 blacks had served in the army during the Civil War, and many of them were eager to enlist. Possibly a majority believed soldiering with steady pay to be a good way of life. Some looked forward to learning to read and write while in the army under the tutelage of literate Negroes and whites. To obtain Civil War veterans, Shafter sent Capt. Orville Burke to Cincinnati and 1st Lt. Lewis Johnson to Nashville. The bulk of the troops, however, were recruited from New Orleans, Baton Rouge, and Shreveport, Louisiana. The men enlisted for a minimum of five years for the basic pay of thirteen dollars a month plus quarters, meals, and uniforms.

Officers of the new black regiments represented an extraordinary lot. Like Shafter, many had sought reappointment or reapplied for commissions. But keen competition for the few places available in the postwar army forced a large number of veteran officers to enlist in the ranks. The ranking officers did not earn the respect of their men by logistical planning in the post or field headquarters, but rather by better shooting, harder riding, or faster improvisation when in trouble. Like Shafter, they often wore a mustache, sometimes a beard, and usually displayed a certain unshaven look. One contemporary believed officers of the black troops were, "as a rule, a very superior set of men."[9]

Officers of black troops along the frontier had more routine responsibilities than those commanding white soldiers. Because educated sergeants and clerks were always available to relieve them of wearisome duties, the officers of white regiments dealt with very little

[8]Board of Examination for Officers, Louisville, Ky., Report on William R. Shafter, Feb. 2, 1867, ACP File, AGO, RG94, NA; Post Returns, Baton Rouge, Feb., 1867, Roll 86, MC617, NA; U.S. Dept. of War, Returns from Regular Army Infantry Regiments, June, 1821–Dec., 1916, Forty-first Infantry, Feb., 1867, Roll 296, Microcopy No. 665, National Archives (hereafter Regimental Returns, MC665,NA).

[9]William H. Leckie, *The Buffalo Soldiers: A Narrative of the Negro Cowboy in the West*, p. 9; H. H. McConnell, *Five Years a Cavalryman; or, Sketches of Regular Army Life on the Texas Frontier, Twenty Odd Years Ago*, p. 213.

clerical work. This was not usually the case with Negro commands, where only rarely in the frontier years did one find a black soldier able to perform such tasks. "Every detail of duty," including sanitation, clerical work, checking the books and supplies, and the many other routine chores, was "attended to by the officers themselves."[10]

With the arrival at Baton Rouge in May, 1867, of Col. Ranald S. Mackenzie, an aggressive young officer who had made a remarkable record in the Civil War, Shafter quit his responsibilities of post and regimental commander. Named superintendent of the regimental recruiting service, he transferred Lieutenant Johnson to Detroit and sent Maj. George W. Schofield to Chicago. He continued some recruiting in the South, but after May, 1867, he concentrated on northern cities.[11]

A month later the Forty-first Infantry moved to Texas. Consisting of eight companies totaling 577 officers and enlisted men, the regiment arrived on June 27 at Brownsville, its new headquarters in the extreme Lower Rio Grande Valley. During the next two weeks several companies scattered to other posts, including Brazos Santiago near modern-day Port Isabel, Fort McIntosh at Laredo, and Ringgold Barracks, a small post at Rio Grande City about 102 miles above Brownsville, where Shafter took command. Other troops under Mackenzie's charge remained at Fort Brown. Detachments of the Fourth, Sixth, and Ninth cavalries helped man the Valley posts.[12]

Shafter's regiment faced several difficulties in the Rio Grande Valley. Bands of Mexican and American thieves, murderers, arsonists, and cattle rustlers raided on both sides of the international border, and occasional clashes between American and Mexican troops occurred. Smuggling was common, and Indian raids added to the friction. The United States charged Mexico with failure to control Indian activities originating in her territory, and Mexico placed responsibility for the depredations on the United States, where government policy had forced many Indians southwestward.[13]

Another difficulty was unhealthful conditions. A few months after

[10]Ibid. Also see L. F. Sheffy, ed., "Letters and Reminiscences of General Theodore A. Baldwin: Scouting after Indians on the Plains of West Texas," *Panhandle-Plains Historical Review* 11 (1938): 13, 15, 25.

[11]Regimental Returns, Forty-first Infantry, May–June, 1867, Roll 86, MC617, NA.

[12]Post Returns, Baton Rouge, May, 1867, Roll 86, MC617, NA; Regimental Returns, Forty-first Infantry, May–June, 1867, Roll 86, MC617, NA.

[13]Paul Schuster Taylor, *An American-Mexican Frontier: Nueces County, Texas*, pp. 49–53; Clarence C. Clendenen, *Blood on the Border: The United States Army and the Mexican Irregulars*, pp. 6–15, 45–60; James M. Callahan, *American Foreign Policy in Mexican Relations*, pp. 341–50.

arriving in the Valley, Shafter wrote to a friend at Galesburg that Ring-gold Barracks "is a fearful place to live." He noted that a quartermaster clerk and two assistant surgeons had died of yellow fever, that he had been sick, and that nearly half the population of Rio Grande City had died. The post medical reports consistently mentioned the various diseases that prevailed, especially yellow fever, venereal diseases, and acute diarrhea.[14]

Finally, there was the problem of racial prejudice. Because a hurricane had demolished some buildings at Fort Brown, most enlisted men lodged in town, where several rough encounters between white civilians and black soldiers occurred. The troopers defended themselves well, but the clashes led whites to harass and even kill black civilians. The fighting annoyed Lt. Gen. Philip H. Sheridan, commanding the military district of which Texas was a part. In his report to the secretary of war in 1867, Sheridan wrote that "an Indian killing of a white man on the frontier caused [violent] concern and anger, etc., but the white man's killing of scores of freedmen in so called civilized areas aroused no great concern, [nor] excitement as if to say the latter event was common place."[15]

Charged with maintaining peace in the lower Valley, Shafter and Mackenzie did their part to help ease the threatening international problems. Their troops guarded important river crossings to curb border violations by both Mexican and American desperadoes. Scouting expeditions by detachments of the Fourth, Sixth, and Ninth cavalry regiments helped reduce the number of Indian raids and the amount of cattle stealing.

Shafter and Mackenzie themselves confronted the problems of racial prejudice and unhealthful conditions. By alternating the regimental headquarters between Fort Brown and Ringgold Barracks, moving the troops about the district, and carefully handling the administration of post and garrison duties, they helped ease much of the tension between white citizens and black troops. To improve unhealthful conditions, the officers exercised more effort to secure a good water sup-

[14]Shafter to Charles [Clement?], Nov. 27, 1867, in Cousins, "Unsung Hero of Galesburg," Shafter Collection, WMU; U.S. Dept. of War, Post Medical Reports, Fort Brown, July–Aug., 1868, Books No. 731-732-734; and Fort Ringgold Barracks, July–Aug., 1868, Books No. 725-726-727, Old Records Division, Adjutant General's Office, National Archives [hereafter Post Medical Reports, ORD, AGO, NA]. Also see McConnell, *Five Years a Cavalryman*, pp. 158–59, 212–15, 292–93, 307–309.

[15]Philip H. Sheridan to Secretary of War, Nov. 25, 1867, U.S. Secy. of War, *Annual Report of the Secretary of War*, 1867, 40th Cong., 2d sess., H. Exec. Doc. 1, 2 (pt. 1): 379. Also see James Smallwood, *Time of Hope, Time of Despair*, pp. 140–45.

ply and to provide adequate water drainage and runoff. They also increased efforts to protect the troops from all kinds of communicable diseases.[16]

Early in March, 1868, seven months after arriving in Texas, the Forty-first Infantry moved again. With Mackenzie absent on military leave, Shafter, acting on orders, transferred the regimental headquarters and all troops to Fort Clark near modern-day Brackettville.

During the march to Fort Clark, two events occurred that subsequently brought Shafter before a military court of inquiry. In one of the incidents, during a heated exchange with some of the troops, Shafter swore at and publicly upbraided several of the men. Although he quickly restored order, the angry men did not forget the humiliation and a year later filed several serious misconduct charges against their lieutenant colonel. The charges included not only harassment, but also unlawful behavior both at Ringgold Barracks and Fort Clark.

The second incident related to a party and celebration at Fort Duncan. During a four-day rest there, March 24–27, 1868, while en route to the new headquarters, Shafter granted permission for his troops to hold a fandango in the hospital building. He allowed the post ambulance to be used for hauling citizens from Eagle Pass to the post on the day before the fandango and carrying them back the day afterward. Although the affair seemed innocent, the illegal use of both the ambulance and the hospital were among the specifications brought against Shafter.

Because of the nature of the charges, Shafter appeared on January 25, 1869, at San Antonio before a court of inquiry. The court, presided over by Bvt. Brig. Gen. James Oakes, colonel of the Sixth Cavalry, considered four general charges: conduct to the prejudice of good order and military discipline, conduct unbecoming an officer and a gentleman, disobedience of orders, and violation of the law. Each charge included from two to four specifications, ranging from accusations that he had cursed at and "damned" Lt. Thomas Sharpe to allegations that in November, 1867, he had proposed to Samuel J. Steward of Rio Grande City that they enter into a contract for supplying fresh beef to the troops at Ringgold Barracks on the condition that Steward and Shafter share in the profits.[17]

Two months later, after considering the charges and allegations, the

[16]Regimental Returns, Forty-first Infantry, July, 1867–March, 1868, Roll 296, MC617, NA; Post Returns, Fort Ringgold Barracks, July–Aug., 1867, November, 1867–March, 1868, Roll 1020, MC617, NA.

[17]"Case Examined by Court-of Inquiry," San Antonio, Tex., March 31, 1869, ACP File, AGO, RG94, NA.

court announced its decisions. It reasoned that Shafter used unwarranted language, that he inappropriately negotiated with Steward, and that, while at Fort Duncan in March, 1868, he misused the hospital and ambulance. But the prosecution, the court found, had not provided sufficient evidence in the first two charges, and in the last two the circumstances showed no criminal intent. In each of the four charges and all of the specifications, the court ruled that no further action should be taken.[18] Shafter resumed his duties.

Although judged inappropriate, the fandango at Fort Duncan illustrated Shafter's capacity to maintain regimental morale. The celebration, which took place after three exhausting and confining weeks on the march, relaxed strained nerves, allowed the troops to rest briefly, and provided the troops, women, and children with some color and excitement for the first time since leaving the lower Rio Grande.

On March 29, the Forty-first Infantry reached Fort Clark. Located 140 miles west of San Antonio, the post had been established in 1852 to guard the Rio Grande border. When the Forty-first arrived, Fort Clark also protected nearby settlers from Lipan, Kickapoo, and Comanche Indians. Strategically situated on a mesa about twenty miles from the Rio Grande, it provided a fine view of the almost limitless mesquite-covered plains that surrounded it. In contrast to Ringgold Barracks, the post also enjoyed a splendid supply of fresh water from Las Moras Spring and healthful conditions.[19]

For Shafter and his family, however, Fort Clark was an uncomfortable home. "This country on the Rio Grande is a [queer?] place," Shafter wrote to a friend a few days after his arrival. "There are but few Americans and they mostly men brought here by the Mexican War. I should judge that at least nine/tenths of the population between the Rio Grande and the Nueces River are Mexicans. Only the official business is done in English. Everyone speaks Spanish and all the interests of the people are with Mexico." Besides the language barrier, Shafter found the living quarters inadequate for even his small family, and living costs were high.[20]

Fort Clark, Shafter discovered, was a wretched installation. Although the water supply was good, Col. Edmund Shriver, who made an inspection of Texas frontier posts, reported that nearly all troops were quartered in huts, no administrative building for offices existed, the regimental adjutant's office was a tent, there was no chapel or suit-

[18]Ibid.
[19]Shafter to Gen. John Coburn, April 4, 1868, ACP File, AGO, RG94, NA.
[20]Ibid.

able room in which to hold courts-martial, and the servants and laundresses lived in miserable shanties. Shriver also indicated that public stores were improperly protected from the weather, theft, and damage.[21] Most companies of the Forty-first continued to other posts.

Nor did Shafter remain long at Fort Clark. After receiving orders to transfer the headquarters of the Forty-first to nearby Fort Duncan, he relinquished command on April 18, 1868, and reached his new post two days later. Fort Duncan, situated on the Rio Grande a mile below Eagle Pass, 40 miles south of Fort Clark, and 156 miles southwest of San Antonio, was a small post first occupied in 1849. Its sandstone and adobe buildings in 1868 were all more or less badly damaged or destroyed.

Duties at Fort Duncan were light. In addition to the routine garrison duty, parades, and drills, there was a little work on the repair and construction of post buildings. Detachments of the Ninth Cavalry handled the few lackadaisical scouts against Indians and rustlers, leaving detachments of the infantry to guard mail routes and to perform escort duty. During his first ten months at Fort Duncan, Shafter led a routine garrison life. He saw the post adequately policed, held garrison courts-martial, and traveled to San Antonio twice to appear before a board of inquiry.[22]

Late in February, 1869, however, Shafter had an opportunity to lead troops in the field for the first time since the Civil War. Ranchers in the region about the headwaters of the Nueces had been complaining of horse stealing and cattle rustling for several months. On February 25, news arrived at Fort Duncan that Indian raiders the day before had killed some white men. Taking Lt. Charles Parker and twenty-two enlisted men of the Ninth Cavalry, Shafter galloped in pursuit. Leaving on the twenty-sixth, he and the hardy black troops scoured the mesquite-covered plains between the Nueces and the Rio Grande, crisscrossing Maverick and Zavala counties, as well as the western portions of Dimmit, for over 260 miles. Although it saw no Indians, the command recovered some horses, saddles, and bridles from white smugglers it overtook in Maverick County near the Rio Grande.[23]

After returning to Fort Duncan, Shafter followed up his disappointing scout by sending out additional expeditions. When none were suc-

[21] Walter C. Conway, ed., "Colonel Edmund Shriver's Inspector-General's Report on Military Posts in Texas, November, 1872–January, 1873," Southwestern Historical Quarterly 67 (April, 1964): 579.

[22] Post Returns, Fort Duncan, April, 1868–Feb., 1869, Roll 336, MC617, NA; Regimental Returns, Forty-first Infantry, April, 1868–Feb., 1869, Roll 296, MC665, NA.

[23] Post Returns, Fort Duncan, Feb.–March, 1869, Roll 336, MC617, NA.

cessful, Shafter planned further scouts through the country lying south and east of the post. Before he could put his plans into operation, however, he went to Fort Jefferson, Texas, to serve as a member of a special military commission.[24]

In the autumn of 1868 a large mob had killed George B. Smith, a carpetbagger, at Jefferson in northeast Texas. The incident had caused such an uproar in the city that the army had to restore order. The army's troops had built a stockade, about seventy by one hundred feet, with walls fifteen feet high and broad enough on top for soldiers to walk. They had placed many prominent men of Jefferson in the prison, where life was reputed to have been cruel and unbearable. A few of the captives had died. Citizens of the vicinity, outraged over the stockade and the general treatment they had received from the Federal troops, had complained. In the spring of 1869 Shafter's special military commission met to investigate the charges of harsh treatment and the army's operation of the stockade.[25]

For four months the commission investigated. Meeting almost daily, it interviewed citizens of Jefferson, stockade prisoners, and authorities at the jail, and examined many of the events relating to Smith's death. At the close of its deliberations, Shafter's group made no ruling either on the stockade, which continued to be used throughout the Reconstruction era, or on Smith's death. It found that a permanent post at Jefferson was unnecessary, however, and two years later, in 1871, the army abandoned the fort.[26]

Upon completing his tour of duty at Jefferson, Shafter took a sixty-day leave of absence and at the end of September, 1869, returned with his wife and daughter to Galesburg. On his first visit home in nearly three years, Shafter renewed old acquaintances and friendships. Perhaps also, because it was the busy fall season, he assisted his father with the autumn harvest. He would have enjoyed such change from army life, where he was steeped in paper work and addicted to form.[27]

While Shafter vacationed in Michigan, the United States Army re-

[24]Ibid., April, 1869; Regimental Returns, Forty-first Infantry, May, 1869, Roll 296, MC665, NA.

[25]Betty J. Sandlin, "The Texas Reconstruction Constitution Convention of 1868–1869" (Ph.D. diss., Texas Tech University, Lubbock, 1971), pp. 83–85; Joseph H. Toulouse and James R. Toulouse, *Pioneer Posts of Texas*, pp. 77–79; Post Medical Reports, Fort Jefferson, Aug., 1870, Book No. 110, ORD, AGO, NA.

[26]See William L. Richter, *The Army in Texas during Reconstruction*, pp. 177–80; Allen W. Trelease, *White Terror: The Ku Klux Klan Conspiracy and Southern Reconstruction*, pp. 140–47.

[27]Regimental Returns, Twenty-fourth Infantry, Aug.–Oct., 1869, Roll 245, MC665, NA.

organized. As part of the reorganization, it cut its rolls to about 25,000 enlisted men and consolidated the Forty-first with the Thirty-eighth to form the Twenty-fourth United States Infantry Regiment. As early as August 23, two companies of the Thirty-eighth Infantry had affiliated with the Twenty-fourth; other companies joined later. Troops of the Forty-first transferred in October. With headquarters for the new regiment at Fort McKavett, Texas, both Shafter and Mackenzie remained as the Twenty-fourth Infantry's ranking officers.

To administer the reorganized army, the United States War Department created a system of geographic commands: the divisions of the Atlantic, Pacific, and Missouri. The latter division, which included the Great Plains, was subdivided into the departments of the Dakota, Platte, Missouri, and Arkansas. Reorganization shortly afterward added the Department of Texas, which from time to time the army subdivided into two or more districts. The headquarters of the Division of the Missouri coordinated most of the Indian campaigns on the western frontier. The whole system provided a centralized but loose chain of command.[28]

Combating western Indians put a premium upon the United States cavalry and a discount on infantry. The Indians fought a guerrilla-style hit-and-run war in which heavy infantry columns were too slow and cumbersome to be effective. Of the over nine hundred estimated engagements with Indians between 1865 and 1890, only a few called together masses of three or four thousand men. Regiments of infantry, as a result, rarely assembled, but scattered to the western frontier posts. Companies of Shafter's Twenty-fourth dispersed to several posts along the Rio Grande frontier, including, in 1870, Forts Bliss, Clark, Davis, Duncan, McKavett, Quitman, and Stockton.[29]

Army posts in the West remained small, scattered, and usually unfortified. Often constructed in a large rectangular pattern, they included barracks and officers' quarters facing each other across a parade ground in the center. Small and crowded buildings of logs, boards, or adobe predominated. As a rule, the commanding officer of a post enjoyed a comparatively spacious home, while most other officers had small houses. Lieutenants' quarters consisted of two or three rooms. Conditions within the quarters and barracks were often primitive and cheerless. Low ceilings and high double bunks, which consisted of a rough

[28] Russell F. Weigley, *The History of the United States Army*, p. 267; Robert M. Utley, *Frontier Regulars: The United States Army and the Indian, 1866–1890*, pp. 13–14.

[29] Russell F. Weigley, *History of the United States Army*, pp. 267–68; Regimental Returns, Twenty-fourth Infantry, Aug., 1870, Roll 245, MC665, NA.

board bottom and a mattress filled with hay, impeded the circulation of fresh air. Rain falling on leaky roofs of adobe quarters created dirty conditions that could not be repaired until the sun had dried the mud. The buildings had no bathrooms, no running water, no central heat, no plumbing. Candles or oil lamps provided the lighting.

The infantry in these scattered outposts did little fighting. Instead, it provided escort duty of various kinds, guarded important river crossings, protected the mails and telegraph lines, and performed routine fatigue duty that included policing the grounds, hauling water, carrying garbage, gathering fuel, and repairing the post. For officers and men of the Twenty-fourth Infantry stationed at some of the more remote outposts on the Texas frontier, life was dull and monotonous. In addition to the usual fatigue duties the men drilled, practiced target firing, and cared for weapons and horses.

For diversion the troops often had a band, a library, a chapel, and a school, usually presided over by the chaplain. But the chief off-duty pastimes included gambling, drinking, and sampling the pleasures of the towns and villages near the military reservations. More wholesome forms of amusement occurred in the celebration of various annual holidays, with Independence Day bringing the most excitement. On such occasions baseball games, wrestling matches, shooting contests, and footraces formed part of the festivities.[30]

Arrival of the paymaster always initiated excitement. Although the troops were to be paid every two months, at remote posts where black soldiers labored generally three or four months passed between paydays. For the last few weeks preceding the paymaster's arrival at the post, little money changed hands. During the few days following his departure, scenes of roaring debauchery broke the otherwise monotonous post life. Men who had endured a prolonged spell of enforced abstinence from whiskey at once made up for lost time by either congregating in the post sutler's store or quietly going off by themselves. "Gambling broke loose in every corner" of the post, either "quiet games of poker" or a homemade layout (a betting device) spread by some fellow smoother and slicker than the rest. "Others either got an order on the commissary and gorged" themselves on officers' stores or else laid in a supply of delicacies from the post trader. "Now and then some

[30]Post Medical Reports, Fort Davis, May, 1873; June, 1875, and June, 1876, Books No. 7-9-12, ORD, AGO, NA; Don Rickey, Jr., *Forty Miles a Day on Beans and Hay: The Enlisted Soldier Fighting the Indian Wars*, pp. 186–89; Arlen L. Fowler, *The Black Infantry in the West, 1869–1891*, pp. 92–139; Erwin N. Thompson, "The Negro Soldier on the Frontier: A Fort Davis Case Study," *Journal of the West* (April, 1968): 225–33.

man saved his money and increased it by trading and lending it, and occasionally one sent his pay home to a relative." As the men squandered their money, they also usually produced a long list of offenses or conduct "to the prejudice of good order and military discipline." As a result, payday nearly always led to a number of garrison courts-martial.[31]

At the end of his leave of absence, William Shafter proceeded to Fort Concho, Texas. Established in 1867, Fort Concho, stood like a prairie sentinel near the junction of the three forks of the Concho River, where it formed the center of a line of posts extending from the Rio Grande at Eagle Pass to the Red River directly north of Jacksboro. Beginning from the south, the garrisoned positions were Forts Duncan, Clark, McKavett, Mason, Concho, Griffin, and Richardson. The three northern posts secured the western line of frontier settlement against Indians who raided from the Texas Panhandle and Indian Territory.

Arriving at Fort Concho on January 7, 1870, Shafter set to work. Assuming command, he pressed his troops, Company F, Twenty-fourth Infantry, and Company E, Ninth Cavalry, into fatigue duty. The energy and restlessness with which he attacked his garrison chores amazed the post surgeon, William Notson. In his report for January, 1870, Notson wrote that Shafter "has displayed an abundance of energy, devoting the first days of his arrival to thoroughly policing the post . . . [and] seeing a large corral . . . in the process of construction." The next month Notson reported that "work upon the guard house and corral is progressing with unprecedented rapidity, and will be completed early in [March]."[32]

Shafter faced several other more serious problems. Indians were unusually troublesome during January and February. Both settlers and soldiers almost daily reported small parties of two to five warriors in all directions from the post. In mid-February only a quarter of a mile from the fort one citizen found a dead settler scalped and with five arrowheads in his body. With a view to stationing pickets, sending out scouts, and patrolling the region, Shafter and Ranald Mackenzie, who had been summoned from Fort McKavett to investigate the depredations, made an inspection tour. For five days they surveyed the region north and west of the post. Upon completing the tour, they dispatched

---

[31]McConnell, *Five Years a Cavalryman*, pp. 156–60; Rickey, *Forty Miles a Day*, pp. 168–73.

[32]Post Medical Reports, Fort Concho, Jan. and Feb., 1870, Books No. 401-403-404-407, ORD, AGO, NA.

83082

Fort Concho in the 1870's. *Courtesy Southwest Collection, Texas Tech University, and Fort Concho Museum*

two scouts northward into the colorful breaks of the Colorado River and ordered several parties westward to well-known water holes in the rough, broken country below the wind-swept Llano Estacado. After Mackenzie's departure, Shafter continued the scouting at a feverish pace, usually with small parties of ten to twenty men, through March and early April, when larger groups rode out less frequently. Although few Indians were seen, the activity reduced the number of raids, encouraged the development of a town near the fort, San Angelo, and kept the Indians on the move and away from the settlers.

At the post, however, trouble erupted. Although Shafter allowed the soldiers a good deal of license in their festivities, including music, dancing, and various exhibitions in their quarters once or twice a week, a general condition of discomfort and uneasiness developed. In February Shafter arrested two officers for brawling and threatened others with confinement. Among the enlisted men, the difficulties related to overcrowding in the barracks, but there was also some misunderstanding concerning duties and orders. During times of considerable scouting activity, conditions improved as many men were absent from the fort, but when scouting dropped off in May, disharmony increased again.[33]

In spite of the bickering, Shafter retained his energy and industry and directed several post improvements. The surgeon reported in April that Shafter's "attention to the post police, in its details, is shown in the improved cleanliness of the parade and surrounding grounds." The troops laid out and filled with gravel the walks and drainage between officers' quarters and barracks; converted an old shed, once used for adjutant and quartermaster officers but more recently abandoned, into a clean and neat cottage building; and gave regular attention to the removal of the garbage and police debris. Greater precision in the delivery of water to the fort improved sanitary conditions. In May and June, however, as rumors of a change is command increased, less and less work occurred on Shafter's other projects; some he never completed.[34]

The rumors of a change in command proved true. Ordered by Joseph J. Reynolds, commander of the Department of Texas, to Fort McKavett, Lt. Col. Shafter rode out of the Concho River country on June 10, 1870. As he left, Shafter could look back upon three outstanding years on the Rio Grande frontier. With Mackenzie, he had turned the Forty-first and Twenty-fourth infantries, which had the lowest desertion rate of any regiments of infantry, into two of the finest commands in the army. He had participated in restoring order temporarily to the lower Rio Grande border, had helped to relieve a tense situation in Jefferson, and more than any other commander had improved the living conditions at Fort Concho. Although he had not always enjoyed the love of his troops, he had consistently displayed his energy and efficiency in leading men.[35]

Although probably unaware of it on that hot June afternoon, Shafter would receive through his command at Fort McKavett his first important opportunity to lead black troops in pursuit of Indians. He was about to embark on a new phase in his frontier military career.

[33]Ibid., Feb., March, and May, 1870.

[34]Ibid., April, 1870.

[35]Regimental Returns, Twenty-fourth Infantry, May–June, 1870, Roll 245, MC665, NA; Fowler, *The Black Infantry in the West*, pp. 92–139; Leckie, *The Buffalo Soldier*, pp. 8–13.

CHAPTER FIVE

With Black Troops in Texas

I N MANY INSTANCES, such as the settlement of Virginia, the Old Northwest, and the Dakotas, armed forces supported and carried forward the westward extension of American civilization. In some instances the military force exercised its power by force of arms; in others, its mere presence served as a stabilizing influence to prevent Indian outbreaks. In the settlement of West Texas, including the Trans-Pecos region, for more than a decade it exerted a dominant role. This state of affairs was due to several causes, chiefly the character of the native Americans, the Comanche and Kiowa tribes of the Texas Plains, the Lipan and Mescalero Apache nations of both Mexico and the United States, and the Kickapoos. These Indians presented special problems to Anglo settlement of the Southern Plains and the Rio Grande border area and to the United States Army.

The Comanche and Kiowa were typical Plains Indians. Well-armed and mounted on horseback, they were powerful warriors who, according to one scholar, were "far better equipped for successful warfare in their country than" the soldiers who came against them.[1] The southern Great Plains was their revered homeland, and they meant to defend it against American intrusion.

Although they show some Plains influence, the Lipan and Mescalero were people of the mountains equally at home in the desert. The Mescaleros roamed the mountains of Texas and Mexico, but they moved about freely, wintering on the Rio Grande or farther south and ranging to the buffalo plains in the summer. The Lipans ranged over northern Mexico below the Rio Grande and raided both Mexico and Texas ranches for food and horses.

[1] Walter Prescott Webb, *The Great Plains*, pp. 67–68.

The Kickapoos, originally living south of the Great Lakes, were newcomers to the Southwest. In 1839 one band had fled to Mexico. During the Civil War at least two other discontented groups joined the refugees where Mexican officials gave them land in return for a pledge to defend the northern frontier. The Kickapoos came to rely for their livelihood on Texas plunder.

Indian resistance to western settlement had often been a problem for pioneers, but in Texas about 1870 it became a serious difficulty. Running short of vacant hunting land, Indians turned increasingly to raiding farms and ranches along the frontier. At the same time pressure from Eastern groups forced the federal government to adopt more peaceful practices in its relations with Indians.[2]

In response to the Eastern pressure, Pres. Ulysses S. Grant in 1869 inaugurated a policy designed to divorce the War Department from Indian activities. Sometimes called the Quaker peace policy, it provided that churchmen serve as Indian agents, that military personnel stay away from reservations, and that officials follow a humanitarian approach to Indian relations.

Although well meant, these and other provisions failed to secure peace. Instead, Comanche and Kiowa reservations from the first became sanctuaries for warriors who disliked the idle, monotonous reservation life. Placed in 1867 on a reserve in what is today southwest Oklahoma, they raided into West Texas with increasing success in the months after adoption of Grant's peace policy. After a raid they would return to the sanctuary of the reservation.[3]

Consequently, when he arrived at Fort McKavett in June, 1870, Lt. Col. William R. Shafter faced an unenviable dilemma. He had to lead scouts and other expeditions against raiders who could flee to regions prohibited to the United States Army. In addition, he had to chase cattle rustlers, horse thieves, and border ruffians from both sides of the Rio Grande. Carried out in hot, semi-arid regions of Texas, the responsibilities involved fierce, exhausting work.

Because Colonel Mackenzie had left on extended leave in April, Shafter commanded both the regiment and the post. Fort McKavett,

[2] Ernest Wallace and E. Adamson Hoebel, *Comanches: Lords of the South Plains*, pp. 13–91; Hugh D. Corwin, *The Kiowa Indians: Their History and Life Stories*, p. 67; Walter Prescott Webb, *The Great Plains*, pp. 67–68; C. L. Sonnichsen, *The Mescalero Apaches*, pp. 3–5; Jack D. Forbes, *Apaches, Navaho, and Spaniard*, p. xvii; Arrell M. Gibson, *The Kickapoos: Lords of the Middle Border*, pp. 3–10; Ernest Wallace, *Ranald S. Mackenzie on the Texas Frontier*, pp. 93–95.

[3] Robert W. Utley, *Frontier Regulars: The United States Army and the Indian, 1866–1891*, pp. 188–214.

located on the San Saba River in modern-day Menard County, 180 miles northwest of San Antonio, was part of the chain of garrisons stretching from the Rio Grande to the Red River designed to secure the westward advancing frontier.[4]

Two months after arriving at Fort McKavett, Shafter directed his first important military campaign in West Texas. Having received word of horse thieves camping on the southern reaches of the plains, he determined to give chase. Hurriedly plans, including the drafting of a last will and testament, took shape. Realizing the seriousness of any expedition into the isolated region, Shafter arranged with his brother John, who had returned with Shafter to Texas and was farming nearby, for the care of his little family.[5]

Preparations completed, the Pecos River campaign began. Early on August 22, a humid dog-day morning, Shafter with four officers and 128 enlisted men of the Ninth Cavalry, two lieutenants of the Twenty-fourth Infantry, and two surgeons, left the fort. Fully armed and equipped, each man carried two canteens, two hundred rounds of ammunition, a poncho and blanket, and extra horseshoes and nails. Twenty pack mules and two escort wagons carried forty days' rations of flour, salt, and sugar and half days' rations (that is, twenty days worth) of coffee and bacon.[6]

After moving nearly due south to the South Llano River, the expedition turned west and headed toward Beaver Lake near modern-day Juno, where it was to meet a detachment of troops, including guides, with a wagonload of corn from Fort Clark. Pushing westward, the command, misreading a compass, veered too far south and marched through a canyon that led to Devil's River, twelve miles below Camp Hudson. From here, to correct its error, the expedition proceeded northward along the Fort Hudson road, finally reaching the rendezvous several days late.

Because the detachment from Fort Clark had already left Beaver Lake, apparently heading back to its post, Shafter, believing he needed the guides, rushed off messengers with orders for the party to return.

[4] Wallace, *Ranald S. Mackenzie*, pp. 25–28.

[5] Shafter to his wife, Aug. 22, 1870, William R. Shafter Papers, Stanford University Library, Stanford, Calif., photocopy in Southwest Collection, Texas Tech University, Lubbock (hereafter Shafter Papers); U.S. Dept. of War, Returns from United States Military Posts, 1800–1916, Fort McKavett, Aug., 1870, Roll 689, Microcopy No. 617, National Archives (hereafter Post Returns, MC617, NA).

[6] Special Orders No. 125, Post Records, Fort McKavett, Aug. 18, 1870, RG 393, NA, in Jerry Sullivan, ed., "Lieutenant Colonel W. R. Shafter's Pecos River Expedition of 1870," *West Texas Historical Association Year Book* 47 (1971): 146–52; Post Returns, Fort McKavett, Aug., 1870, Roll 689, MC617, NA.

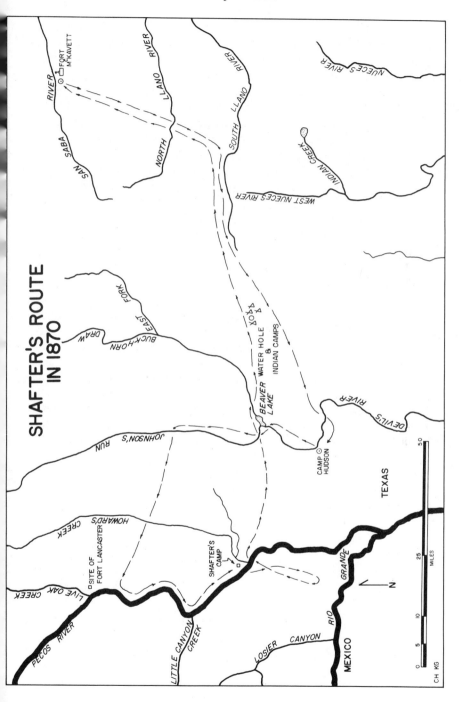

SHAFTER'S ROUTE
IN 1870

The messengers with the detachment rejoined Shafter, and four days later, with the expedition fully organized, he struck for the Pecos. He rode north and then west to reach the river near the site of Fort Lancaster. He then headed down the river.

To expedite his operations in the largely unexplored country, Shafter divided his command. Leaving most of it at the Pecos about thirty miles below modern-day Sheffield, he and Capt. Edward M. Heyl with fifteen men crossed to the west bank, climbed onto the tablelands, and marched due south for twenty miles, keeping all the time within four miles of the stream. Using his field glasses to examine each ravine, Shafter discovered no indications of Indians or other thieves. He then left the Pecos to ride southwestward for six miles to Painted Rock Arroyo, named for a nearby rock painted with hieroglyphics, only ten miles from the Rio Grande, before returning to the main camp.

For more than a week afterward the command continued its work. Although a few patrols probed beyond the Pecos, the expedition concentrated its efforts in the region to the east, where in February Capt. John N. Bacon had sighted some Apaches. No Indians were seen. Neither were there trails or other indications of Indians or cattle rustlers having passed through the country since Bacon's scout. Eight ponies, which Shafter believed had been near the Pecos for six months, were caught.

Unable to locate either thieves or recent signs of them, Shafter on September 18 decided to return to Fort McKavett. Sending the detachment from Fort Clark to its post, he ordered his troops into their saddles. On the return march, two days later, his scouts reported the location of several large trails running in a north-south direction and from two to six months old about thirty-five miles west of the headwaters of the North and South Llano and the San Saba rivers. While examining them, the scouts discovered some abandoned Indian villages. One had been deserted only three or four months earlier and had contained as many as 150 Indians.

One mile southwest of this site, two men found a large, permanent pond of water about two hundred yards long and deep enough to swim horses. For years the army had heard reports of a water pond in the area, but its location had been known only to Indians. Since there were as yet no cattle in the vicinity, neither the cattlemen nor the army frequented the region. As Shafter indicated in his report, the pond was a convenient and secure rendezvous for raiders to strike at ranches and settlements near the headwaters of the Nueces River.[7]

[7]The details of the expedition are found in Shafter to H. Clay Wood, Asst. Adj.

The scout was significant. Having marched 473 miles in thirty-five days, it showed that no Indians were present in the vicinity of the Pecos and the headwaters of the Llano rivers. Eight horses had been captured. A strategic and favorite camping place had been located, and no longer would Indians be able to use the water hole as a safe rendezvous. Moreover, in the psychological warfare that figured vitally in Indian fighting, the expedition demonstrated that black troops could campaign successfully in an area the Indians previously had thought inaccessible to the army.

Anxious to follow up the expedition but with his troops needing rest, Shafter waited until November 1 to dispatch another unit. For two months afterwards several scouts probed westward.[8] Cold weather in January, 1871, slowed explorations, and early in February reconnaissance activity halted when Shafter heard rumors of a change in command. Colonel Mackenzie had been transferred to the Fourth Cavalry Regiment.

Shafter continued to head the Twenty-fourth Infantry until April, when Col. Abner Doubleday relieved him at Fort McKavett. Doubleday, often given credit for perfecting the popular sport of baseball, was a West Point graduate from New York who had served with distinction during the Civil War. After the war he had been assigned to the Thirty-fifth Infantry, but since the reorganization of the army in 1869 he had been unassigned. When Mackenzie left, Doubleday became the Twenty-fourth Infantry's commanding officer.[9]

At the end of April, Shafter, having been ordered to a new post, left for Fort Davis, Texas, in the Trans-Pecos country. Fort Davis, named for Jefferson Davis, who was secretary of war when it was established in 1854, was located near Limpia Creek in Presidio County and stood about 475 miles northwest of San Antonio and 220 miles southeast of El Paso. The site had been selected because of its location on the main road connecting San Antonio and El Paso, its healthy climate, its defensibility, and its proximity both to the favorite lands of the Mescalero Apaches and to the Comanche war trail to Mexico.

Assuming command at Fort Davis in May, 1871, Shafter set to work. He directed repairs on the roofs of a storeroom and the post hospital

Gen., Dept. of Texas, Oct. 10, 1870, Post Records, Fort McKavett, RG393, NA, in Sullivan, ed., "Shafter's Pecos River Expedition," pp. 140–52; Shafter to his wife, Aug. 22, 1870, Shafter Papers; Post Returns, Fort McKavett, Aug.–Oct., 1870, Roll 689, MC617, NA.

[8] Post Returns, Fort McKavett, Nov., 1870–Feb., 1871, Roll 689, MC617, NA.

[9] Paul H. Carlson, "Baseball's Abner Doubleday on the Texas Frontier," *Military History of Texas and the Southwest* 12, no. 4 (Spring, 1976): 236, 239.

Fort Davis in the 1880's. It was among the largest military installations in the West at the time. *Courtesy National Park Service, Fort Davis National Historic Site*

and clapped several disorderly troops in the guardhouse. In less than twenty days the repairs on the storeroom were completed, those on the hospital were in progress, and order among the troops had been restored. He then turned to such duties as the construction of stables and corrals for the horses and other responsibilities.[10]

One of the responsibilities included guarding stagecoach lines. Duty as station guards was generally quiet work but appreciated because it afforded an escape from the tedium of garrison life. At the end of such a tour of duty men returned to the post on an inbound stage. But the Negro troops were often kept off the stages and forced to walk back to the post.

Shafter would not tolerate the prejudice. When the El Paso Mail

[10]Post Returns, Fort Davis, May–June, 1871, Roll 297, MC617, NA.

Lines station keeper at Leon Hole, about eight miles west of Fort Stockton, refused to provide food and shelter for the guards, Shafter warned company officers against the discrimination. When the black guards were put off the stage, he wrote, they were obliged to walk to Fort Stockton and along the way to obtain their rations "by their wits." He demanded that his troops should "be fed by the company or allowed facilities at the stations for cooking their own rations." He would "be glad to furnish mail escorts as long as they wanted," he concluded, "but they must be properly treated."[11] Apparently his letter got results, for the records show no further complaints against the stage company.

Sometimes guard duty proved dangerous. On the evening of June 17, fifteen Comanches attacked a station at Barrilla Springs between Forts Stockton and Davis and ran off some forty-three horses and mules. Although no one was killed in the exchange of gunfire during the raid, the theft led to a torturous expedition in pursuit of the thieves.

Shafter led the pursuit. As soon as news of the raid reached him at Fort Davis on June 18, he dispatched Lt. Isaiah McDonald of the Ninth Cavalry and ten enlisted men with forty mules to replace those captured. A few hours later, he mounted all his available cavalry and with surgeon David Weissel set out for Barrilla Springs, where two days later Capt. Michael Cooney and a detachment of black troops from Fort Stockton joined him. The combined command, totaling eighty-six officers, guides, and enlisted men, set out on the trail. They would be gone three weeks.[12]

From Barrilla Springs, Shafter followed the trail to Toyah Creek and thence northeast to within five miles of the Pecos River. On June 23 he crossed the river and the next morning took the trail northeastward to the virtually unknown White Sands region (Monahans Sand Hills), reaching a water hole in the Sand Hills late that evening. Shafter reported that the Sand Hills, consisting of a range of low hills of very white sand without vegetation, extended northwest and southeast for about twenty-five miles and were almost impassable except for horses.

---

[11]Shafter to F. C. Taylor, Agt., El Paso Mail Lines, ca. Jan. 4, 1872, U.S. Dept. of War, Records of United States Army Commands, Letters Sent, Fort Davis, Record Group 98, National Archives (hereafter USAC, RG98, NA). Also see Arlen L. Fowler, *The Black Infantry in the West, 1869–1891*, pp. 25–26.

[12]Shafter to H. Clay Wood, Asst. Adj. Gen., Dept. of Texas, July 15, 1871, USAC, RG98; NA; Post Returns, Fort Davis, June–July, 1871, Roll 297, MC617, NA; U.S. Dept. of War, Post Medical Reports, Fort Davis, June–July, 1871, Books No. 7-9-12, Old Records Division, Adjutant General's Office, National Archives (hereafter Post Medical Reports, ORD, AGO, NA). Also see J. Evetts Haley, *Fort Concho and the Texas Frontier*, pp. 163–67.

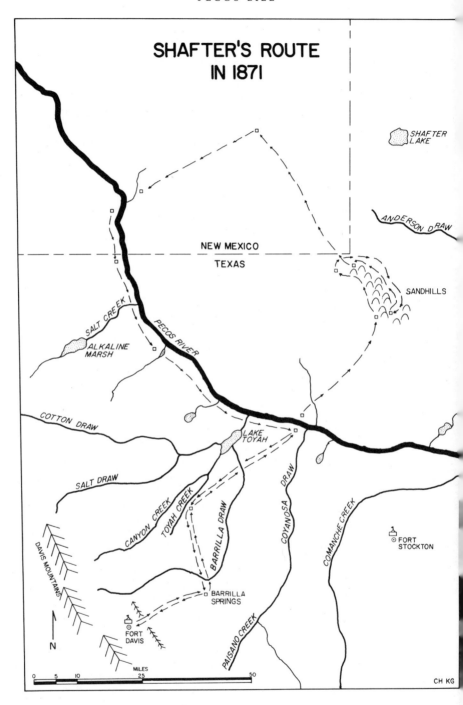

SHAFTER'S ROUTE
IN 1871

He noted that double teams would be required to draw even lightly loaded wagons through the hills, but he also indicated that water could be found by digging from two to four feet in depressions at the bases of the hills. At the water hole he discovered a three-day-old camp of the Comanches.

On the twenty-fifth, Shafter started again. He proceeded northwestward, made a dry camp that evening, and on the twenty-sixth, west of the hills, found fresh tracks left by shod mules, presumably the animals stolen at Barrilla Springs. Following the tracks, he skirted the northern edge of the Sand Hills where the trail headed east. But out of water and knowing that there was no water in that direction closer than the streams emptying into the Colorado and Concho rivers, he turned back toward his camp of the twenty-fourth near the southern edge of the hills. When they reined in to water holes near the old camp, the thirsty and trail-weary troops had been without water for almost two days. They remained here the next day to rest and to graze their horses.

At sundown on June 28 Shafter moved out. Taking his old trail, he marched northward before turning to the northwest. He rode all night. At daybreak, near the future site of Kermit, he rested his command for an hour and then continued until about noon when he arrived a second time at the east-west trail. He discovered that the mules had mysteriously passed again over the trail, this time headed west.

Undaunted, Shafter turned his jaded horses due west. Following the trail, he skirted the Sand Hills on his left, and about four in the afternoon he located a deserted village north of modern-day Wink that, judging from the number of huts, had housed about two hundred Indians. Although his command had already covered forty miles since sundown on the previous day, he was determined to catch the fleeing Indians. After resting until eleven that evening, he ordered his troops into their saddles and followed the trail northwestward into New Mexico. But by daylight on June 30 the mule tracks had disappeared.

Disappointed, Shafter rested his command. About four that afternoon, when on the march again, his scouts spied an Apache camp. A survey of the village revealed a few huts near a herd of horses but no activity. Ordering Lt. William Morgan of the Twenty-fourth Infantry with fifteen men to capture the herd, Shafter charged the camp with the balance of the command. Upon sighting the cavalrymen, the Indians—only three braves were in camp—mounted ponies and fled. After chasing the Indians about four miles through the hills and scattered brush, Shafter realized the futility of pursuit and ordered his troops to rein in and return to the Apache village.

Back in camp Shafter's men had been busy. They had rounded up some ponies and had jumped several Apaches at a second camp about a mile away, but the Indians had escaped. Surveying the results of the activity, Shafter found that his black troops had captured ten horses, five mules, about six months' supply of dried beef, twenty-five or thirty buffalo robes, a large supply of lead, and several flasks of powder. Shafter destroyed the rations and burned the robes and huts.

Turning back on the Apache trail, Shafter moved southwest toward the Pecos. About ten in the morning of July 1, roughly two miles ahead of the column, Shafter and an orderly came upon an old Apache woman riding a slender mule and trying to herd along two broken-down horses. Suspecting that warriors were not far ahead, he turned the woman over to his soldiers, took a detachment of twenty-four picked troops, and went in pursuit. Although he rode at a fast trot until nearly sundown, he failed to overtake the Apaches.

At a small stream about four miles from the Pecos, Shafter set up camp and waited for the main column, which arrived about nine that evening, exhausted from its thirty-two mile ride. The next morning at the Pecos, near modern-day Harroun, New Mexico, Shafter found signs that the party he was following, probably two hundred, having been warned of his presence by the Apaches who had escaped two days earlier, had ascended the river. Taking stock of his own conditions— short rations, jaded horses—and the Indians' movements, he decided to return to Fort Davis, reaching the post on July 9.[13]

The immediate results of the march were salutary. Shafter had discovered and destroyed the abandoned village, two dozen robes, skins, and a large supply of provisions. He had captured about twenty horses and mules and the old woman. The woman informed Shafter that the Comanches and the Lipan and Mescalero Apaches, longtime enemies, had concluded a peace in the Monahans Sand Hills. The lead he found at the Apache camp, stamped with the trademark of a Saint Louis, Missouri, firm, provided important evidence that the Sand Hills was a place of barter for the *comancheros*, traders from New Mexico.

Of greater significance, the long-range results of the march lay in the successful penetration into the Sand Hills of West Texas, where it had generally been believed that soldiers could not operate. The expedition not only had destroyed another Indian sanctuary, but it had brought back geographical knowledge necessary for future operations.

[13]This expedition is described in Shafter to Wood, July 15, 1871, USAC, RG98, NA. See also J. Evetts Haley, *Fort Concho and the Texas Frontier*, pp. 163–67.

Shafter believed that even though no major engagements with the Indians were fought, extensive scouting like that in the Sand Hills produced valuable results. "My experience has been that Indians will not stay where they consider themselves liable to attacks," he informed his superiors, "and I believe the best way to rid the country of them . . . is to thoroughly scour the country with cavalry."[14] Because his scout in 1870 to the Pecos and his recent one to the Sand Hills seemed to support his thesis, he applied the technique to the Big Bend region of Texas where, it had been reported, Apaches were camping.

On October 5, 1871, Shafter headed south. Leading thirty-nine men of the Ninth Cavalry, thirty men of the Twenty-fifth Infantry (part of which was stationed at Fort Davis), and several officers, he rode to the Chisos Mountains and beyond to the Rio Grande. He struck the river below San Vincente, a village on the Mexican side of the river about twenty-five miles above its great bend. Here, near the lower end of Mariscal Canyon, he reported that because the river banks were several hundred feet high, it was impossible to get down to the water with animals. Shafter and four others succeeded in reaching the water by climbing down a ravine.

Because signs indicated that Indians were almost constantly in the Big Bend, Shafter and the black troops scoured the country, crossing and recrossing trails, noting important water holes and marking the sites of old Indian camps. At San Vincente they discovered an important Apache crossing on the river. They found an abandoned Indian encampment southwest of Peña Blanca and noted signs of many recent camps. The grass for grazing horses or other livestock along their lines of march was excellent.[15]

When it returned to Fort Davis on November 5, the expedition had covered five hundred miles. Although it had seen no Indians, it had found abundant evidence that Apaches used the Big Bend as a sanctuary. Perhaps more importantly, it added to the geographical knowledge of the Chihuahuan deserts and Big Bend mountains. The information it gained about the territory and its resources enabled the army later to maneuver more confidently in the region. In addition, it smoothed the way for later settlement.[16]

No sooner had Shafter returned from the Big Bend than he found another problem. One of his black troopers, after getting drunk near

[14]Shafter to Wood, Feb. 12, 1872, USAC, RG98, NA.
[15]Shafter to Wood, Feb. 1, 1872, USAC, RG98, NA.
[16]Ibid.; Post Returns, Fort Davis, Oct., 1871, Roll 297, MC617, NA; Post Medical Reports, Fort Davis, Oct.–Nov., 1871, Books No. 7-9-12, ORD, AGO, NA.

Fort Davis, had struck a civilian. When Henry Tinkhouse, sheriff of Presidio County, attempted to serve a civil process on the soldier, Shafter intervened. He and Tinkhouse got into a bitter verbal fight over who in this affair possessed the higher authority. The argument concluded only when Shafter had the sheriff thrown off the post. Tinkhouse swore that he would kill Shafter the next time they met. To protect himself and his soldiers from the sheriff, Shafter ordered that Tinkhouse was not to be allowed on the post for any reason. The same day, November 6, he wrote twice to S. R. Miller, justice of the peace for Presidio County, stating that, although he was required by the articles of war to deliver to civil authorities upon proper demand any person belonging to his command charged with a crime, Miller in this instance would have to send another constable. He indicated that Tinkhouse had not been politic in performing his duties. Because of Shafter's timely intercession, the trooper was never arrested. Miller did not send another official.[17]

Shortly afterward Shafter got results from his Big Bend campaign. An Apache chief who frequented the Big Bend and who had gone to Presidio del Norte (Ojinaga, Mexico) to negotiate with the Mexican authorities for release of some children of his band held captive, sent word to Fort Davis that he wished to surrender. Shafter sent Lt. Isaiah McDonald to receive his surrender. But perhaps because the residents there, who gained their living by supplying United States army posts, did not welcome complete harmony between Indians and Americans, the *alcalde* of Presidio del Norte warned the chief that his departure would prejudice release of the children. Whatever the reason, McDonald returned to Fort Davis empty-handed. Shafter agreed with his lieutenant that "the local authorities at Del Norte do not want [the Apache] to make or keep peace with the United States."[18]

Having scouted the Big Bend on the theory that scouring the region was the best way to "rid the country" of Indians, Shafter led his black troops on another expedition in pursuit of Indians. This time he rode into the mountains northwest of his post. Taking nineteen enlisted men and three officers, he marched on December 28 into the heart of the Davis Mountains, hoping to overtake a small band who had been committing depredations in the vicinity. After riding only two days,

[17]Shafter to S. R. Miller, Justice of the Peace, Presidio County, Nov. 6, 1871, USAC, RG98, NA.

[18]Shafter to Lt. Isaiah H. McDonald, Ninth Cavalry, Dec. 8, 1871, copy with Shafter to Wood, Jan. 4, 1872, USAC, RG98, NA.

however, bad weather and perhaps a desire to be at the post for a New Year's Eve celebration caused him to turn back.[19]

Early in 1872 Shafter laid plans to continue his scouting of isolated areas. If he received proper authority from his superiors, he intended to spend a month in the spring searching the Guadalupe Mountains and another two months exploring the long stretch of broken country along the Rio Grande west of the Pecos.[20] Through March and April, a number of small patrols combed the regions, but Shafter was ordered back to Fort McKavett before he could lead the extended expedition. To the east Ranald S. Mackenzie was organizing an offensive against hostile Indians believed to be on the Llano Estacado, and he wanted his former lieutenant colonel and the black troops to form one arm of the campaign.[21]

Shafter returned on June 12, 1872, to Fort McKavett. From there, barely a week later, with three companies of the Twenty-fourth Infantry including five officers and 177 enlisted men and five six-mule wagons, he left to join Mackenzie on July 1 along the Freshwater Fork of the Brazos.[22] Rain, swollen streams, and general bad weather slowed his march. He encountered further delay at Fort Concho, where he stopped to obtain additional wagons, three ambulances, and a surgeon. On July 6, he reached the rendezvous, but too late to aid in trapping a band of Comanches in Blanco Canyon from which the waters of the Freshwater Fork gushed.[23]

Three days later, when he left camp for the Palo Duro, a deep canyon cut into the High Plains by the Prairie Dog Town Fork (Main Fork) of the Red River, Mackenzie instructed Shafter to lead his black troops on a short scout in the vicinity of the headwaters of the Salt Fork (Main Fork) of the Brazos. With difficulty Shafter carried out the orders. Heavy rains during the march slowed the command, but it reached its destination before returning to the supply camp in Blanco Canyon on July 21.[24]

[19]Shafter to Wood, Feb. 12, 1872, USAC RG98, NA; Post Returns, Fort Davis, Dec., 1871, Roll 297 MC617, NA.

[20]Ibid.

[21]Special Orders No. 102, Dept. of Texas, May 31, 1872, Shafter Papers; Post Returns, Fort McKavett, June, 1872, Roll 689, MC617, NA.

[22]Special Orders No. 102, Dept. of Texas, May 31, 1872, Shafter Papers; Post Returns, Fort McKavett, June, 1872, Roll 689, MC617, NA.

[23]Brig. Gen. C. C. Augur, Commanding Dept. of Texas, to Shafter, June 12, 1872, Shafter Papers; Ranald S. Mackenzie to Wood, July 6, 1872, in Ernest Wallace, ed., *Ranald S. Mackenzie's Official Correspondence Relating to Texas, 1871–1873*, p. 101.

[24]Shafter, Report of Scout, July 22, 1872, and Wentz C. Miller, Report of Scout, Sept. 2, 1872, in Wallace, ed., *Mackenzie's Correspondence, 1871–1873*, pp. 120–23.

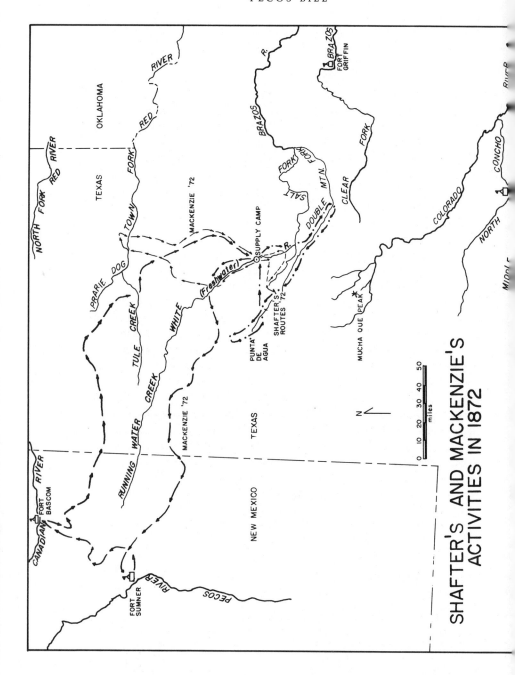

SHAFTER'S AND MACKENZIE'S
ACTIVITIES IN 1872

Ranald Mackenzie. *Courtesy Southwest Collection, Texas Tech University*

One week after Shafter's return, Mackenzie, who had arrived back at the supply camp on July 19, left again. Taking along sixty-three men of the Twenty-fourth and five companies of cavalry, he departed on July 28 on a daring venture across the Llano Estacado that took him to Fort Sumner, New Mexico, and beyond. He mapped the region, marking water holes and fuel supplies. Returning by way of the Red River, Mackenzie noted that there was good water and grass along both routes.[25] Shafter meanwhile remained to guard the camp. For a month his men probed the Caprock north and south of the rendezvous.

After returning on September 2 from New Mexico, Mackenzie laid plans for yet another expedition north to the Red River. When he left he again took men of Shafter's regiment. The black troops rode with six companies of the Fourth Cavalry, two surgeons, and nine Tonkawa scouts, nearly three hundred men in all. The bluecoats proceeded north, splashed across the Prairie Dog Town Fork of the Red River, and rode to the Salt Fork at a point in today's Donley County. On September 29, they moved northward to McClellan Creek and followed it. After marching two miles they discovered the trail of a mule. Guessing it would lead to an Indian camp, they gave chase and soon came upon a large Comanche village containing an estimated 262 lodges on the North Fork of the Red. Mackenzie ordered a charge. After a brisk and at times hand-to-hand fight, the troops took the village, killing about 30 warriors, capturing more than 120 women and children, and driving off the rest. The soldiers, who suffered four casualties, burned the lodges, destroyed the camp equipment, and rounded up several horses and mules that had been stolen the year previous in a bloody attack at Howard's Wells. After the fight, Mackenzie returned to the supply camp.[26]

Upon his return, Mackenzie broke camp and sent his men to their respective posts. As they rode southward, Shafter and his black troops could point with pride to several important consequences of the recent campaign. They had aided in sweeping the northern rim of the Llano Estacado clear of Indians for a time, mapped the region westward to Fort Sumner, noted sources of water, explored thoroughly the Double Mountain Fork of the Brazos River, and gained valuable knowledge needed for further operations on the southern High Plains. Their recent operations had scattered the Indians.[27]

Results of the Mackenzie-Shafter expedition changed for a time military operations in Texas. Driven from their camps along the canyons and ravines that cut sharply into the Llano Estacado, the Indians returned to their reservations or moved farther west into New Mexico. Consequently, the attention of Texas military leaders turned to the Rio Grande border between Laredo and Presidio. For many years the area, called the Upper Rio Grande Border Region, had been raided by Kickapoos, Lipan and Mescalero Apaches, other Indians, and cattle

[25]Mackenzie to Wood, Sept. 19, 1872, ibid., pp. 134–35.
[26]Mackenzie to Wood, Oct. 12, 1872, ibid., pp. 141–45.
[27]Wallace, *Ranald S. Mackenzie*, pp. 77–89.

rustlers who used Mexico as a base for operations against Texas frontier settlements, for a refuge from pursuit, and for a market for their plunder. The Kickapoos were especially troublesome. They ravaged the country from Del Rio and Laredo northward as far as Uvalde and almost to San Antonio. Shafter and many of the black troops now headed for Fort Duncan on the Rio Grande.

When he arrived at Fort Duncan in December, 1872, Shafter found a deteriorating situation. Indian raids and cattle rustling were increasing in both number and severity. Citizens of the vicinity complained and demanded military protection. Although he could do little without proper authority, the impatient but sedulous officer in January directed several important scouts. His troops spent two weeks searching the Rio Grande for Indians and thieves. When they sighted neither Indians nor recent signs of them, Shafter kept his troops home through the remainder of the cold winter.[28]

In the spring of 1873 military operations increased. Gen. William T. Sherman, commanding the United States Army, wrote Brig. Gen. Christopher C. Augur, a veteran Indian campaigner who commanded the Department of Texas, that President Grant wanted Mackenzie with his Fourth Cavalry to join Shafter in the Upper Rio Grande Border Region.[29] During the same month General Augur visited the region, stopping at Fort Duncan on February 25 and 26. Less than fifty days later, William Worth Belknap, the secretary of war, and Lt. Gen. Philip Sheridan, commander of the Division of the Missouri, spent two days at Duncan. All important officials in the chain of command—Augur, Sheridan, Sherman, Belknap, and Grant—wanted a swift end to the Indian depredations. By the end of April, Mackenzie was at Fort Clark laying plans with Shafter for a campaign against the Kickapoos, an expedition designed to curb their border crossings.[30]

Three weeks later the celebrated raid took place. On the night of May 17, with six companies of the Fourth Cavalry and thirty-four Indian scouts, Mackenzie crossed the Rio Grande, marched all night at a quick pace, and about seven the following morning reached three camps of the Kickapoo and Lipan at Remolino near the head of the San Rodrigo River. During the ensuing engagement, Mackenzie's troops burned the lodges of all three villages with their accumulated property, killed nineteen Indians, and captured forty women and children.

[28] Post Returns, Fort Duncan, Dec., 1872, Roll 336, MC617, NA.

[29] Sherman to Augur, Feb. 5, 1873, in Wallace, ed., *Mackenzie's Correspondence, 1871–1873*, pp. 161–62.

[30] Post Returns, Fort Duncan, April, 1873, Roll 336, MC617, NA; Wallace, *Ranald S. Mackenzie*, pp. 104–107.

In addition, they took Costilietos, a principal Lipan chief, prisoner. After several hours' rest, the command returned, marching all through what Lt. Robert Goldthwaite Carter called "a long, long night" of terror.[31]

Although he did not cross into Mexico with Mackenzie, Shafter performed valuable service for the expedition. He aided Mackenzie in preparing the troops for the raid and provided important information on the Mexican population, the location of villages, and the whereabouts of Mexican troops. Mackenzie stated that he was under great obligation to Shafter for his cordial cooperation and active support through the campaign.[32]

The Mackenzie raid aroused anger and resentment among Mexican citizens. The Mexican government was also excited but did not wish to make the affair an international issue. In the United States some observers reacted favorably, but many people charged the United States with trying to precipitate another war with Mexico. Most Texans were pleased. Significantly, the number of border depredations dropped.[33]

The border raids, however, did not stop. Some of the Kickapoos and Lipans planned a retaliatory attack. In preparation for such an attack Shafter established scouting outposts up and down the river. Upriver about twenty-five miles from the post he established Camp Shafter. About thirty miles downstream, he located a camp at an important river crossing. The retaliatory raid never developed. Border crossings continued, but their number and severity diminished enough that Shafter needed to send fewer and fewer scouting parties on patrol. In July, satisfied that the border was quiet, he took a seven-day leave to visit San Antonio.[34]

Although the summer passed quietly, in the fall border violations again increased. Colonel Doubleday, seriously ill, had returned to New York in midsummer. In response to the renewed outbreaks, Shafter, who had assumed command of his regiment, ordered two large scouting parties out of Fort Duncan. One searched the region along the Rio

---

[31]Post Medical Reports, Fort Duncan, May, 1873, Books No. 86-87, ORD, AGO, NA; Robert Goldthwaite Carter, *The Mackenzie Raid into Mexico*, pp. 17–50.

[32]General Orders No. 6, Dept. of Texas, June 2, 1873, Shafter Papers.

[33]Wallace, *Ranald S. Mackenzie*, pp. 105–107; Ernest Wallace and Adrian S. Anderson, "R. S. Mackenzie and the Kickapoos: The Raid into Mexico in 1873," *Arizona and the West* 7 (Summer, 1965): 105–26.

[34]Shafter to Mackenzie, May 21, 1873, and May 26, 1873, in Wallace, ed., *Mackenzie's Correspondence, 1871–1873*, pp. 177–78, 182–83; Post Returns, Fort Duncan, June, 1873, Roll 336, MC617, NA; Regimental Returns, Twenty-fourth Infantry, May, 1873, Roll 246, MC665, NA.

Grande between Fort Duncan and Camp Shafter. It discovered no thieves and returned a week later. The second left shortly afterward with orders to intercept and capture Pedro Cespide, governor of Coahuila, who, private citizens reported, had crossed the Rio Grande in the vicinity of Camp Shafter with an armed force. It returned in a few days without finding signs of Cespide.

During the winter Shafter continued the heavy scouting. In February, 1874, no less than ten patrols left Fort Duncan, and he sent others from Forts Clark and McIntosh. In the spring, he reduced the activity only slightly. Before Indian raids could be stopped, however, Shafter left Texas, and, with Mackenzie also absent on an extended furlough, the Department of Texas in the summer of 1874 found itself without two of its most energetic field officers.[35]

In early June, the United States War Department ordered Shafter to report to Fort Leavenworth, Kansas, to serve as president of a military equipment board. The five-member board was to consider and report upon the subject of a proper gear and outfit for the infantrymen and to recommend the adoption of equipment best suited for soldiers. Furthermore, it was to determine what materials and supplies were necessary for the efficient outfit of infantry troops in the field and garrison.[36]

William R. Shafter convened the infantry equipment board on July 1, 1874. But the board at first accomplished little, for Fort Leavenworth, lacking adequate equipment and weapons experiment facilities, was not a suitable meeting place. Shafter requested another post to hold the sessions.

While awaiting a response, the board held preliminary sessions to establish how it would conduct its proceedings. During the next two weeks it outlined the order in which it would examine the materials and decided that the meeting room would be prepared with racks and appliances to permit display of all patterns of gear submitted for investigation. All equipment submitted would be studied; none would be discarded prior to a full inquiry. When the gear had been examined, the board would read and scrutinize all pertinent reports from offi-

---

[35]Post Returns, Fort Duncan, Oct., 1873–June, 1874, Roll 336, MC617, NA; U.S. Department of War, Returns from Regular Army Infantry Regiments, June, 1821–Dec., 1916, Twenty-fourth Infantry, Oct., 1873–June, 1874, Roll 246, Microcopy No. 665, National Archives. See also U.S. Congress, House, *Testimony Taken by Committee on Military Affairs in Relation to Texas Border Troubles*, 45th Cong., 2d sess., 1879, H. Exec. Doc. 64, pp. 1–10; Wallace, *Ranald S. Mackenzie*, pp. 105–11.

[36]"Proceedings of the Board of Officers," Special Orders No. 120, AGO, 1874, in *Infantry Equipment 1874, Ordnance Memoranda No. 19,* p. 9.

cers, soldiers, and citizens. Finally, a practical test of each item would be conducted. Shafter's committee would be thorough and systematic.

On July 15 Shafter again complained about insufficient facilities at Fort Leavenworth. This time he requested permission to change the place of meeting to Watervliet Arsenal at West Troy (Watervliet today), New York. Three days later, upon receipt of a favorable reply, he adjourned the board to meet August 19 at Watervliet Arsenal.[37]

En route to the arsenal, Shafter and his family stopped in Galesburg, Michigan. They found his father, who was still active in local politics, in good health and operating the little farm on which he had settled forty-one years earlier. They also visited with Hattie's relatives near Athens before continuing to the East.[38]

Shafter and other members of the infantry equipment board arrived in mid-August in New York. West Troy, located on the west bank of the Hudson River about ten miles upstream from Albany, was a city of about eight thousand inhabitants whose principal business was to serve the arsenal. Watervliet Arsenal, an extensive place in 1874, produced heavy weapons, and it included enough land for its technicians to test the big guns and ammunition manufactured there.

At Watervliet the board met daily except Sunday for three and one-half months. It examined everything an infantry soldier used, including guns, cartridges, cartridge boxes and their linings, canteens, mess kits, shoulder straps, haversacks, belts, and other gear. It inspected hundreds of different pieces of equipment. It read reports, took testimony, and tested samples before deciding which supplies were best.

Shafter on December 2, 1874, adjourned the final meeting. In a detailed and illustrated report to the chief of ordnance, the board submitted its findings. Three of the many recommendations stood out. First, the board argued that the mess kit should be issued by the army, not provided by the soldier himself, and should contain a tin cup, fork, spoon, knife, knifesheath, tin plate, and meat can. It also reasoned that the sword should no longer form part of the gear of company sergeants. In perhaps the most significant recommendation, it suggested that private "foot lockers" should replace the common boxes then being used to store clothes and other personal items in permanent barracks.[39]

More than most members of the board, Shafter had labored diligently. He had missed no sessions, had demanded a thorough examination

[37]Ibid., pp. 7–9; Regimental Returns, Twenty-fourth Infantry, July–Aug., 1874, Roll 336, MC617, NA.
[38]"Proceedings of the Board of Officers," p. 9.
[39]Ibid., pp. 7–49.

of all equipment, and with one member, Capt. May H. Stacy, had remained at Watervliet several days after the others to answer late correspondence and complete last-minute details.[40]

With the board's work finished in December, Shafter went to Poughkeepsie, New York. Having been granted a delay before rejoining the Twenty-fourth Infantry, he and his family inspected Lyndon Hall, a boarding school, as a possible place to enroll his daughter Mary. From Poughkeepsie, he took his family to Washington, D.C., for a vacation before returning by train to Texas.[41]

Back in Texas in February, 1875, Shafter found the military situation changed. With settlers clamoring for Indian lands and demanding that federal officials remove the Indians from open territory on which the Indians hunted, Congressmen from western territories and states, including Texas, were pressed, at the risk of their congressional seats, to support legislation favoring pioneers. The subsequent congressional erosion of Indian legal rights returned responsibility for many Indian affairs to the War Department and led to a partial abandonment of President Grant's peace policy.[42] In response Gen. Philip Sheridan had ordered a major offensive against Indians off their reservations and living in the Texas Panhandle. The campaign had been a military success, and Shafter, as a finale, was to sweep the Llano Estacado clear of holdouts. His expedition resulted in the most thorough exploration of the region to that time.

[40]Ibid.

[41]Shafter to Adjutant General, United States Army, in United States, William R. Shafter, Letters Received, Appointments, Commissions, and Personal Branch, Adjutant General's Office, Record Group 94, National Archives.

[42]Robert M. Utley, *The Indian Frontier of the American West*, pp. 129–55; Thomas C. Leonard, "Red, White, and Army Blue: Empathy and Anger in the American West," in Peter Karsten, ed., *The Military in America: From the Colonial Era to the Present*, pp. 215–16; William H. Leckie and Shirley A. Leckie, *Unlikely Warriors: General Benjamin H. Grierson and His Family*, pp. 164–65.

CHAPTER SIX

Scouting the Llano Estacado

F ROM THE TIME the first Europeans reached the region with Coronado in the sixteenth century until well into the second half of the nineteenth century, people referred to the Great Plains as the "Great American Desert." Contemporary observers applied the description particularly to the treeless and windswept Llano Estacado in the Southern Plains which, it was commonly believed, would be uninhabited for hundreds of years if, indeed, it would ever be suitable for civilization.

The surface of the Llano Estacado, or Staked Plains, in 1875 presented an almost limitless ocean of waving grass, sunshine, and space nearly unbroken by rolling hills or gully-washed river valleys. Virtually flat, the plains had been built up through thousands of years by streams carrying debris eastward from the Rocky Mountains in a process nearly identical with that of delta formations that create coastal plains.

Because it was void of timber, had only scattered water holes, and lacked adequate landmarks, white settlers tended to stay clear of the Llano Estacado. Even Indians frequented the Staked Plains only to hunt buffalo or to cross it. The Texas–Santa Fe Expedition, designed to establish the jurisdiction of Texas over Santa Fe, had crossed the Llano Estacado in 1841. Capt. Randolph B. Marcy crossed and recrossed it by different routes in 1849 and explored the headstreams of the Red River in 1852. Capt. John Pope of the United States Army, later to win fame in the Civil War, visited the region three years later, and in 1872 Shafter's former colonel, Ranald Mackenzie, had crossed the northern portions to Forts Sumner and Bascom, New Mexico. As late as 1875, however, travelers still looked upon the Llano Estacado with trepidation. Those bound for California through Texas usually followed the Old Butterfield Trail that swung south around the High Plains.

Even the cattlemen, who by 1875 had spread westward on the Texas plains to the Caprock escarpment and were well established along the slopes of the Rockies farther west, avoided the region. Not for almost another decade would they drive their cattle to graze on the Llano Estacado.

The existence and location of the Staked Plains was well known. The Great American Desert myth had been perpetuated for decades by school histories, geographies, and popular atlases. Moreover, descriptions of the Great Plains made by men who traveled through it, including Coronado, Lewis and Clark, Stephen H. Long, and others, were widely circulated. Captain Marcy, whose report was published by Congress, vividly portrayed the plains as a "natural barrier between civilized man and the savage, as, upon the east side are numerous spring-brooks, flowing over a highly prolific soil . . . while on the other side commence those barren and desolate wastes, where but few small streams greet the eye of the traveller, and these are soon swallowed up by the thirsty sands over which they flow. . . ." As late as 1859, the keenly observant Horace Greeley, editor of the *New York Tribune,* described the plains as "a desert indeed."[1]

No one, it now seems clear, did more to dispel the desert myth attached to the Llano Estacado than William R. Shafter. For over five months in 1875 his troops ranged over the vast tableland from the tributaries of the Red River south to the Rio Grande and from the eastern Caprock west to the Pecos River. In selecting Shafter to lead the expedition, Brig. Gen. Edward O. C. Ord, who had recently replaced Augur as commander of the Department of Texas, made a wise choice. Standing five feet eleven inches tall and weighing almost 230 pounds, Shafter was corpulent, but nevertheless considered the most energetic man of his rank in the department. As in his Civil War experiences, however, he was still something of an anomaly, enjoying the respect but rarely the affection of his men, who viewed him as coarse, abusive, and gruff—the "terror of his subordinates."[2] To many men he was a volatile martinet, but to those who knew him well he was a "splen-

[1] Randolph B. Marcy, *Exploration of the Red River of Louisiana in 1852,* 32d Cong., 2d sess., 1854, Exec. Doc. 54, pp. 84–85; Horace Greeley, *An Overland Journey from New York to San Francisco in the Summer of 1859,* pp. 128–30. Preceding discussion drawn from Robert F. O'Connor, ed., *Texas Myths,* p. 19; Walter Prescott Webb, *The Great Plains,* pp. 8, 14–17; and Del Weniger, *The Explorers' Texas: The Lands and Waters,* pp. 15–22.

[2] Robert M. Utley, "'Pecos Bill' on the Texas Frontier," *American West* 6 (Jan., 1969): 4–6; James Parker, *The Old Army: Memories, 1872–1918,* p. 100; Charles J. Crane, *Experiences of a Colonel of Infantry,* p. 64.

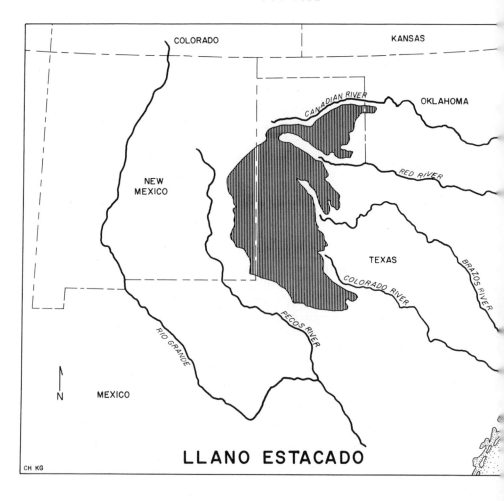

LLANO ESTACADO

did, handsome, jovial, helpful man," regarded with "admiration and love."[3]

In selecting Shafter's troops, Ord likewise chose well. All black, organized into Companies A, C, F, G, I, and L of the Tenth Cavalry, Company A of the Twenty-fifth Infantry, and Companies D and F of Shafter's Twenty-fourth Infantry, the troopers numbered nearly 450 men. Supporting the black troops was a company of Seminole-Negro Indian scouts. These remarkable warriors were descendants of Seminole Indians and runaway slaves of the Florida swamps who during the 1840's were removed from the Everglade state. Many had been transported to Indian Territory, but one band under the leadership of Chief Wild Cat had fled to the Mexican side of the Rio Grande near Piedras Negras. In subsequent years others had joined the band in northern Mexico. In 1870 the Seminole-Negro Indians below the Rio Grande were invited to enlist as scouts in the United States Army. Many of them agreed, bringing their families and settling on the government military reservation at Fort Clark. For the next eleven years they were attached to various commands in the Southwest.[4]

There were several purposes for the scout. First, the frontier line of settlement was pushing through West Texas, approaching the Caprock escarpment. Before pioneers moved out onto the High Plains, Ord wanted the region thoroughly explored and mapped, water holes marked, and fuel supplies noted. In addition, he asked Shafter to record all pertinent information relating to resources and flora and fauna of the plains. Finally, there were military reasons. A year earlier, under political pressure, the federal government had abandoned the peace policy and turned loose the troops. General Sheridan, commanding the Division of the Missouri, thereupon had ordered a five-pronged attack against Indians in the Texas Panhandle. The fighting that followed, called the Red River War, had occurred in the fall and winter of 1874–75. In the spring of 1875, because the campaign had been successful for the army, only a few Indians roamed free on the Southern

[3] Quote from unsigned and undated letter to Mary Shafter McKittrick (Shafter's daughter), William R. Shafter Collection, Michigan Historical Collections, University of Michigan, Ann Arbor. See also Frank D. Reeve, ed., "Frederick E. Phelps: A Soldier's Memoirs," *New Mexico Historical Review* 25 (Summer, 1950): 203; William H. Leckie and Shirley A. Leckie, *Unlikely Warriors: General Benjamin H. Grierson and His Family*, p. 231; John Coburn to [?], Dec. 31, 1899, William R. Shafter Papers, Stanford University Library, Stanford, Calif., photocopy in Southwest Collection, Texas Tech University, Lubbock (hereafter Shafter Papers).

[4] Kenneth W. Porter, "The Seminole-Negro Scouts, 1870–1881," *Southwestern Historical Quarterly* 55 (Jan., 1952): 358–77. Also see Frost Woodhull, "The Seminole Indian Scouts on the Border," *Frontier Times* 15 (Dec., 1937): 118–21.

A rare photograph of the famous Seminole Negro Scouts. *Courtesy Archives of the Big Bend, Sul Ross State University, Alpine, Texas*

Plains. Fully aware of this fact, Ord planned for Shafter to pursue any Indians still in the region.[5]

Orders for the Shafter expedition went out at the end of May, 1875. Participating soldiers were to rendezvous before June 21 at Fort Concho. Accordingly, on June 19, Shafter set up a temporary camp along the Concho River near the fort and waited for his troops. Two days later he received orders temporarily suspending the operation. No reason was given. When July came and still no instructions had arrived for starting, Shafter and others began to question the necessity of the expedition. Forgetting momentarily its important nonmilitary purposes, one officer, Benjamin H. Grierson, colonel of the Tenth Cavalry, former commander of Fort Sill near the Comanche and Kiowa reservations, and an apostle of the ill-fated peace policy, remarked that there were no Indians to go after since the young malcontent

[5]Special Orders No. 106, Dept. of Texas, May 31, 1875, Shafter Papers; Robert W. Utley, *Frontier Regulars: The United States Army and the Indian, 1866–1890*, pp. 213–14, 219–21, 230–33.

Quanah Parker in June had led his Comanche band from its hiding place and surrendered. Shafter also concluded that the campaign, estimated to cost between $300,000 and $500,000, would be a "wild goose chase."[6]

Nevertheless, on July 11 orders to start arrived, and three days later in steaming heat Shafter left Fort Concho with one of the largest scouting expeditions ever assembled in West Texas. In addition to the black troops and Seminole-Negro scouts, there were a handful of Tonkawa scouts, several medical officers, blacksmiths, packers, teamsters, and other civilian employees. Twenty-five wagons drawn by six-mule teams and a pack train of approximately one hundred mules carried supplies for a four-month campaign. Moreover, the command drove along a beef herd to provide a ready supply of fresh meat. The long, striking column headed north for the Freshwater Fork of the Brazos River some 180 miles away.[7]

Not expecting hostile action, Shafter planned to break his command into units of two or three companies. He wanted each to scout as much country as possible, making notes about the high tableland with a view to locating water holes and fuel supplies for future settlement. In accordance with his plan of operation, Shafter, on the way north, left Capt. Nicholas Nolan and two companies of his Tenth Cavalry, about ninety men, at Rendlebrock Springs. Shafter wanted them to search westward before rejoining him in Blanco Canyon. As the main command continued toward the Brazos, the scouting column pushed west. Before noon on the second day, its guides picked up an Indian trail and by midafternoon sighted a large body of Apaches. By the time Nolan brought up the striking force, however, the Indians had abandoned their camps and fled toward the Monahans Sand Hills. Nolan burned seventy-four lodges, cooking utensils, robes, and a six-month supply of food, but before he could give chase, a hard rain made trailing conditions so difficult that he decided to give up pursuit. The next day he headed his command northeastward for the Blanco Canyon supply camp, arriving there early in August.[8]

[6]Frank M. Temple, "Colonel B. H. Grierson's Texas Commands" (Master's thesis, Texas Tech University, Lubbock, 1959), pp. 83–84.

[7]J. Evetts Haley, *Fort Concho and the Texas Frontier,* pp. 231–34; William H. Leckie, *The Buffalo Soldiers: A Narrative of the Negro Cavalry in the West,* pp. 143–47; Leckie and Leckie, *Unlikely Warriors,* pp. 226–27.

[8]Capt. Nicholas Nolan, Tenth Cavalry, to Shafter, Aug. 1, 1875, U.S. Dept. of War, Records of United States Army Commands, Letters Sent, Fort Davis, Record Group 98, National Archives (hereafter USAC, RG98, NA); John R. Cook, *The Border and the Buffalo,* p. 261.

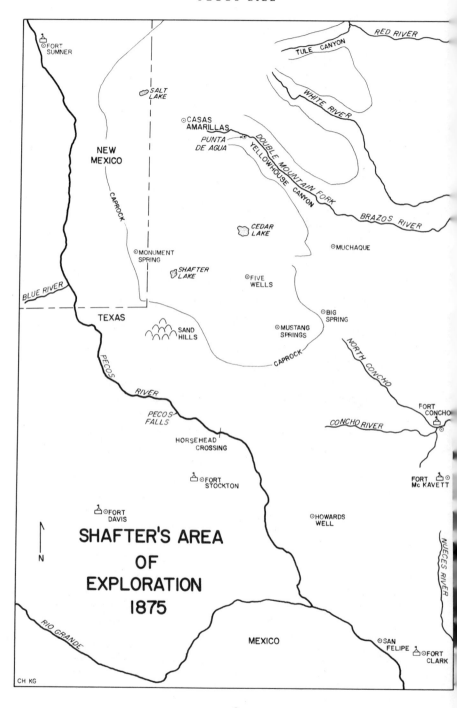

SHAFTER'S AREA
OF
EXPLORATION
1875

Although pleased with Nolan's destruction of the camps, Shafter was angry over what he regarded as Nolan's lack of vigorous pursuit. A hard-driving, quick-tempered man, harshly intolerant of associates who displeased him, he relieved Nolan of his command and ordered him to Fort Concho to await a court-martial. At the post, Nolan appealed to Grierson, his colonel, to intercede on his behalf. Grierson, knowing that Nolan had led recruits just assigned to the Tenth Cavalry from the East, consented to the request. Because of Grierson's friendly intervention, the court-martial was never held; Nolan received only a sharp reprimand.[9]

Intending to run down the Indians Nolan had jumped, Shafter temporarily changed his plans. On August 5, he left his supply camp with 220 officers and men plus a detachment of 20 Seminole Negro scouts commanded by Lt. John L. Bullis, a tough, wiry campaigner of the Twenty-fourth Infantry. Taking a single wagon to carry medical supplies and the sick and with rations on pack mules, the command moved up Blanco Canyon, climbed the Caprock onto the Llano Estacado, and headed northwest. Then, making a giant semicircle, it proceeded due south. Near modern-day Lorenzo, it overtook nine *comancheros* mounted, armed, and with several pack mules. Although the traders knew or at least would say nothing as to the whereabouts of Indians, Shafter took them into his service as guides. From here the command continued south, crossed the Double Mountain Fork of the Brazos, then turned and marched northwest to Punta del Agua, within the modern-day city of Lubbock. Thence following the Yellowhouse Canyon, it moved forty-two miles farther west to Casas Amarillas Lake, an old *comanchero* campground and watering place. From this prominent landmark, it headed toward the southwest into a torrid region absolutely unknown to black troops.[10]

Upon leaving Casas Amarillas Lake, the column marched thirty miles each day over an ocean of waving grass. Day after day it moved through buffalo herds where hundreds of thousands of the beasts lumbered off to each side, fleeing to a safe distance and turning to gaze in bewilderment at the strange intruders. Although no buffalo hunters were seen during the march, within three years the buffalo would be eradicated from the Great Plains. During the march the men saw a horse running with one of the buffalo herds. A detachment captured

[9]Shafter to J. H. Taylor, Asst. Adj. Gen., Dept. of Texas, Aug. 5, 1875, USAC, RG98, NA; Leckie, *The Buffalo Soldiers*, p. 157.

[10]Shafter to Taylor, Sept. 29, 1875, Shafter Papers; L. F. Sheffy, ed., "Letters and Reminiscences of General Theodore A. Baldwin: Scouting after Indians on the Plains of West Texas," *Panhandle-Plains Historical Review* II (1938): 9–12.

the animal, an old army mount, and Shafter, who adjusted his saddle blanket to avoid chafing the horse's old saddle galls, rode it on alternate days throughout the remainder of the march. Although several lighter-weight cavalry officers lost their private mounts, Shafter's captured steed was in good condition when the command returned to its base.[11]

After leaving Casas Amarillas, Shafter had hoped to find sufficient water in the large circular depressions called playa lakes that characterized the High Plains. During the first two days he was successful, but, having found no water by the end of the third day, he concluded that he must either make for the Pecos River fifty miles distant or turn back. Typically he struck for the Pecos. During the next thirty hours the troops suffered, and after a dry supper on the last evening many officers and men began to give out. Shafter cajoled and harangued his troops, forcing them to follow the trail. About eight that evening the advance troops at last reached the Pecos. Two hours later the main body of troops arrived, and some time after midnight everyone was encamped along the river near today's Carlsbad, New Mexico.[12]

There were no casualties. Some of the command, upon reaching the refreshing Pecos, had been without water for forty hours. Although the officers had grumbled and bickered, the durable black enlisted men had registered few complaints. Noting Shafter's intense drive to reach the river, however, they had dubbed their commander "Pecos Bill," a name he carried through the remainder of his career.[13]

In the morning two problems developed as the command headed downriver. The first was irritating but not serious. To avoid following several wide bends of the river, Shafter moved in as straight a line as possible, and in doing so his command made several dry camps along the way, a fact of which the critical cavalry officers, who resented being under the leadership of an infantry officer, made special note.[14] The second affected Shafter. Along the route, while swimming in the Pecos, he severely cut the shin of his right leg on a sharp rock, probably of gypsum. Unwilling to travel by wagon, he rode on horseback during the scout, about six hundred additional miles, his leg at times

[11]Col. George W. Adair, "Diary," in Percy M. Ashburn, *A History of the Medical Department of the United States Army,* p. 107; William G. Muller, *The Twenty-fourth Infantry, Past and Present,* pp. 1–8.

[12]Shafter to Taylor, Sept. 29, 1875, Shafter Papers; Sheffy, ed., "Letters and Reminiscences of General Baldwin," pp. 11–16.

[13]Edward H. Plummer to Mrs. Mary McKittrick, Jan. 5, 1918, Shafter Papers; Stewart H. Holbrook, *Lost Men of American History,* p. 285.

[14]Sheffy, ed., "Letters and Reminiscences of General Baldwin" pp. 16–21.

tied to his horse. Although the wound appeared to heal, subsequent injuries to the leg caused an occasional ulcer that lasted from ten days to three months. The injury disabled him twice afterward, and in 1891 it was an important reason Shafter was denied promotion to brigadier general.[15]

The command rode downriver to Horsehead Crossing. After resting a few days, it backtracked upriver to Pecos Falls and from there proceeded northeastward to the lower end of the Monahans Sand Hills, still looking for the Apaches that Nolan had flushed. The hunt was rewarded. On September 9, near modern-day Odessa, the Seminole-Negro scouts struck an Indian trail. Pursuing it westward eight miles, they discovered an abandoned camp that had contained one hundred families and a large horse herd. The main command joined the chase and followed tracks to water holes at the upper end of the Sand Hills, where it rested and watered horses. After midnight the men rode northwestward until sunrise, when they rested two hours before continuing. As water supplies disappeared, pursuit proved impossible; thirst, dust, and heat took a heavy toll on men and animals. On the twelfth advance troops located another spring where the Indians had stopped. Prospects of catching the elusive quarry brightened, and Shafter brought the main body of his troops to the water hole.

Here, at Three Wells, or Dug Spring, as Shafter called it, the Indians took the offensive. At 2:00 A.M. a party of thirty Apache warriors struck the camp but scattered when guards returned the fire. The only losses were four horses run off. At dawn Shafter with forty-five picked troops went after the Apaches. Twenty miles to the north, near a large water hole afterward called Monument Spring, south of modern-day Hobbs, New Mexico, he found an abandoned camp. Bringing up the main command, he ordered lodges and other camp equipage of the isolated sanctuary destroyed. He also dispatched some troops to build a rock monument on a low hill about a mile and a quarter to the southwest. The white stone marker, eight feet at the base, four at the top, and seven and a half feet high, could be seen for several miles in every direction.

Shafter gave up the chase. His rations were low, his animals were worn, his supply camp was two hundred miles away, and the Indians had scattered in all directions. On the sixteenth he headed due north,

---

[15]Shafter, endorsement of "Report of Post Surgeon on Physical Condition of Officers at Angel Island," April 11, 1891, and Shafter to Adj. Gen., U.S. Army, March 29, 1893, both in United States, William R. Shafter, Letters Received, Appointments, Commissions, and Personal Branch, Adjutant General's Office, Record Group 94, National Archives (hereafter ACP File, AGO, RG94, NA).

struck his outward trail, and returned by way of Yellowhouse Canyon and Punta del Agua to Blanco Canyon, where he arrived on September 25 after an absence of fifty-two days and a march of 860 miles.[16]

It was a tough march. The men lost twenty-nine horses and much of their equipment. Boots, leggings, and blouses were worn thin or in some cases completely missing. The men were exhausted.[17] Although it had captured no Indians, the expedition had wrecked an Indian sanctuary, destroyed camp equipment, and located several previously unknown water holes. Moreover, the durable black soldiers had shown again that troopers could penetrate successfully an area once known only to the Indians.

Upon returning to Blanco Canyon, Shafter rested and refitted his men. At the same time, he considered anew his initial plans to break his command into smaller units of two or three companies each. In fact, he had not abandoned the strategy. While he had pursued the Apaches, Capt. Charles C. Viele, Tenth Cavalry, leading ninety men, had made sure no Indians camped in the north. In two separate scouts Viele had explored the Panhandle from Tule Canyon to Portales Spring in eastern New Mexico. He had sighted neither Indians nor recent signs of them.

Convinced that most Indians had gone onto their reservations, Shafter divided his command. Knowing the Panhandle was clear, he ordered infantry troops to remove the supply camp to Tobacco Creek, a headstream of the Colorado River, and on October 12 with his cavalry troops he headed a second time onto the High Plains.

At Punta del Agua he dispatched Capt. Theodore A. Baldwin, Tenth Cavalry, with 120 men to scout south to Big Spring. Baldwin, a prodigious braggart and one of Shafter's chief critics, rode by way of Tahoka Lake and the Muchaque ("Moo-cha-ko-way," as Shafter spelled it) to Sulphur Springs near modern-day Ackerly. He continued southward, keeping close to the High Plains escarpment on his right. Unable to locate water, he rode eastward and then southward in search of the headwaters of the Concho rivers. After having gone thirty-eight hours without water, he found the Middle Concho River. Three days later he arrived at Big Spring. Baldwin, who sighted no Indians, scouted the

---

[16]Shafter to Taylor, Jan. 4, 1876, in M. L. Crimmins, ed., "Shafter's Exploration in West Texas," *West Texas Historical Association Yearbook* 9 (Oct., 1933): 82–96; Shafter to Taylor, Sept. 29, 1875, Shafter Papers; Leckie, *The Buffalo Soldiers*, pp. 143–47; Haley, *Fort Concho and the Texas Frontier*, pp. 231–34.

[17]Shafter to J. H. Taylor, Asst. Adj. Gen., Dept. of Texas, Sept. 29, 1875, Shafter Papers; Shafter to Taylor, Jan. 4, 1876, in Crimmins, ed., "Shafter's Explorations in West Texas," pp. 82–96.

country south and west of Big Spring and recorded topographical features.[18]

Baldwin opened roads between the upper North Concho River and Mustang Creek and between the upper North Concho and Beals Creek. He showed that the Big Spring, where there was permanent water, lay in a high dry tableland that would support large herds of livestock. And he connected the well-known water supply at Big Spring with previously unknown Sulphur Springs and the famous landmark of Muchaque Peak near modern-day Gail. Though punishing, his march proved helpful. His information made it easier for cattlemen later to locate water for their herds, and the area he covered soon filled in with ranches.

Meanwhile, Shafter and the remaining troops rode from Punta del Agua in a southerly direction to Lagunas Cuartes, also Lagunas Quartras (Four Lakes), currently known as Double Lakes. Here he detached Lieutenant Bullis and the Seminole-Negroes. Bullis and the scouts proceeded south to Lagunas Sabinas, now called Cedar Lake. Approaching the lake on October 17, they spied an Apache encampment. To rest and plan an attack, they withdrew a short distance and waited for daylight. Charging the camp early the next morning, they succeeded in capturing twenty-five horses and mules and destroying all the supplies, including fifty packs of mesquite beans, three or four thousand pounds of buffalo meat, about one hundred undressed buffalo hides, one hundred good lodge poles, and a quantity of cooking utensils. The Indians escaped. Sending word of the engagement to Shafter, Bullis and the scouts waited at Cedar Lake.

After the arrival of the scouts' courier, Shafter hurried to join the scouts. From Cedar Lake, anxious to overtake the Apaches, he followed the Indians due south for thirty miles to five large wells near modern-day Andrews. Here he dispatched Lt. Andrew Geddes with two companies of the Tenth Cavalry, some wagons, and a detachment of the scouts, with orders to continue on the trail as long as possible.

Taking Shafter literally, Geddes dogged the Indian trail for a month. He followed it over a long, twisting path that covered much of the southern Llano Estacado before turning westward to cross the Pecos and heading south toward the Rio Grande and Mexico. Within two and

[18] U.S. Dept. of War, "Map of the Country Scouted by Colonels Mackenzie and Shafter, Capt. R. P. Wilson and others in the Years 1874 and 1875," drawn by Alex. L. Lucas, 2832 Adjutant General's Office 1876, Record Group 94, National Archives (hereafter Lucas Map, 2832 AGO 1876, RG94, NA); Haley, *Fort Concho and the Texas Frontier*, p. 234; Sheffy, ed., "Letters and Reminiscences of General Baldwin," pp. 16–21; David J. Murrah, *C. C. Slaughter: Rancher, Banker, Baptist*, pp. 35–36.

one-half miles of the Rio Grande, at a point almost directly south of modern-day Dryden, Geddes on November 2 finally sighted some of the Apaches he had been chasing. Charging them, he killed the only brave there and captured four women and a young boy. The women informed him that the chief and the rest of the party had gone toward the settlements in Texas. Geddes's weary command turned back the next day. It recrossed the Pecos, struck the San Antonio–El Paso Road, and followed it to Fort Clark. After resting for three days, it took the military road toward its home post at Fort Concho, which it reached on November 26.

Geddes's march was significant. It had captured five Indians and had destroyed their camp. It had noted the availability of grass, fuel, and wild game along the 650 miles it covered. Southeast of modern-day Midland, it located a large salt lake now known as Peck's Springs. The lake was dry, but the Indians had been getting water at a spring on the south side that showed signs of a much-frequented camp where rustlers had been holding a herd of cattle. It discovered Mustang Springs between the present-day cities of Big Spring and Midland. Human bones found there indicated the place at some time had been a favorite Indian camp. Geddes reported that good grass and mesquite abounded and that a large mass of rocks had been piled high in the shape of a fort. The information helped to encourage cattlemen later to push their herds up the three forks of the Concho river.[19]

Meanwhile, Shafter and the other black troops crisscrossed the Llano Estacado over a veritable maze of trails. From Five Wells they scouted west, discovering new water holes, lakes (one named Shafter Lake), and two abandoned camp sites. Once again they explored the Sand Hills, examined Dug Spring, searched the rim of the Pecos valley west of Monument Spring, and noted the excellent ranching potential of the region. Because day after day they rode through buffalo herds, Shafter suggested in his report that cattle might be fattened where the buffalo grazed.[20]

The command found only a few traces of Indians. The abandoned camps, where some tepee poles were left behind, were old, and no signs indicated that Indians had returned to their camps in the Sand Hills–Monument Spring vicinity. The Indians had scattered in so many directions that Shafter knew not which band to chase. He followed the

[19]Hans Gasman, 2d Lt., Tenth Cavalry, "Itinerary of Scout," Nov. 26, 1875, U.S. Dept. of War, Records of United States Army Commands, Letters Sent, Dept. of Texas, Record Group 93, National Archives (hereafter USACDT, RG93, NA); Lucas Map, 2832 AGO 1876, RG94, NA.
[20]Shafter to Taylor, Jan. 4, 1876, 4688 AGO 1876, LR, RG94, NA.

trail of one until it pointed in the direction of Baldwin's area of operations. Giving up pursuit, he returned to Cedar Lake. To follow another he sent Lt. Thomas C. Lebo, Tenth Cavalry, with Company A in the direction of Casas Amarillas. Lebo found no Indians, but he located additional water and fuel supplies north of Casas Amarillas and reported the presence of excellent grass in the area. He showed that the region, although not thoroughly watered, was not as barren as previously believed.[21]

As Lebo rode north, Shafter sent out several scouts. The troops charted the distance between recently located water holes and well-known landmarks. They opened wagon roads between the supply camp at Tobacco Creek and Cedar Lake and from Punta del Agua across the Colorado River to Big Spring. At the same time, Shafter concentrated the bulk of his command at Cedar Lake. On November 15, planning again to cross the Llano Estacado, he divided his remaining troops. Leading the main column, Shafter rode due south to Five Wells and turned west to check Shafter Lake. Finding no Indians, he marched to Monument Spring, reaching it on the evening of the twenty-first. For a week afterward he scouted in the vicinity of the old Indian sanctuary.

Lt. C. R. Ward, Tenth Cavalry, led the smaller force. From Cedar Lake he marched west-southwest to an arroyo, afterward called Seminole Draw, arriving there on November 19. He discovered a remarkable series of wells, evidently a favorite Indian rendezvous. Henceforth known as Ward's Wells, the shallow holes, dug in the sand and ranging from fifteen feet deep at the lower end of the draw to only four feet at the upper, contained an abundance of excellent water capable of providing for several thousand horses or cattle. There were about fifty in all within a distance of a mile and one-half, scooped out with sloping walls so that horses could walk down to drink.

Ward located other wells. In a draw three and one-half miles west of the site that commemorates his name, he found about twenty similar to the first group, and in another draw about three miles to the south his scouts discovered several additional water holes. Grass in the vicinity was good, and mesquite roots were fairly abundant. Old trails and the scattered cattle skeletons suggested that the area was a favorite refuge for Indian raiding parties. After completing his notes about the wells and the nature of the adjacent region, Ward continued his

[21]Thomas C. Lebo, "Itinerary of Scout made by 'A' Company, Tenth Cavalry," Nov. 15, 1875, USACDT, RG93, NA; Lucas Map, 2832 AGO 1876, RG94, NA; Haley, *Fort Concho and the Texas Frontier*, pp. 230–45.

march for forty miles across an unwatered country to Monument Spring, reaching it on the second morning behind Shafter.[22]

Satisfied that no Indians were in the vicinity of Monument Spring, Shafter rode back to investigate Ward's Wells. Here, during the last few days of November, he received an order by courier from General Ord to break up his scout. He thereupon led his troops to Fort Concho, reaching the post on December 9. The campaign ended. Nine days later Shafter was at Fort Duncan, his own post on the Rio Grande, working on the report of his finale to the Red River War.[23]

Knowing that Indians no longer ranged over the Llano Estacado, settlers, close on the heels of the Shafter expedition, invaded the empty land. Sheepmen, cattlemen, merchants, and others pushed first into the canyons and river valleys of the High Plains before spilling onto the tableland. The Canadian River Valley in 1875 and 1876 attracted the first migrants, but one sheepherder, Jesús Perea, grazed his flocks of thirty thousand sheep to Blanco Canyon, Yellowhouse Canyon, and Tahoka Lake. He scattered his animals widely and took them wherever good grass and water could be found on the plains. Charles Goodnight, a cattleman, moved his herd of 1,500 cattle from Colorado to the Panhandle. After wintering among sheepmen along the Canadian, in 1876 he entered Palo Duro Canyon to establish the JA Ranch. In the same year other cattlemen came to the High Plains.[24] Most of the early settlers entered the region as a result of the success of Shafter's campaign.

Clearly, Shafter's Llano Estacado campaign had been remarkable. Covering 2,500 miles, Shafter and his black troops had dispelled the dreary myth of the Staked Plains—the dreaded Sahara of North America. They had explored, mapped, and charted topographical features of the High Plains from the Caprock on the east through the Sand Hills to the Pecos on the west, and from below Fort Concho and Horsehead Crossing on the south to Tule Canyon on the north. They had observed the extreme western range of the buffalo and had noted the region's excellent potential for ranching and farming. They had connected by wagon roads previously unknown water holes on the Llano Estacado

[22]Shafter to Taylor, Jan. 4, 1876, 4688 AGO 1876, LR, RG94, NA.

[23]Ibid.; U.S. Dept. of War, Returns from United States Military Posts 1800–1916, Fort Duncan, Dec., 1875, Roll 336, Microcopy No. 617, National Archives.

[24]José Ynocencio Romero, "Spanish Sheepmen on the Canadian at Old Tascosa," ed. Ernest R. Archambeau, *Panhandle-Plains Historical Review* 19 (1946): 45–72; J. Evetts Haley, *Charles Goodnight: Cowman and Plainsman*, pp. 280–90; J. Evetts Haley, "Pastores del Palo Duro," *Southwest Review* 19 (April 1934): 279–94; Paul H. Carlson, *Texas Woollybacks: The Range Sheep and Goat Industry*, pp. 86–100.

with well-known trails at Punta del Agua, across the Colorado River, at the Big Spring, and along the Concho River.

Shafter and his black troops had dramatically fulfilled their orders to sweep the Llano Estacado clear of Indians. They had found only a few traces of them on the plains, killed but one warrior, and captured only five Indians. Captain Viele's scouts showed that no Indians were, or recently had been, in the northern part of the plains. Other than the trail he followed, Lieutenant Geddes discovered no recent signs of Indians in the south. Neither Baldwin nor Ward found Indians. The band Lebo chased was tiny. In short, the Indians who had been on the Llano Estacado after the Red River War had scattered, most to their reservations in Indian Territory or to New Mexico.

Although successful, the campaign had not been easy. Stern and demanding, Shafter had demonstrated an enormous ability to get the utmost out of his soldiers. At one stretch during the expedition he had marched his troops three hundred miles in ten days. Because they were seldom in camp for more than one night, the men in addition to marching thirty miles a day had to pack their tents and other field equipment each morning and unpack it again each night. The subsequent wear and tear on both men and animals was severe. The black troops had proved equal to the task. During five long months in the field they had demonstrated the readiness and proficiency of a crack army command. In the pursuit of Indians they had been tireless and aggressive. Their finale to the Red River War marked an end to the magnificent horse-and-buffalo days of the proud Southern Plains Indians.[25]

When the campaign was completed and his reports were written, Lt. Col. William R. Shafter left on detached service for San Antonio and a well-deserved rest. In the spring of 1876, however, he was back in the field leading his black troops and organizing a daring raid against Indians in Mexico.[26]

---

[25]Leckie, *The Buffalo Soldier;* Haley, *Fort Concho and the Texas Frontier,* pp. 235–55; Shafter to Taylor, Jan. 4, 1876.

[26]Post Returns, Fort Duncan, Jan.–Mar., 1876, Roll 336, MC617, NA; Regimental Returns, Twenty-fourth Infantry, Jan.–March, 1876, Roll 246, MC665, NA.

CHAPTER SEVEN

With Black Troops in Mexico

A FTER his extended campaign on the Llano Estacado, William R. Shafter returned to the Rio Grande. During his absence the border raiders from across the river had continued their plundering operations. Ranald Mackenzie's celebrated 1873 raid into Mexico was decisive against the Kickapoos, but it had no lasting effect on lawless Mexicans and Americans who still regarded the ranches and farms of Texas as fair prey and easy sources of loot. Moreover, the perennial Juan Nepomuceno Cortina, a prominent Mexican-American who had been raiding periodically across the river since 1859, had reappeared on the border. Many people believed him responsible for most of the cattle rustling and horse stealing that occurred in 1874 and 1875.

Below Eagle Pass the internal state of Mexico intensified the borderland turbulence. After independence in 1821, civil disorder was common in Mexico, and after the French left in 1867, the country contained large numbers of men whose lives had been filled with violence and warfare. In 1871, soon after the reelection of Pres. Benito Juárez, Gen. Porfirio Díaz, a hero of the Mexican resistance against the French, attacked the Juárez government. His revolution failed, but in 1876 he revolted against the government of Pres. Sebastián Lerdo de Tejada. Successful in the second attempt, Díaz in 1877 made himself President.

Because Díaz initiated his 1876 revolt from the United States, northern Mexico was the scene of much of the early fighting. The subsequent disorder created confusion along the Rio Grande border and encouraged banditry, especially across the river in the United States, that included cattle rustling and horse stealing. As the Díaz revolution ended and discharged soldiers without work returned to their

88

homes in northern Mexico, the banditry intensified. Indians and out-laws from both sides of the border made raiding during the period a profitable enterprise along the Rio Grande below Eagle Pass.[1]

Above Eagle Pass, in the Upper Rio Grande Border Region through today's Big Bend National Park to old Fort Leaton, few bandit raids succeeded because the adjacent regions on both sides of the river were almost uninhabited and virtually unexplored. The region, however, served as a natural haunt and even highway for bands of Lipans and Mescaleros who slipped across the Rio Grande at any one of a dozen crossing places and moved through the chaparral until they reached a place far from the river where cattle and horses grazed. Any luckless cowboy or traveler who got in the way they killed. With hard riding the Indians returned to the river and vanished, often before news of their foray became known. The upriver Indian menace now became Shafter's principal concern.[2]

Pleased with the results of the Llano Estacado expedition, Brig. Gen. Edward O. C. Ord wanted Shafter to lead another campaign. He planned for Shafter in the spring of 1876 to scout along the Rio Grande near the mouth of the Pecos, where he was to search out and punish Indian raiders and cattle thieves. To work out details for the campaign, Ord on two occasions called Shafter to San Antonio. He also wanted Shafter to have the leg he had injured in 1875 examined by doctors at the de-partment headquarters.[3]

By the end of March, 1876, with plans completed, Shafter was back at Fort Duncan waiting only for orders to start. Despite the leg injury and his excessive weight, the medical officers had given the robust Pecos Bill a clean bill of health. He was a stout man, his long body set upon short legs. His blue eyes peered out, grimly for the most part,

[1]Lyman L. Woodman, *Cortina: The Rogue of the Rio Grande*, pp. 99–100; William J. Hughes, *Rebellious Ranger: Rip Ford and the Old Southwest*, pp. 160–62, 222–25, 257–59; Clarence C. Clendenen, *Blood on the Border: The United States Army and the Mexican Irregulars*, pp. 70–74; Robert M. Utley, *Frontier Regulars: The United States Army and the Indian, 1866–1890*, pp. 344–56.

[2]Shafter testimony, Jan. 7, 1878, in *Testimony taken by Committee on Military Affairs in Relation to Texas Border Troubles*, 45th Cong., 2d sess., 1879, H. Misc. Doc. 64, pp. 154–57, 164–67; Robert M. Utley, "'Pecos Bill' on the Texas Frontier," *American West* 6 (Jan., 1969): 10.

[3]U.S. Dept. of War, Returns from United States Military Posts, 1800–1916, Fort Duncan, Jan.–March, 1876, Roll 336, Microcopy No. 617, National Archives (hereafter Post Returns, MC617, NA); U.S. Dept. of War, Returns from Regular Army Infantry Regiments, June, 1821–Dec., 1916, Twenty-fourth Infantry, Jan.–March, 1876, Roll 246, Microcopy No. 665, National Archives (hereafter Regimental Returns MC665, NA).

from shaggy and heavy dark brows. His full head of short cropped hair showed only a trace of white. Although clean-shaven on the chin, he wore a great walrus mustache that joined with long, thick sideburns on each cheek. Just over forty years of age, he was aggressive, determined, and, perhaps most important for his new assignment, utterly unafraid of responsibility.[4]

Closely teamed with Shafter was the highly competent John L. Bullis, who had been on the Llano Estacado campaign. A Civil War veteran whose service had been with black troops, Bullis had found civilian life distasteful after the war and had elected to become a career soldier. Small and wiry, he wore a black mustache on his thin, sunburned face. According to a contemporary, when Bullis, a tireless marcher, wanted to be luxurious in scouting, he took along one can of corn.[5] Bullis's indefatigable Seminole-Negro Indians spearheaded Shafter's efforts to stop Mescalero and Lipan raids and to protect the Texas frontier.[6]

Shafter did not wait long for marching orders. On April 7 Ord wired him to proceed to Camp Hudson on Devil's River. Leaving Fort Duncan two days later, Shafter led a contingent of two companies of his Twenty-fourth Infantry, five companies of cavalry, and a detachment of Bullis's scouts, perhaps 350 officers and men. Wagons hauled a four months' supply of simple rations of coffee, flour, salt, and bacon, and a long pack train of mules carried other supplies, and civilian employees trailed along a small beef herd to provide fresh meat.[7]

Fully aware that Indian raiders crossed the river at night, stole horses, and were back in Mexico before the end of the second night, General Ord agreed that troops on a "fresh trail" should pursue thieves wherever they might go, even into Mexico.[8] The order delighted Shafter. He preferred to strike the Indians at places where they believed them-

[4] Stewart H. Holbrook, *Lost Men of American History*, pp. 284–95; Utley, "'Pecos Bill' on the Texas Frontier," pp. 4–10; Regimental Returns, Twenty-fourth Infantry, Roll 246, MC665, NA.

[5] Frank D. Reeve, ed., "Frederick E. Phelps: A Soldier's Memoirs," *New Mexico Historical Review* 25 (Summer, 1950): 203.

[6] Edward S. Wallace, "General John Lapham Bullis, Thunderbolt of the Texas Frontier," *Southwestern Historical Quarterly* 55 (July, 1951): 77–85.

[7] Brig. Gen. Edward O. C. Ord to Shafter, May 15, 1876, in William R. Shafter Papers, Stanford University Library, Stanford, Calif., photocopy in Southwest Collection, Texas Tech University, Lubbock (hereafter Shafter Papers); Post Returns, Fort Duncan, April, 1876, Roll 336, MC617, NA; Regimental Returns, Twenty-fourth Infantry, April, 1876, Roll 246, MC665, NA.

[8] Ord testimony, Dec. 6, 1877, in *Texas Border Troubles*, 45th Cong., 2d sess., 1879, H. Misc. Doc. 64, p. 103.

John L. Bullis. *Courtesy National Park Service, Fort Davis National Historic Site*

selves safe from attack, in this instance their retreats across the Rio Grande in Mexico.

Crossing the river and getting to the Mexican mountains, however, was no easy task. The topography of the Rio Grande near the mouth of the Pecos for several miles each way presented a vast wasteland of canyons, gorges, chasms, and countless arroyos. Sandbars choked the river channel, making it difficult to bridge during rainy weather be-

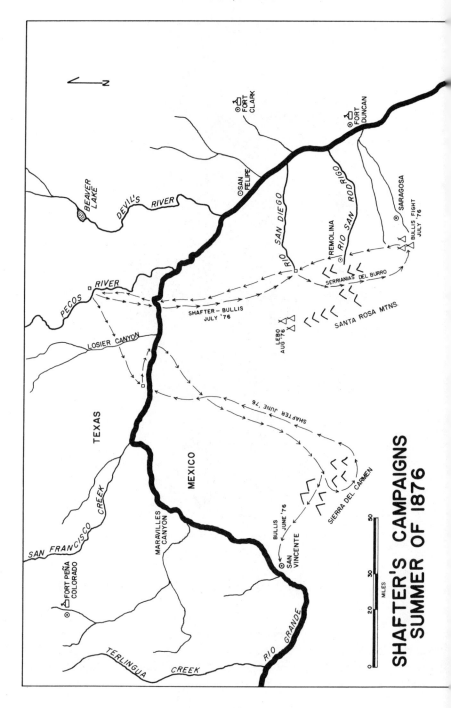

SHAFTER'S CAMPAIGNS
SUMMER OF 1876

cause of shifting beds of quicksand. The mesas and buttes remained barren and rocky, the basins and high tablelands almost devoid of vegetation. The desolate country for miles on each side of the river contained poison wells, alkali sinks, and stretches of blinding salt marshes. Both camp life and movement of troops in the region proved tough and undesirable.[9]

After stopping at Camp Hudson, Shafter cut west to the Pecos River. Here, near modern-day Pandale, he established a permanent supply camp for the summer operations. A few weeks later, at the end of May, 1876, he left with the cavalry for the Rio Grande to a point about sixty miles west of the Pecos. He sent out scouting parties, but they located no fresh signs. Undismayed, Shafter, adopting a broad interpretation of Ord's term "fresh trail," ordered a scout into Mexico. He sent Lieutenant Bullis with seven men to locate Indian villages rumored to be in the Sierra del Carmen, or Carmen Mountains, southeast of modern-day Big Bend National Park. Bullis rode sixty to eighty miles into the unexplored Mexican deserts without discovering any villages but finding plenty of other signs, including evidence of an old Indian camp in the foothills of Sierra del Carmen. Returning to the United States on June 7, he made his report, and Shafter on the same day started for Mexico with the cavalry and a company of Seminole-Negro scouts.

After a hard march across the Coahuila deserts in over 100°F heat, the last sixty-five miles without water, Shafter reached Sierra del Carmen on June 11. Disappointed in not finding Indians, after four days in the mountains Shafter turned back, arriving on June 18 at the supply camp on the Pecos. Results of the expedition had been meager. No Indians had been found. The only fresh trail led westward to the Big Bend, and it had been followed unsuccessfully. Shafter had succeeded, however, in opening a wagon road connecting Camp Hudson, the supply camp on the Pecos, and the Rio Grande.[10]

A month later Shafter again crossed into Mexico. His destination this time was an Indian Village in the vicinity of Saragosa (Zaragoza). Taking a force of 210 officers and enlisted men and Lieutenant Bullis with a party of twenty Seminole-Negro scouts, he left camp for the Rio Grande to await the return of two Mexican guides whom he had sent ahead to spot the Indians. On July 24, after the guides had re-

[9]Clendenen, *Blood on the Border,* pp. 72–75; Shafter testimony, Jan. 7, 1878, in *Texas Border Troubles,* 45th Cong., 2d sess., 1879, H. Misc. Doc. 64, pp. 154–57, 164–67; Utley, *Frontier Regulars,* pp. 344–50.

[10]Shafter to J. H. Taylor, Asst. Adj. Gen., Dept. of Texas, June 20, 1876, Shafter Papers.

ported, Shafter, leaving the infantry troops at the river, crossed the Rio Grande and hit a trot for the Indian camp.

After he had pushed southeastward for five days to a point near the head of the San Diego River, Shafter called a halt. Fearing that a Mexican force might cross his back trail and cut off his return to the river, he decided to bivouac, proposing that Bullis with the Seminole-Negro scouts, Lt. George Evans, Tenth Cavalry, and twenty picked troops storm the Lipan village.[11]

Bullis and Evans needed little urging. In a long night march they covered fifty-five miles and located the village of twenty-three lodges some five miles southwest of Saragosa. About dawn on July 30 they rushed the village. After the first volley a savage hand-to-hand fight swirled among the lodges. For fifteen minutes the soldiers and scouts used their carbines as clubs to combat the Indians, who used lances. When it was over, the Lipans headed in full flight toward Saragosa. They left twelve dead warriors, four women, and nearly one hundred horses and mules behind. Bullis's loss numbered three wounded troopers.

After capturing the women and all the animals, Bullis quickly destroyed the camp, including all the equipment and supplies. Then, slowed somewhat by the wounded troopers, he retreated toward Shafter's camp with a force of Mexican troops from Saragosa in pursuit. Having gotten a good head start, he outdistanced the small Mexican force and reached camp without further incident. The detachment had covered 110 miles and fought a successful battle while remaining in the saddle for twenty-five hours without rest. The entire command then filed back to the Rio Grande and recrossed it on August 4 to the safety of American soil.[12]

Shafter had not finished, however. Hoping to find a second Indian camp, reported by one of the captive women to be in the Santa Rosa Mountains, he dispatched Capt. Thomas C. Lebo, Tenth Cavalry, back to Mexico. Taking 110 cavalry troops, Lebo on the same day forded the river and headed southwestward. After an eight-day march, he surprised and destroyed a small Kickapoo camp of ten lodges, located a few miles north of the Santa Rosa Mountains, and captured sixty horses and mules.[13] As Lebo rode into Mexico, Shafter directed scouting activi-

[11] Ibid.

[12] Shafter to Taylor, Aug. 27, 1876, Shafter Papers; Frost Woodhull, "Seminole Indian Scouts on the Border," *Frontier Times* 15 (Dec. 1937): 122; William H. Leckie, *The Buffalo Soldiers: A Narrative of the Negro Cavalry in the West*, pp. 150–51; Kenneth Wiggins Porter, "The Seminole Negro Indian Scouts, 1870–1881," *Southwestern Historical Quarterly* 55 (Jan., 1952): 370.

[13] Shafter to Taylor, Aug. 27, 1876, Shafter Papers.

ties on the Texas side of the Rio Grande, but the soldiers located no Indians.[14]

While thus engaged, Shafter received congratulations from General Ord for his expedition to Saragosa. In the same letter Ord authorized Shafter anew to "scout into Mexico when ever you can follow a trail successfully." Disregarding the rights of the Republic of Mexico in the matter of border crossings, Ord further instructed Shafter to punish marauders in Mexico. "I am perfectly sure," he wrote to Shafter, "that the President will make 'no ado' over our crossing, so that you can follow up these Lipans and Kickapoos, until they are entirely beyond reach" of the Texas settlements.[15]

Fifteen days later, however, Ord sent Shafter back to his post. In his communication, Ord expressed his complete satisfaction with the manner in which the Saragosa expedition had been carried out. Noting that the country covered and scouted presented major difficulties to the successful operations of troops, he was gratified at the cheerful and energetic spirit displayed by both the officers and enlisted men. He gave no reason, however, for the unexpected decision to abandon the summer campaign. Shafter was back at Fort Duncan on September 19, 1876.[16]

Six days later Shafter went by horseback to San Antonio to huddle with General Ord. In this presidential election year Shafter's invasion of Mexico had created a politically sensitive situation on three levels, and Ord, as department commander, found himself under heavy pressure to end Indian depredations, restore peace, but keep his troops out of Mexico. First, citizens along the Rio Grande worried about lack of protection. They got support from Texas governor Richard Coke, who complained that organized bands of marauders from Mexico had invaded the country between the Rio Grande and Nueces River and killed many Americans. Second, the Mexican government protested each military violation of its country, complaints that taxed already strained relations between the United States and Mexico. And third, members of the United States House of Representatives, led by Edward S. Bragg of Wisconsin, criticized Ord's policy and Shafter's raids. The sharp criticism from Washington had caused Ord to bring Shafter back from the summer expedition early.[17]

[14]Lt. William Beacom, Twenty-fourth Infantry, to Shafter, Aug. 22, 1876, and Shafter to Taylor, Aug. 27, 1876, both in Shafter Papers.

[15]Ord to Shafter, Aug. 14, 1876, United States, William R. Shafter, Letters Received, Appointments, Commission, and Personal Branch, Adjutant General's Office, Record Group 94, National Archives (hereafter ACP File, AGO, RG94, NA).

[16]General Orders No. 10, Dept. of Texas, Aug. 29, 1876, Shafter Papers.

[17]*Special Committee of the House of Representatives to Investigate Texas Fron-*

Ord was in a tough position. To satisfy his critics, he must stop Indian raids and cattle rustling without angering Mexican authorities.
He wanted an officer of discretion and ability who, when entering Mexico, could start at night, go fast, move quietly, and return as soon as
a blow was struck.[18]

Shafter, never one to underestimate his own ability, believed that
he could solve Ord's dilemma. On October 21, just four days after his
return from San Antonio, Shafter suggested that, although it would
give him a command four times the size to which he was entitled by
rank and place him above two full colonels, he be given control of the
troops at the posts of Forts Clark, Duncan, and San Felipe. The following day in a longer letter to Ord, he again asked for the authority.[19]

On October 27, Ord agreed. He created the District of the Nueces,
which embraced the Upper Rio Grande Border Region and included
the three forts Shafter had mentioned, and appointed the bold and
confident lieutenant colonel commander of the district. He telegraphed
Shafter to proceed with preparations for an immediate crossing of the
Rio Grande as a bluff to keep the Indians in Mexico. He told his trusty
field officer to organize a campaign consisting of eight companies of
cavalry and ten of infantry and to carry several Gatling guns — far more
troops than necessary to chase Indians.[20]

Meanwhile, Ord wrote again to Washington for permission to pursue
Indians into Mexico. After consulting with Secretary of War James D.
Cameron, Gen. William T. Sherman, commanding the United States
Army, consented in mid-November, but only on the condition that a
fresh trail had been discovered. Recognizing that the large contingent
of troops Ord mentioned was unnecessary against Indians in Mexico,
Sherman feared that Ord and Shafter might be planning to seize northern Coahuila from Díaz and hold it until it could be turned over to
the Lerdo government. Therefore, he declined to offer unlimited support. (Unknown to Sherman, the Lerdo government had already fallen
to Díaz on November 21.)[21]

tier *Troubles*, 44th Cong., 1st sess., 1876, H. Rept. 343, pp. 73–74; Bernarr Cresap, *Appomattox Commander: The Story of General E. O. C. Ord*, pp. 306–15.

[18]Ord, "Annual Report," Oct. 1, 1877, in *Annual Report of the Secretary of War*,
1877, 45th Cong., 2d sess., H. Exec. Doc. 1 (pt. 2), 2:80–81; Cresap, *Appomattox Commander*, p. 307; Ord to Shafter, Aug. 14, 1876, ACP File, AGO, RG94, NA.

[19]Shafter to Ord, Oct. 22, 1876, Shafter Papers; Shafter testimony, Jan. 7, 1878, in
Texas Border Troubles, 45th Cong., 2d sess., 1879, H. Misc. Doc. 64, p. 165.

[20]Taylor to Shafter, Oct. 27, 1876, Shafter Papers.

[21]Ord to Shafter, Nov. 23, 1876, Shafter Papers; Utley, *Frontier Regulars*, p. 351;
Clendenen, *Blood on the Border*, p. 79.

The new orders delighted Shafter. Just before the full moon in December, when raiding was most likely to occur, he stationed four detachments of twelve men each with good horses and excellent "trailers" near ranches along the river where Indians, desperadoes, or cattle thieves would be most likely to strike. He made certain that in event of a protracted stay forage, feed, and fresh meat could be purchased. His patrols waited for the full moon.

The plan worked. On the night of December 30, 1876, thieves stole about sixty horses from a rancher who lived about seven miles west of Fort Clark. They drove the animals to the Rio Grande near San Felipe, where between two hundred and three hundred cattle stolen from nearby ranchers had been gathered for herding across the river into Mexico. As soon as the patrol discovered the absence of the stock and the fresh trail, it sent word to Shafter at Fort Clark, headquarters for the District of the Nueces. Shafter ordered Bullis and Capt. Alexander B. Keyes to lead troops in pursuit.

Bullis and Keyes, leading 112 officers and men, followed the trail across the Rio Grande and rode about 125 miles into Mexico. At an Apache camp in the Santa Rosa Mountains they found horses and the drying meat of one hundred head of cattle stolen from the United States, but the Indians had fled. After burning the village, the troops took the horses and some of the cattle that could be rounded up and returned to Fort Clark on January 23, 1877, having been in Mexico three weeks. The Bullis-Keyes raid had a sobering effect on border thieves, and depredations slackened for a time.[22]

Shafter, influenced by the inauguration of new administrations both in Mexico City and in Washington, kept his troops in check. Porfirio Díaz assumed charge in Mexico in early February, and on March 4, Rutherford B. Hayes became the United States president. Both civilian and military leaders in Texas hoped the new presidents could solve the border conflicts. They were disappointed. Unable to establish firm control over the northern Mexican states, Díaz used the border trouble as a means to gain diplomatic recognition for his government from the United States. In the United States the bitter 1876 presidential election, the Indian wars, and the presence of other problems explain the indecisive federal policy toward events along the Rio Grande.

The documents reveal that a most turbulent state of affairs existed in the Upper Rio Grande Border Region. On March 9, 1877, Shafter re-

[22]Bullis testimony, Jan. 8, 1878, in *Texas Border Troubles*, 45th Cong., 2d sess., 1879, H. Misc. Doc. 64, pp. 188–90; Post Returns, Fort Clark, Jan., 1877, Roll 214, MC617, NA.

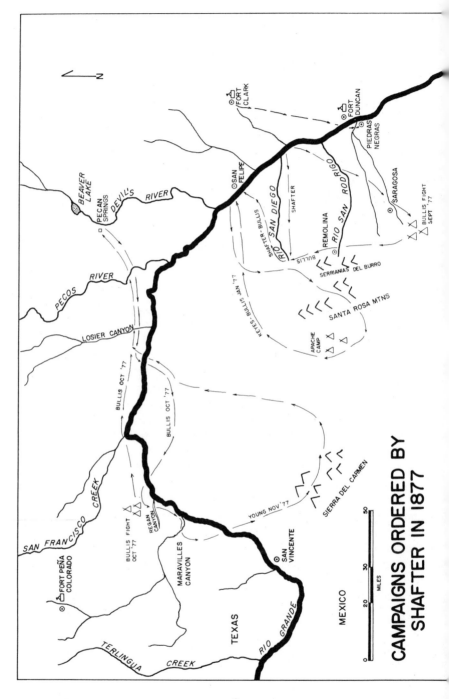

CAMPAIGNS ORDERED BY
SHAFTER IN 1877

ported new raids. "Not the slightest attempt," he wrote, "was being made by the Mexican government to stop the depredations." To the contrary, the bandits found refuge and a market for their stolen goods in Mexican towns. Shafter recommended the adoption of his favorite tactic: attack the raiders in their lairs.[23]

Although he received no immediate reply, Shafter again crossed into Mexico. At the end of March, General Ord had received word that Julian Longina and Pedro Rodríguez were confined in jail at Piedras Negras. Considered traitors by local authorities, they were charged with having guided United States troops in Mexico. The men had guided Shafter and Bullis during their 1876 raid near Saragosa. Because the prisoners were in danger of being executed, Ord had protested, unsuccessfully, to the governor of Tamaulipas. The *alcalde* of Piedras Negras, in reply to a demand for the release of the two men, had stated that his orders were to arrest any person who guided American troops in Mexico. Ord thereupon telegraphed Shafter to rescue the captives.[24]

Shafter acted quickly. He marched to Fort Duncan, arriving at 10:00 P.M. on April 2. Early in the predawn hours of the following day, he moved with three companies of cavalry, perhaps 140 men, across the river to a position southwest of Piedras Negras and sent Maj. George W. Schofield, Tenth Cavalry, with two companies of infantry directly toward the village on the opposite bank of the river. Although threatened by a small party as he waded the river, Schofield reached the south bank without loss and occupied the town plaza. Simultaneously, Shafter and his troopers arrived.

The raid had been for naught. Shafter found the doors of the jail swinging open and the jail deserted. The prisoners had been removed during the previous night. The Mexican authorities, having learned that a rescue attempt was planned, had hustled the prisoners southward. Shafter and the entire command returned to the United States without having fired a shot. Mexican authorities had taken the prisoners to Saltillo to try them for treason.[25] After the raid Ord kept Shafter in Texas.

Encouraged by the lack of military action, raiders through April and May grew bolder, their depredations more numerous. In response to the increasingly intolerable border situation, Secretary of War George W. McCrary took action. Replying to Shafter's recommenda-

---

[23]Shafter to Taylor, March 9, 1877, Shafter Papers. Also see *Mexican Border Troubles*, 45th Cong., 1st sess., 1878, H. Exec. Doc. 13, pp. 4–5.

[24]Ord's telegram cited in Taylor to Shafter, April 1, 1877, Shafter Papers; Clendenen, *Blood on the Border*, p. 79.

[25]Taylor to Ord, April 5, 1877, Shafter Papers. Also see Shafter testimony, Jan. 7,

tion of March 9, McCrary issued on June 1, 1877, an official order through General Sherman to the border troops under General Ord. "You will," he wrote to Sherman, "direct General Ord that in case the lawless incursions continue he will be at liberty . . . when in pursuit of a band of marauders and when his troops are either in sight of them or upon a fresh trail, to follow them across the Rio Grande, and to overtake and punish them" and recover stolen property.[26]

The order, a subtle but significant change in American policy, was denounced by the entire Mexican press as an insult to Mexican sovereignty. It embittered the Díaz administration, already angry toward the United States for withholding recognition. The Mexican minister of foreign affairs, Lauro Vallarta, claiming that the United States had treated Mexico "as savages, as Kaffirs of Africa," charged that a scheme had been concocted to bring about war. Later, the American minister to Mexico, John Watson Foster, recalled that there was indeed some foundation for the charge that a scheme had been formed to bring on a war through the Texas border troubles.[27]

With the two countries on the verge of an open break, Secretary of State William Evarts instructed Foster to suggest to the Mexican government that its troops cooperate with American forces in maintaining peace on the border. Díaz replied that it was an excellent plan but that he could not spare the necessary troops. Díaz insisted on United States recognition before cooperation, a step Evarts was not yet prepared to take. Thus, the summer of 1877 brought no changes. Indian raiding continued along the border, and, except for one insignificant campaign in July led by Bullis, Shafter's troops remained north of the Rio Grande.

Shafter was unhappy with the restraints, and when raiding increased in the fall, he became impatient. Acting on the McCrary order of June 1,

---

1878, in *Texas Border Troubles*, 45th Cong., 2d sess., 1879, H. Misc. Doc. 64, pp. 179–80; Shafter to Taylor, March 9, 1877, Shafter Papers; Arlen L. Fowler, *The Black Infantry in the West, 1869–1891*, pp. 34–35; J. Fred Rippy, *The United States and Mexico*, p. 295; *Mexican Border Troubles*, 45th Cong., 1st sess., 1878, H. Exec. Doc. 13, pp. 1–10.

[26]George W. McCrary Secy. of War, to William T. Sherman, Commanding the U.S. Army, June 1, 1877, quoted in Taylor to Shafter, June 8, 1877, Shafter Papers. Also see Robert D. Gregg, *The Influence of Border Troubles on Relations between the United States and Mexico, 1876–1910*, p. 51.

[27]Vallarta quoted by John W. Foster, *Diplomatic Memoirs*, cited in James Parker, *The Old Army: Memories, 1872–1918*, pp. 85–86; and Utley, "'Pecos Bill' on the Texas Frontier," p. 12. Also see "Mexican Border Grievances," *The Nation* 27 (Aug. 29, 1878): 125; William G. Muller, *The Twenty-fourth Infantry, Past and Present*, pp. 5–10.

1877, but under his own authority, at the end of September he boldly crossed his troops to Mexico. Having discovered a faint trail but giving a broad interpretation to the June 1 order, Shafter and Bullis with four hundred men on September 28 waded the Rio Grande. In Mexico Shafter divided his command. Knowing that a Mexican contingent of two hundred soldiers, as well as dozens of thieves and outlaws in the area, would be watching for an opportunity to strike the Americans, Shafter with the main force would protect the rear. Bullis with the striking force would ride to an Apache village nera Saragosa, close to the site of his July, 1876, raid.[28]

Starting after dark, Bullis rode all night. He reached the Lipan and Mescalero camp about eight in the morning and attacked. The Indians fled, but the soldiers captured four women and a boy. After burning the village and destroying the camp equipage, they turned back and headed due north to meet the main force. On the following morning, September 30, a little after sunrise, they rejoined Shafter.

As the combined command headed for the Rio Grande at San Felipe, they discovered a Mexican force at their rear. Col. Innocente Rodríguez with ninety troops from Saragosa followed about a mile behind for a distance of ten miles but disappeared when Shafter began to maneuver his larger force for battle.[29] No engagement took place nor were any shots fired, and, when Shafter again headed for the Rio Grande, some of the officers grumbled about running from "a handful of Mexicans." After wading the river near San Felipe about midnight, Shafter rested his command before returning to Fort Clark, where he arrived on October 4.[30]

The Shafter-Bullis raid brought unfavorable reaction in the capitals of both countries. In Mexico City the newspapers, exaggerating its significance, indicated that the American troops had flagrantly violated international law. They also boasted of how a small Mexican force of

[28]Bullis testimony, Jan. 8, 1878, in *Texas Border Troubles*, 45th Cong., 2d sess., 1879, H. Misc. Doc. 64, pp. 191–93; Edward O. C. Ord, "Annual Report of the Department of Texas," Oct. 1, 1877, in *Annual Report of the Secretary of War, 1877*, 45th Cong., 2d sess., H. Exec. Doc. 1 (pt. 2), 2:81. Also see Cresap, *Appomattox Commander*, pp. 306–307; and Utley, *Frontier Regulars*, pp. 347–56.

[29]Bullis testimony, Jan. 8, 1878, in *Texas Border Troubles*, 45th Cong., 2d sess., 1879, H. Misc. Doc. 64, pp. 191–93; Shafter to Taylor, Oct. 1, 1877; and Bullis to Helenus Dodt, Twenty-fourth Infantry, Post Adj. at Fort Clark, Oct. 12, 1877, all in Shafter Papers. Also see Rippy, *The United States and Mexico*, pp. 264–95; Utley, *Frontier Regulars*, pp. 347–56.

[30]Turner testimony, March 2, 1878, in *Texas Border Troubles*, 45th Cong., 2d sess., 1879, H. Misc. Doc. 64, p. 269; Post Returns, Fort Clark, Oct., 1877, Roll 214, MC617, NA.

only ninety men had easily repelled an American command four times its number. In Washington the raid became an important factor in the decision of Congress to investigate the Texas border troubles.[31]

In Texas the raid caused Shafter trouble. After recrossing the Rio Grande, the troops encamped near San Felipe. Largely because Shafter's order to proceed northward to the border had created the appearance that Shafter was fleeing from a force of only ninety Mexicans, camp talk turned against him. One group of troopers questioned his courage, complained of his hard march, and traded rumors about his personal life. In response to the malicious gossip, an angry Shafter verbally assaulted 2d Lt. Edward P. Turner and several other malcontents. It was a brutal scene. Turner and twenty-three enlisted men of the Twenty-fourth Infantry and Tenth Cavalry thereupon drafted a set of court-martial charges against him. They handed the charges, dated October 10, 1877, to Shafter, who sent them to Ord. For the moment nothing else occurred.

Undaunted by the personnel problem or the political and diplomatic reaction to the raid, Shafter ordered another river crossing. He directed Bullis to patrol the Rio Grande and to follow the trail if he located fresh tracks. On October 28 Bullis crossed into Mexico and rode toward the Sierra del Carmen before the trail turned westward across northern Mexico to the Rio Grande. Four days later, when Indians took the offensive at their village along the river, Bullis turned back, reaching the Pecos about November 7.

When Bullis returned, Shafter sent Capt. Samuel Young, Eighth Cavalry, and Bullis with 120 men back to Mexico. During the month of November Bullis and Young crisscrossed the deserts of northern Mexico between the mouth of the Pecos River and the Rio Grande in the vicinity of the mouth of Boquillas Canyon near modern-day Big Bend National Park. On the twenty-ninth, Thanksgiving Day, in weather cold enough to freeze water in the canteens, they surprised some Mescaleros in Sierra del Carmen. In the blazing fight that followed, two Indians died and the soldiers wounded three others. As the remaining Indians fled, Young and Bullis rounded up thirty head of horses and mules and destroyed the village, including a large quantity of robes, hides, dried meat, saddles, and ropes. After resting their command one day, they started for the Rio Grande, following the trail Shafter had

[31]"Charges and Specifications against William R. Shafter," Oct. 10, 1877; Lt. Edward Turner, Tenth Cavalry, to Adj. Gen., U.S. Army, Jan. 11, 1878; and Turner to Adj. Gen., Jan. 16, 1878, all in ACP File, AGO, RG94, NA; Clendenen, *Blood on the Border*, pp. 80–83; Utley, *Frontier Regulars*, pp. 352–53; Gregg, *The Influence of Border Troubles on Relations between the United States and Mexico*, pp. 51–61.

made in 1876. They recrossed the river on December 3, turned east, and rode into Fort Clark on December 16.[32]

As soon as the command got back to American soil, Young sent one of the scouts ahead with a report. The courier, in addition to delivering the report to Shafter, was instructed to inform Mrs. Frederick E. Phelps, wife of Young's adjutant who had been injured slightly in the fight in Sierra del Carmen, that her husband's injury was healing fine. Arriving at the post in the predawn hours when only a few troopers were out, the courier delivered his report to Shafter and took his horse to the stable to await a more convenient time to see Mrs. Phelps. At the stable a trooper asked him whether anyone had been killed in the fight. Unable to speak or understand English well and interpreting the word to be "wounded" he replied, "Yes, adjutante." The word that Adjutant Phelps had been killed reached Mrs. Phelps before she had an opportunity to talk to the scout. Upon hearing the gossip, she turned ghastly white, took her daughter, went into her home, and closed the door. Shafter, who had Young's official report that Phelps's injury was healing satisfactorily, was unaware of the rumor. About thirty minutes after Mrs. Phelps had closed her door, he called upon her and, before noticing the tears streaming down her cheeks, said to her in a loud, jovial manner, "Madam, allow me to congratulate you."

Mrs. Phelps straightened up and replied sharply, "Since when, Colonel Shafter, has it been the custom of the army for the commanding officer to congratulate the widow?"

Chagrined for only a moment, Shafter replied, "If Mr. Phelps is dead, he is a mighty lively corpse, for here is a letter from him."

Mrs. Phelps fainted. As she fell to the floor, Shafter caught her, possibly saving her from injury, and placed her on the carpet. He then summoned Pvt. George Pond, whose quarters were next door, and the two lifted the stout woman onto the bed. A few moments after the application of a wet towel to her face and neck, Mrs. Phelps revived. Afterward, she and Shafter enjoyed many laughs over the incident.[33]

Meanwhile, Congress took a hand in the Rio Grande border troubles. At a special session of the Democrat-controlled Congress in October, 1877, some members, trying to embarrass the Republican administra-

[32]Bullis testimony, Jan. 8, 1878, in *Texas Border Troubles*, 45th Cong., 2d sess., 1879, H. Misc. Doc. 64, pp. 194–97; Shafter to Taylor, Nov. 9, 1877, ibid., pp. 85–86; Capt. Samuel B. M. Young, Eighth Cavalry, to Act. Asst. Adj. Gen., District of the Nueces, Fort Clark, Dec. 18, 1877, in Affairs on the Rio Grande and Texas Frontier, Letters Received, (1653 AGO 1878), AGO, RG94, NA; Post Returns, Fort Clark, Nov., 1877, Roll 214, MC617, NA.
[33]Reeve, ed., "Frederick E. Phelps" pp. 215–16.

tion, showed considerable hostility to Pres. Rutherford B. Hayes's Mexican policy. Especially critical were Sen. Roscoe Conkling of New York and Sen. Simon Cameron, chairman of the Senate Committee on Foreign Relations. These two urged a congressional investigation of the border difficulties. The House Committee on Foreign Affairs eventually spent months on the problem, forcing Secretary of State William Evarts to appear and defend the administration's policy and calling Minister John Watson Foster from Mexico to testify on the border crisis. The House Committee on Military Affairs also made an investigation of the border troubles. It was tough. When neither President Hayes nor Secretary of State Evarts could be discredited, the committee tried to find fault with Ord and Shafter.[34]

Called to Washington in December, Shafter began his testimony on January 6, 1878. Little progress was made during the first day, but he was on the stand all the next day. After the preliminary routine questions, the committee concentrated on three main topics. First, the members asked about the McCrary order of June 1, 1877, which had been denounced by Mexico as offensive to its national honor. The Mexicans, Shafter suggested in response, were quick to see that the order of June 1 was really a departure in American policy. Previous invasions of Mexican territory had been made under orders of local military commanders on the border, and then in 1875 General Ord at the department level had begun giving orders to enter Mexico and assuming responsibility in specific instances. The War Department by remaining silent had extended tacit consent for such crossing, he said, but had not given official approval until June 1, 1877. When the committee wanted to know the reaction to the order of Mexican citizens along the border, Shafter indicated that the border inhabitants were annoyed more by the spirit of the order than by the American raids it inspired. He said that many leading Mexican citizens encouraged the American raids as a means of ridding Mexico of outlaws and desperadoes. He further pointed out that he and Gen. Anacleto Falcón, one of the commanders of Mexican troops along the border, were friends who on several occasions had exchanged personal gifts and had visited many times in one another's homes.

A second area of questioning focused on the number and severity of Indian raids. The committee wanted a brief history of border crossings. Its members also wanted to know what Indians committed them, why the Indians were so often successful, and why the raids occurred

---

[34]Chester L. Barrows, *William M. Evarts: Lawyer, Diplomat, Statesman*, pp. 351–54, 357; James M. Callahan, *American Foreign Policy in Mexican Relations*, pp. 190–93.

at all. They asked Shafter to provide a summary of United States military movements in Mexico. Shafter responded to each question courteously, giving the committee as much information as he could without referring to the official reports.

The final area of questioning was personal and harsh. Pointing to some sentences from Shafter's reports and official letters, two of the interrogators in effect accused Shafter of trying to start a war with Mexico. Particularly damaging, they suggested, was a letter Shafter had written in August, 1876, to General Ord. One sentence seemed to indicate that Shafter hoped for an Indian raid to give him an excuse to cross into Mexico. The committee also suggested that perhaps the Shafter-Bullis raid of September, 1877, to Saragosa was an attempt to provoke a war. One member asked Shafter if he did not have "a latent disposition" to cross the border into Mexico on any pretext. Shafter admitted that although he took care to avoid engaging Mexican troops, he welcomed each chance to strike in their homes Indians who plundered ranches in Texas. He made it clear that, in his opinion, the best solution to the border trouble was to demand that Mexico stop the raids and, if she failed, to declare war.[35] He liked to rattle the sabers in support of diplomacy.

Shafter's testimony ended on January 8. In the event that he might again be needed, the committee instructed Shafter to remain in Washington until further notice. He did not appear before the committee again, but on January 13 and 14, 1878, he testified before the House Committee on Foreign Affairs, which was investigating relations between the United States and Mexico. Questions from the second committee remained official and revealed no new information.[36]

Now Lt. Edward Turner's charges surfaced in Washington. When they did, Shafter, who in September had considered court-martial proceedings against Turner but had not filed them, encouraged General Ord to issue the appropriate documents.[37] Concerned about the unfriendly attitude of the congressional investigation, he asked Gen. William T. Sherman, commanding general of the army, to intercede on his behalf. Sherman, happy to do so, watched developments in the investigations and discussed the situation with his trusty field officer Shafter. When the House Committee on Military Affairs considered inviting Turner

[35]Shafter testimony, Jan. 6, 7, 8, 1878, in *Texas Border Troubles*, 45th Cong., 2d sess., 1879, H. Misc. Doc. 64, pp. 152–87.

[36]*Report and Accompanying Documents of the Committee of Foreign Affairs on the Relations of the United States with Mexico*, 45th Cong., 2d sess., 1879, H. Rept. 701, pp. 21–30.

[37]Special Orders No. 13, Dept. of Texas, Jan. 16, 1878, ACP File, AGO, RG94, NA.

to testify, Sherman, on January 18, wrote to the committee. He indicated that Turner was under sentence of a general court-martial for breach of discipline and, now that Shafter had filed his charges against Turner, "is further ordered for trial for another and greater breach of discipline." To order Lieutenant Turner to Washington at this time, he suggested, would have a bad effect on the army "whose laws and rules he has defied, and would be construed as an escape from just punishment which will likely terminate his service. . . ."[38]

In response, Rep. Edward S. Bragg of Wisconsin, apparently hoping that he had uncovered fraternal corruption in the army, on February 5, introduced a resolution in the House that called upon the secretary of war, George W. McCrary, to furnish information on the charges and specifications against Shafter. Bragg believed Shafter's charges against Turner had been filed simply because Turner had preferred them against Shafter. Bragg also believed that the army feared Turner's testimony, not because of the bad effect it might have on discipline, but because of the corruption and presumed incompetence it might unearth.[39]

Bragg could not be denied, and Turner appeared on March 2 before the House Committee on Military Affairs. Wanting to portray his commander as a coward, Turner complained that the previous September, after the expedition to Saragosa, Mexico, Shafter had left "the country to escape a handful of Mexicans," but facts elicited in his testimony substantiated the accounts of both Shafter and John L. Bullis, who indicated that Shafter's army left Mexico to keep the peace, not out of cowardice. None of his evidence on the events that transpired on the border was new, only his opinion of the motives that influenced Shafter. Realizing the futility of his testimony, the committee questioned Turner for only a few minutes.[40] It discovered neither military collusion to protect Shafter nor any evidence to suggest the lieutenant colonel was trying to start a war.

Shafter, who in mid-February had arrived by train back in Texas, moved to end the Turner affair. He asked for and got a court of inquiry to investigate Turner's charges against him. The court met in April at San Antonio and considered two charges, lying to the prejudice of good order and military discipline and conduct unbecoming an officer and gentleman. Each charge contained several specifications, rang-

[38]William T. Sherman to [House Committee on Military Affairs?], Jan. 18, 1878, ACP File, AGO, RG94, NA.
[39]Barrows, *William M. Evarts*, p. 357; Callahan, *American Foreign Policy in Mexican Relations*, pp. 190–93.
[40]Turner testimony, March 2, 1878, in *Texas Border Troubles*, 45th Cong., 2d sess., H. Misc. Doc. 64, pp. 268–70.

ing from allegations that Shafter had gossiped to accusations that he had entered into an illegal and corrupt partnership with a local post sutler. Most of the specifications were flippant, malicious, and unfounded attacks upon his personal life, including one in which he had allegedly taken licentious liberties with a black woman at Eagle Pass and another that he had allegedly paid fifty dollars to a father of a girl in San Antonio to keep from being accused of having attempted to seduce the man's daughter.[41]

Ranald S. Mackenzie presided at the inquiry. He asked Turner and his confederates to present documentary evidence. None was provided. Then he called all the people whose names appeared on the list of charges and specifications to appear as witnesses. Upon examination of all the witnesses, Mackenzie and the other members of the inquiry board recommended dissolution of the court. There was no documentary evidence. "The whole matter," they said, "grew out of irresponsible camp talk and an insubordinate spirit towards Lieutenant Colonel Shafter." A few days later, on April 18, military authorities dissolved the court. The court of inquiry proved damaging to Turner, who remained only briefly in the Tenth Cavalry. No longer trusted by his colonel, Benjamin Grierson, on June 25 he resigned from the army.[42]

Shafter, exonerated by the court, once again turned his full attention to the Rio Grande. And as Congress in Washington searched for someone to blame for the troubles with Mexico, Shafter in Texas was again a participant in even larger and more significant efforts to stop international banditry and murder along the border.

[41]"Charges and Specifications against William R. Shafter," Oct. 10, 1877, ACP File, AGO, RG94, NA.

[42]General Orders No. 7, Dept. of Texas, April 18, 1878, ACP File, AGO, RG94, NA; Francis B. Heitman, *Historical Register and Dictionary of the United States Army,* 1:876.

CHAPTER EIGHT

The Last Years in Texas

I N THE UNITED STATES civilian authority often controls, as it should, the armed services. In the decade of the 1870's the relationship was characterized by the Quaker peace policy, the reduction in size of the army, and the military's struggle to secure from Congress adequate financial support. In 1877 no money was appropriated to the army until November 30. In a scramble to avoid emasculation, military officials had to comply with demands of small but crucial congressional groups.

The Democratic congressional delegation from Texas represented one such group. As a result of the long history of border banditry and Indian hostility in the state, it was actively pro army and could be counted by the War Department for support of critical legislation. In early 1878, as Rio Grande border violations continued and even increased, William T. Sherman, commanding general of the army, was quick to accede to the delegation's wishes when it demanded that Ranald S. Mackenzie with his Fourth Cavalry be returned to the Mexican border.[1] Consequently, on February 9, 1878, William R. Shafter, relieved by Mackenzie of his command of the District of the Nueces, went to Fort Duncan where again he closely teamed with the popular Texas hero.[2]

Shafter had scarcely relinquished command when a murderous raiding party from Mexico slipped into Texas. According to the lucid report of an army officer in the area, on Sunday, April 14, a band of

[1] Russell F. Weigley, *The History of the United States Army*, p. 271; C. Wright Mills, *The Power Elite*, p. 179.

[2] U.S. Dept. of War, Returns from Regular Army Infantry Regiments, June, 1821–Dec., 1916, Twenty-fourth Infantry, Feb., 1878, Roll 246, Microcopy No. 665, National Archives (hereafter Returns, MC665, NA).

Kickapoo, Lipan, and Mescalero Indians, Mexican desperadoes, and an American outlaw, estimated to be forty in number, waded the Rio Grande at a point about forty-five miles northwest of Laredo. Within minutes of their arrival in Texas, the band had killed two *vaqueros* and headed southeastward along the main road that meanders down the Rio Grande toward Laredo. At dusk the raiders killed Gorgea Garcia within hearing distance of his wife and friends on his ranch. After stealing Garcia's goatskin leggings, horse, saddle, and other *chivarras* (accoutrements), as well as a nearby drove of gentle horses, they resumed their course.

Two days later, within fourteen miles of Fort McIntosh, the thieves turned northeastward toward the Nueces River. After stealing enough horses to mount all their party, they divided into smaller raiding groups. With near-perfect organization, they appeared simultaneously at several ranches in the vicinity, taking the best horses and devastating the territory in a wide sweep. They then reunited and, after killing a hapless cowboy, rode eastward for sixty miles to old Fort Ewell on the Nueces River in La Salle County.

From abandoned Fort Ewell the group descended the Nueces River to a point where it swings northward in McMullen County. At this place, long a favorite rendezvous for raiders from Mexico, the marauders celebrated their success. Drunk from too much liquor, they "held high carnival," butchering John Steele, murdering Mrs. William H. Steele's eight- and twelve-year-old sons by mangling and mutilating them with knives, and killing two *vaqueros*. Here also they wounded Venturo Rodríguez with a rifle bullet and arrows, stripped two sheepherders naked, and compelled the *pastores* to run footraces.[3]

Following two more days and nights of looting, burning, and killing as they moved through Duval County, the raiders fled for Mexico. Reaching the Rio Grande at a point twenty-five miles below Laredo late at night on April 19, they escaped with their plunder on hastily improvised wooden rafts to the safety of foreign soil.

For six days the bandits had been in the United States. Covering 265 miles during the period, they had been within fourteen miles and again within twenty-five miles, of government troops at Fort McIntosh, had passed within thirty miles of federal troops at San Diego, in Duval County, and had been at no time during the week over sixty

[3]Capt. John O. Elmore, Twenty-fourth Infantry, to Act. Asst. Adj. Gen., District of the Rio Grande, Fort Brown, May 23, 1878, Affairs on the Rio Grande and Texas Frontier (Consolidated File No. 1653 AGO 1878) Letters Received, Attorney General's Office, Record Group 94, National Archives (hereafter LR 1805–89, AGO, RG94, NA).

miles from a military post. Nevertheless, they had escaped any notice of the army. Well armed with modern rifles, the raiders had killed eighteen people, including men, women, and children, and stolen two hundred horses plus rifles, money, clothes, camp equipment, saddles and blankets, and other items along the line of their march. They had burned some buildings and homes and damaged wells.[4]

After crossing the Rio Grande, the band scattered. Since they had been driven deep into Mexico by Shafter's feverish activity of 1877, Indians in the raiding party probably returned to their villages in the Santa Rosa highlands. Spies operating below the border had informed United States military officials about the Santa Rosa camps where American cattle were butchered, horses traded, and beef dried.

The bloody foray convinced Shafter and Mackenzie that only by destroying the Santa Rosa villages could border depredations be curtailed. Sending a *comanchero* to spy out the region, the duo began making plans to strike there as soon as they could gather the necessary information and secure approval from General Ord. Although they soon obtained the information about the villages, several weeks passed before they heard favorably from Ord. At the end of May, 1878, assured by Ord of full support if they crossed on a fresh trail, they started at once for Mexico.

The hard-driving but thorough Mackenzie, concerned that his force might encounter opposition from Mexican troops, organized the command into two columns. The smaller scouting column consisted of four companies of the Eighth Cavalry, two of the Fourth, and a group of Seminole-Negro Indian scouts under John L. Bullis, in all perhaps three hundred men led by Mackenzie and Capt. Samuel B. Young, and was to search the region between the Rio Grande and the Serranias del Burro (Burro Highlands).[5]

Shafter led the larger supporting column. His command consisted of three battalions of the Twenty-fourth Infantry, two companies of cavalry, and three batteries of artillery equipped with six field pieces and two Gatling guns, in all about seven hundred men. In addition, he carried along forty wagons filled with twenty days' rations for the troops and four days' forage for the horses and mules. He was to march his column to the Rio Grande and there wait temporarily before moving 150 miles to Santa Rosa, Mexico, to establish a supply base.[6]

[4]Ibid.

[5]Ernest Wallace, *Ranald S. Mackenzie on the Texas Frontier,* pp. 176–77.

[6]Ibid. Also see Charles J. Crane, *The Experiences of a Colonel of Infantry,* p. 74; James Parker, *The Old Army: Memories, 1872–1918,* p. 104; and General Orders No. 7, District of the Nueces, June 11, 1878, William R. Shafter Papers, Stanford Univer-

Leaving Fort Duncan on June 3, Shafter proceeded to Sycamore Creek, twenty miles west of Fort Clark, where he set up his temporary camp. Eleven days later he was instructed by courier from Mackenzie to wade the Rio Grande and to scout southeastward, reclaiming as much stolen stock as possible in the vicinity of the San Diego River. From there he was to lead his command to Santa Rosa.[7] On June 15, he led his force across the river and for two days searched as instructed, camping the second night on the San Diego. Proceeding up the river on the seventeenth, he met Mackenzie with the scouting column. Because of incompetent guides who had failed to find either water or the way, Mackenzie had been forced to modify his plans.

Planning now to scour the region between the San Diego and San Rodrigo rivers, Mackenzie directed the combined command to proceed to Remolino, where in 1873 he had destroyed a Kickapoo and Apache village. Heavy rain on the eighteenth limited the march to six miles. Hoping to surprise the Indians, the force started after midnight on the nineteenth and rode south, reaching Remolino just before noon. Instead of Indians, the troops found a tough-looking squadron of Mexican soldiers commanded by Col. Pedro Valdez (nicknamed "Colonel Winker" by Mackenzie's troops) under orders to repel the Americans. The American command went into camp.

Shortly after lunch, Shafter met with Valdez. He informed the Mexican officer that the American army was in Mexico to punish thieves and Indians, that it was going to move on at 3:00 P.M., and that the Mexican command was in the proposed line of march. When Valdez told Shafter to turn back, the meeting ended. Valdez, reinforced with additional men, did not move. At the appointed hour, the United States squadron started forward. Shafter, leading the main force, proceeded along the right bank of the San Rodrigo directly toward the Mexican troops. Captain Young led another force along the left bank to flank the Mexican host should it attempt to engage Shafter.

No engagement occurred. As Shafter approached, the Mexican forces withdrew. That evening, when the American troops encamped seven miles below Remolino, the Mexican command was nowhere in sight. The following day as the Americans continued down the river toward the Rio Grande, the Mexican cavalry could be seen in the rear, but it approached no closer than five or six miles.[8]

---

sity Library, Stanford, Calif., photocopy in Southwest Collection, Texas Tech University, Lubbock (hereafter Shafter Papers).

[7]General Orders No. 7, District of the Nueces, June 11, 1878, Shafter Papers.

[8]Mackenzie to Asst. Adj. Gen., Dept. of Texas, June 23, 1878, in Ernest Wallace,

The next morning, June 21, the Americans encountered the Mexican troops again. About seven miles from the Rio Grande, near Monclova Viejo, they discovered that Col. Jesús Nuncio, who had brought up reinforcements and assumed command of the Mexican force, had stationed his men on a hill overlooking the American line of march. A parley followed in which the Mexicans threatened an attack. Undisturbed, Shafter at the close of the conference moved to flank the Mexican position while Captain Young advanced toward it. Again the Mexicans retreated without firing a shot. To avoid further incident, the Americans marched to the Rio Grande, scrambled across it without trouble, and continued to their respective stations.[9]

Even though no Indians were sighted or any cattle or horses recovered, the expedition remained significant. It influenced Pres. Porfirio Díaz, who could not afford to have American troops embarrass his army in Mexico, to take more immediate steps to break up cattle-rustling and horse-stealing across the border. Díaz denounced the invasion, but after a note to the United States minister to Mexico, he let the matter drop.[10] He did move to establish law and order along the Upper Rio Grande Border Region, however, and to promote friendship with the United States. Relations between the two countries remained tense for another two years, but within weeks Indian depredations into Texas had declined.[11]

After returning to Fort Duncan on June 22, 1878, Shafter remained busy with regimental and garrison duties. Detachments of the Fourth, Eighth, and Tenth cavalries maintained a few scouting camps in the Nueces Valley and along the border and handled nearly all the scouts. If they entered Mexico, they crossed the river only when they were on a fresh trail and when they could avoid conflict with Mexican troops. Shafter's Twenty-fourth Infantry troops remained at their posts. As Díaz consolidated his strength in northern Mexico, depredations in the Upper Rio Grande Border Region diminished.[12]

In the fall with tension relaxed, Shafter found time for a short hunt-

ed., *Ranald S. Mackenzie's Official Correspondence Relating to Texas, 1873–1879*, p. 205.

[9]Parker, *The Old Army*, p. 109; Wallace, *Ranald S. Mackenzie on the Texas Frontier*, p. 179; Robert M. Utley, *Frontier Regulars: The United States Army and the Indian, 1866–1890*, pp. 350–56.

[10]J. W. Mota, Secy. of Foreign Affairs, Republic of Mexico, to John W. Foster, July 12, 1878, in *Report and Accompanying Documents of the Committee on Foreign Affairs on the Relations of the United States with Mexico*, 45th Cong., 2d sess., 1878, H. Rept. 701, pp. 555–57.

[11]Utley, *Frontier Regulars*, pp. 354–55.

[12]Ibid.; U.S. Dept. of War, Returns from Regular Army Infantry Regiments, June,

ing trip. Taking Lt. Charles Crane, Twenty-fourth Infantry, a recent graduate of West Point, John Harmar, a contract surgeon, Henry Brisco, a company musician and the best field cook in the regiment, and three or four other men, he left on October 27 for a spot on the Nueces River near modern-day Crystal City. About twenty-five or thirty miles from the post, he noticed the fresh hide of a cougar hanging out to dry in a rancher's yard. Pulling his team to a halt, he interviewed the successful hunter. Informed that with the assistance of a half-dozen dogs the big animal had been treed and killed only the day before, Shafter asked the rancher to take him and his companions on a hunt. But the rancher declined, pointing to his dogs' worn and cut feet. Shafter, who appreciated the value of a good hunting dog, understood.

While proceeding to their camp on the Nueces, the hunters killed two turkeys and bagged some quail which Brisco prepared for supper. Shafter, Crane, and Dr. Harmar reached the camp first and, while waiting for the others, Crane and Shafter, both of whom were excellent marksmen, held a shooting contest.

"Put a hole in that cactus leaf," Shafter told Crane, "and we will shoot at the hole."

They soon spoiled the leaf, making a bigger hole as well as several others. With the leaf destroyed, Shafter turned to a more challenging target. "Now, watch me cut off that twig," he said, pointing to a slender twig some ten or fifteen yards distant. His shot was true. "Now, what will you do?" he asked Crane, handing the young lieutenant the rifle.

Crane replied, "My shot is not so hard to make as yours was, for the twig is bigger where I have to aim." The officer cut the twig clean, six inches lower down.

Looking around camp for another target, Shafter sighted a half-grown hog rooting up the camp ground. Pointing to it, he said, "See me cut off that pig's tail." The lieutenant colonel then took careful aim, fired, and watched the pig run away with its tail hanging by a thin thread of skin.

The remainder of the party arrived at camp in time to see Shafter shoot off the hog's tail. Later, when Shafter and Crane were absent from camp, one of the soldiers boasted to Brisco that "I kin cut off a hog's tail, too." Then, taking aim, he fired at a shoat near the edge of camp. The poor hog fell, loudly squealing, with a broken hip. The soldier, fearing Shafter's anger, killed the pig with an axe, buried it among

---

the nearby bushes, and begged Dr. Harmar to say nothing of the incident. The doctor kept his promise. The party enjoyed several days of
good hunting. Before returning to the post on the last day of October,
it had killed an ocelot, along with some ducks, quail, and turkeys.[13]

One month after his return from the hunting trip, Shafter again took
charge of the district. On December 3, 1878, Mackenzie, called to
Washington on military business, relinquished command to Shafter.
The change involved no major alterations. Shafter continued scouting
along the Rio Grande and in the Nueces River valley. In January, 1879,
he enrolled three Lipans as army scouts and assigned them to Bullis's
command. The following month he sent Bullis to scout along the upper Rio Grande and to establish a camp at Lancaster. But there was
no significant action against Indians, and nearly all companies assigned
to the district remained at their stations.[14]

With conditions quiet, Shafter applied for and received a five months'
leave of absence. Leaving Texas in May, 1879, he returned with his
family for the first time in several years to his home in Galesburg,
Michigan. After renewing old acquaintances and reviving ancient
memories, he made plans to send Mary to an eastern boarding school.
Then, accompanying her to Poughkeepsie, New York, with his wife
he enrolled his fifteen-year-old daughter in Lyndon Hall, a school for
girls.[15]

During his visit in Michigan, Shafter, who had been promoted to
colonel on March 4, 1879, accepted assignment with the First United
States Infantry Regiment. The news delighted him. For months he had
expected the promotion, but when his commission did not arrive, he
reasoned that his aggressive but effective action in 1877 along the Rio
Grande had worked to his disadvantage. He was aware that some Democratic congressmen had urged that Lieutenant Turner's old charges
be used against him. Until his commission finally arrived at Gales-

[13]Crane, *The Experiences of a Colonel of Infantry,* pp. 82–85; Regimental Returns,
Twenty-fourth Infantry, June–Sept., 1878, Roll 246, MC665, NA.

[14]U.S. Dept. of War, Returns from United States Military Posts, 1800–1917, Fort
Clark, Dec., 1878–April, 1879, Roll 215, Microcopy No. 617, National Archives (hereafter Post Returns, MC617, NA); Regimental Returns, Twenty-fourth Infantry, Dec.,
1878–April, 1879, Roll 246, MC665, NA.

[15]Shafter to Theodore Vincent, Adj. Gen., Dept. of Texas, April 18, 1879, United
States, William R. Shafter, Letters Received, Appointments, Commission, and Personal Branch, Adjutant General's Office, Record Group 94, National Archives (hereafter ACP File, AGO, RG94, NA); Regimental Returns, Twenty-fourth Infantry, May,
1879, Roll 246, MC665, NA; Samuel W. Durant, *History of Kalamazoo County,
Michigan,* p. 354.

burg in May, he feared that he had again been denied the colonelcy.[16]

Four months later, on October 3, 1879, Colonel Shafter assumed command of his new regiment at Fort Randall, Dakota Territory. The post, established in 1856 to serve as an army supply base and to keep the road open between Fort Ridgely in Minnesota and Fort Laramie in Wyoming, was situated on the right bank of the Missouri River thirty miles above the mouth of the Niobrara near modern-day Pickstown. A typical frontier post, it had no stockade, its buildings formed a rectangle enclosing a large parade ground, and the stables and other outbuildings stood a short distance to the rear of the soldiers' quarters. In 1858 a reservation for the Yankton Sioux had been established east and north of Fort Randall, and later, to the south, a similar reservation had been created for the Poncas. For almost fifty years the post stood between the reservations, holding the Indians to their treaty promises.[17]

The First Infantry Regiment had been organized during the War of 1812 and reorganized in its present form on May 15, 1815. Its troops had fought in both the Mexican War and the Civil War, and its former colonels included Zachary Taylor, later president, who had served from 1832 to 1843. When Shafter became colonel, replacing retiring Thomas G. Pitcher, its high-ranking officers included Lt. Col. Pinckney Lugenbeel and Maj. H. M. Lazelle. Louis Wilhelmi, who became one of Shafter's close personal friends, was adjutant general of the regiment.

When Shafter assumed command of the First Infantry, he found his troops scattered among three posts. Four companies were at Fort Randall, two companies were at Fort Hale about eighty miles up river near modern-day Chamberlain, and three companies were at Fort Meade, far out in the Indian Territory at the northern edge of the Black Hills. The final company was constructing a telegraph line to Fort Bennett in the Sioux reservation on the Missouri River about twenty miles below the mouth of the Cheyenne.[18]

At his new post Shafter faced two major responsibilities. One involved Sioux threats to the Ponca reservation. Because the reservation in 1876 had been pillaged several times by the Yankton Sioux, federal troops under Capt. Fergus Walker, First Infantry, had removed most of the Poncas in 1877 to the Indian Territory (Oklahoma). Two years later, just before Shafter arrived, Chief Standing Bear had led his Pon-

[16]Shafter to Adj. Gen., U.S. Army, April 27, 1879, and General Orders No. 7, District of the Nueces, April 18, 1878, both in ACP File, AGO, RG94, NA.

[17]*The Disposal of a Portion of Fort Randall Military Reservation*, 52d Cong., 1st sess., 1891, S. Rept. 912, 2:1–4.

[18]Regimental Returns, First Infantry, Oct., 1879, Roll 7, MC665, NA.

cas in an escape from the territory to their former reservation near Fort Randall where they were allowed to remain. To avoid a recurrence of the 1876 trouble, Shafter protected the reservation, with good results.[19]

The second problem involved threats to settlers. A few Sioux warriors from the Rosebud agency had struck ranches along the Niobrara River at a point near the mouth of the Keya Paha. Although no one was killed or even injured, settlers in the vicinity complained of the attacks. In response, Shafter established and maintained Camp Keya Paha nearby and sought permission to build a military road to the isolated camp in case it became necessary to move troops quickly in that direction. Receiving proper authority late in the year, he ordered construction of the road to begin as soon as weather permitted. During the long, cold winter, he kept his troops close to their posts.[20]

In the spring of 1880 Shafter set to work. He dispatched Captain Walker with some troops to Camp Keya Paha to build semipermanent quarters. He ordered some under Capt. James D. DeRussy to construct a military road from Fort Randall to the camp on the Keya Paha and from there to a new post, Fort Niobrara, being built near Valentine, Nebraska, about one hundred miles west of Fort Randall. One company resumed construction of the telegraph line to Fort Bennett.[21]

Shafter also directed several improvements at Fort Randall, including construction of twelve new sets of officers' quarters, improvement of the water facilities, and restoration of the post cemetery. He also installed an extra-large bath in his own house so that he might have warm water in which to soak his almost constantly inflamed legs. Perhaps the most conspicuous addition at the post was the erection of a cross-shaped church. Consisting of a chapel, a library, and an Odd Fellows Hall, the building was an unofficial project originated by Lt. Col. Lugenbeel and financed by soldiers and private citizens who in their spare time hauled rock and timber from nearby Cedar Island and constructed the building.[22] The church, built in spare hours and without any nails, although dilapidated, is the only surviving building at the old post.

In mid-April, after making an inspection tour of the new military

[19]Merrill J. Mattes, "Revival at Old Fort Randall," *Military Engineer* 44 (March–April, 1952): 92; Kenneth R. Jacobs, "A History of the Ponca Indians to 1882" (Ph.D. diss., Texas Tech University, Lubbock, 1974), pp. 96–97, 112–16, 127–31.

[20]Post Returns, Fort Randall, Dec., 1879, Roll 989, MC617, NA; Regimental Returns, First Infantry, Dec., 1879, Roll 7, MC665, NA.

[21]Regimental Returns, First Infantry, April, 1880, Roll 7, MC665, NA.

[22]Mattes, "Revival at Old Fort Randall," p. 93.

road to Fort Niobrara, Shafter went on a seven-day hunting trip north-west of Fort Randall in the hills adjacent to the Missouri River. In the spring, when the grass is dark green in color, the rolling hills present a beautiful panorama. Their draws and ravines, covered with brush and small trees, provided excellent shelter for plentiful numbers of timid wildlife, including deer, turkey, and quail. Although the record on the outcome is mute, the hunt provided Shafter with a needed break in his monotonous post routine.[23]

At the end of May, 1880, Shafter with his First Infantry Regiment returned to Texas. During the previous year, Apaches led by the gallant Victorio, called by one historian the master of Apache warfare, had left the reservation at Fort Stanton, New Mexico, and taken to the hills. For over a year afterward, Victorio and his band raided ranches and settlements in their flight for freedom across southern New Mexico and southeastern Arizona. The Victorio War, as efforts to capture Victorio's band were called, raged across the Trans-Pecos region before the Apaches escaped into Mexico. In the summer of 1880, there were clear indications that Victorio's next move would be into Texas, and General Ord wanted Shafter, his trusty and relentless Indian fighter, to help protect the Trans-Pecos.[24]

Taking two steamboats at Fort Randall, Shafter and eight companies of his regiment proceeded by water to Yankton, Dakota Territory, and from there by rail to Texas. Upon their arrival at San Antonio on June 8, Shafter, at Ord's direction, dispatched three companies to Ringgold Barracks on the lower Rio Grande. The five others remained at San Antonio, where four days later Shafter assumed command of the post.[25]

During June and July, Shafter planned for the West Texas campaign. Knowing that his men would guard isolated water holes and lonely river crossings, he pored over maps of the Trans-Pecos region. He determined to make Presidio, deep in the Big Bend country but at an important crossing of the Rio Grande, his temporary headquarters. When Victorio crossed into Texas on July 28, Shafter, whose remaining troops in Dakota had arrived in Texas, left for the Trans-Pecos with six companies of infantry.[26]

---

[23]Post Returns, Fort Randall, April, 1880, Roll 989, MC617, NA; Regimental Returns, First Infantry, April, 1880, Roll 7, MC665, NA.

[24]Robert M. Utley, "Special Report on Fort Davis," mimeographed report for the National Survey of Historic Sites and Buildings, Dept. of Interior, 1960, p. 74. See also Utley, *Frontier Regulars*, pp. 360–63.

[25]Regimental Returns, First Infantry, May, 1880, Roll 7, MC665, NA; Post Returns, Fort San Antonio, May–June, 1880, Roll 1084, MC617, NA.

[26]Regimental Returns, First Infantry, Aug.–Oct., 1880, Roll 7, MC665, NA; Post

As Shafter started westward, Victorio, looking for food and water, rode through the Sierra Diablo, Quitman, Eagle, and Van Horn mountains. Pursued by Tenth Cavalry troops commanded by Col. Benjamin Grierson and Seminole-Negro scouts under John L. Bullis, Victorio on August 4 pushed northeastward to near modern-day Van Horn. Two days later, in attempting to get water, he was repulsed near Rattlesnake Springs but not captured. Although Victorio evaded Grierson near the Van Horn Mountains, on August 7 troops under Capt. Thomas C. Lebo, who had been with Shafter on the Llano Estacado in 1875 and in Mexico in 1876, stumbled onto his supply camp in the Sierra Diablo and destroyed it, including twenty-five head of cattle and a large supply of beef on pack animals. Denied access to water and out of fresh beef, Victorio turned his followers back toward the Rio Grande and on August 11 escaped into Mexico.[27]

As Victorio eluded federal troops, Shafter marched westward. After three weeks on the trail, news reached him that Victorio had escaped. With a view now to keeping Victorio and his followers out of Texas, he scattered his troops at well-known crossings along the Rio Grande and headed directly for Presidio. Eighteen days later, after a march of two hundred miles, he set up his headquarters a few miles north of Presidio on Cibolo Creek.

As Shafter guarded the treacherous Trans-Pecos, the Victorio War ended. During the first days of October, American troops under Col. Eugene A. Carr and Col. George P. Buell and Mexican troops under Col. Joaquín Terrazas converged on Tres Castillas, about eighty miles northwest of Presidio in the Candellaria Mountains of Mexico where the Apaches hid. The international cooperation did not last, and on October 9 Terrazas told the Americans to return to their own country. A few days later, on October 14, Terrazas cornered the Indians, killed Victorio, and slaughtered sixty warriors and eighteen women and children. Within days of Victorio's death, Shafter, turning to other matters, put his troops to work repairing military roads in the region.

Shafter and the First Infantry had played only a small role in the

Returns, Fort San Antonio, Aug., 1880, Roll 1084, MC617, NA; William T. Sherman, "Report of the General of the Army," Nov. 10, 1880, in *Annual Report of the Secretary of War*, 1880, 46th Cong., 3d sess., H. Exec. Doc. 1, pt. 2, p. 307.

[27] Frank M. Temple, "Colonel B.H. Grierson's Texas Commands" (Master's thesis, Texas Tech University, Lubbock, 1959), pp. 134–36; C. L. Sonnichsen, *The Mescalero Apaches*, pp. 159–97; William H. Leckie, *The Buffalo Soldiers: A Narrative of the Negro Cavalry in the West*, p. 228; Clarence C. Clendenen, *Blood on the Border: The United States Army and the Mexican Irregulars*, p. 95; Regimental Returns, First Infantry, Oct., 1880, Roll 7, MC665, NA.

final defeat of Victorio. Nevertheless, stationed at important river crossings along the border and at well-known watering places in the neighboring mountains, they had effectively blocked any plan by Victorio to return to the rugged fastnesses of the Big Bend. With no place to go, Victorio became an easy target for the Mexican troops.[28]

During the Victorio War Shafter had become involved in a silver-mining venture. Within weeks of Shafter's arrival in the Trans-Pecos, John W. Spencer, a freighter and part-time prospector who had come to the Big Bend as a trader and merchant during the Mexican War, found some silver carbonates and other metals in the Chinati Mountains. Because he was broke, Spencer showed the ore to Shafter, and the samples when assayed were found to contain a small but profitable deposit of silver. Shafter, wanting to secure title to as much land as possible near the discovery, encouraged Louis Wilhelmi and John L. Bullis to join him in purchasing several sections of land. Taking Spencer in as a partner, they agreed to split ownership and any profits from the land four ways, one-quarter each. In January, 1881, Wilhelmi and Bullis purchased four sections of land, and two years afterward one of the sections proved to contain a rich deposit of silver.

Lacking the technical skills to operate a mine, the four partners leased the land to a mining firm from San Francisco, California. A subsequent struggle over land and mineral rights ended in the courts when Bullis brought suit to retain ownership of the land and mining profits after Spencer, Wilhelmi, and Shafter had sold their interests to the company. The bitter court fight cost Shafter Bullis's friendship and a promotion in 1891 to brigadier general. Settled in favor of the mining company, which offered the partners shares in the operation, the case also led to substantial gains for Shafter and the others and a secure financial future. Shafter, by the standards of his day, became a wealthy man.[29]

[28]Leckie, *The Buffalo Soldiers,* pp. 226–28; Utley, *Frontier Regulars,* p. 364. A remnant of Victorio's band escaped the dreadful fate of the Indians at Tres Castillas. A few people managed to break through Terrazas's lines, and thirty-nine warriors en route to Victorio's stronghold who had tarried along the Rio Grande survived. The survivors were quick to exact revenge. On October 28 they ambushed a small party of the Tenth Cavalry along the Rio Grande near Ojo Caliente, killing four troopers and stealing four horses and two mules. After the raid, the Indians pushed into southern New Mexico, where for a year afterward they eluded troops under Col. Edward Hatch, Ninth Cavalry, commanding the Department of New Mexico. Utley, *Frontier Regulars,* pp. 364–65.

[29]*Presidio Mining Co.* v. *Alice Bullis,* Court Transcript No. 5909 (now filed as M11633), filed in Texas Supreme Court at Austin, May, 1886; Shafter to Bullis, Nov. 12, 1883, in A. J. Evans, Brief for the Appellees, filed in *Presidio Mining Co.* v. *Alice Bullis,* 68 Tex. 581 (1887), ACP File, AGO, RG94, NA; Paul H. Carlson, "The Discov-

For the first few months following Victorio's death, Shafter suffered. Not only did he weigh some 260 pounds, but he had developed gout, his varicose veins by now made it necessary for him to wear medical stockings, and his district headquarters, only a rough cantonment, offered few physical comforts. Moreover, military developments kept him in the saddle. At the end of November General Ord called him back to San Antonio to report on the Victorio campaign. Placed in command of Fort McKavett on December 16, a few days later Shafter left San Antonio by horseback for his new post, arriving on January 2, 1881. A few weeks later, Shafter transferred again. On February 1, he received orders sending him to Fort Davis. He left near the end of the month and after sixteen days on the trail rode on March 11 into his new post. During the preceding three months, although he was in poor physical health, Shafter had spent more than thirty days on the road.

When he assumed command at Fort Davis on March 12, 1881, Shafter found a peaceful frontier. The defeat of Victorio, the growing power of the Porfirio Díaz regime in Mexico, the extension of railroads into the area, and the forceful confinement of Indians on reservations all played a part. A stable Trans-Pecos encouraged a population boom of sorts. Sheepherders and cattlemen filtered in to establish their ranches near widely spaced water holes or along the meandering streams of the dry land. Small towns sprang up along the tracks of the Southern Pacific and Texas and Pacific railroads. In the beginning, most of the communities appeared as little more than railway stations, whose importance as shipping points attracted settlers. The growing population, although never large, combined with the recent military developments to turn the stark land into a rural commonwealth.

As a result Shafter's duties were largely routine. To vary their commands Shafter moved his troops from one sub-post to another in the district and back again to Fort Davis. From time to time he sent scouting units southward to search the Rio Grande for Indians, but no Indians or recent signs of them were seen. In the spring and summer some of his troops guarded Texas and Pacific Railroad construction

ery of Silver in West Texas," *West Texas Historical Association Year Book* 54 (1978): 55–64. Also see David S. Stanley, Commanding the Dept. of Texas, to Adj. Gen., U.S. Army, July 2, 1887, ACP File, AGO, RG94, NA. Wilhelmi, suffering from chronic ill health, died before he received any significant returns. Spencer sold his shares in the company and squandered the proceeds. The record for Bullis is mute, but he seems to have invested in West Texas lands. Shafter carefully invested his mining income. *San Francisco Call*, Nov. 13, 1906; *San Francisco Chronicle*, Nov. 13, 1906. The Presidio Mining Company began full-scale operations at the close of the court fight in 1887. See Carlson, "The Discovery of Silver in West Texas," pp. 55–64.

gangs who were building a bridge across the Pecos River. At Fort Davis Shafter took steps to complete construction of the post, a major army installation in 1881 with nearly fifty buildings and several long rows of stables for horses and mules. He maintained a bivouac, Camp Pinery, about forty-five miles to the northwest, where he detailed soldiers to cut trees into lumber for building purposes.[30]

Shafter supervised many of the fatigue duties. He visited Camp Pinery to examine the lumbering detail once in August and twice in December. He directed the construction of the post stables, and when new privies were needed he planned the necessary changes.[31] Thus, by close observation of even undistinguished activities, Shafter kept Fort Davis in top shape. The post medical officer reported in October, 1881, that "the general police of the grounds, barracks, hospital, guardhouse, kitchen, [and] mess-rooms . . . have been very well performed. . . ." The water supply, obtained from a well about a mile away along Limpia Creek, was good and ample for ordinary purposes. The general health of the men and officers was excellent. "The quality of rations," the surgeon indicated, "has been very good, and mode of cooking and serving very satisfactory."[32]

To maintain the quality of rations Shafter sometimes used unorthodox methods. One evening in the summer, according to Barry Scobee, while Shafter was sitting on the porch of his home, a soldier walked across the parade ground from the enlisted men's barracks holding a tin plate with a scanty supply of meat and vegetables on it. The trooper saluted and with anger and indignation displayed the food.

"Sir," he complained to Shafter, "this is my dinner!"

Shafter leaned forward in his easy chair, took a look at the meager contents of the plate, and said, "Well, eat it, then; I have had mine." Without a word the soldier saluted and returned to the barracks, presumably cursing Shafter as well as the food.

Shafter quickly took action. After the trooper left, he sent for the captain of the company responsible for the sparse rations. "Sir," Shafter demanded of the captain, "how much money have you in your mess fund?"

The captain, proud that he had been able to cut food expenses, replied, "Eighteen hundred dollars, Colonel."

[30]Post Returns, Fort Davis, March, 1881, Roll 297, MC617, NA; U.S. Dept. of War, Post Medical Reports, Fort Davis, March–April, 1881, Books No. 7-9-12, Old Records Division, Adjutant General's Office, National Archives (hereafter Post Medical Reports, ORD, AGO, NA).
[31]Post Returns, Fort Davis, Aug. 1881–March, 1882, Roll 297, MC617, NA.
[32]Post Medical Reports, Fort Davis, Oct., 1881, Books No. 7-9-12, ORD, AGO, NA.

"Well, sir," returned Shafter, "change the eighteen hundred dollars into provisions for your company and do it damn quick."[33] The complaining soldier never knew that Shafter had with dispatch taken steps to improve the food, and possibly for years afterward he cursed his colonel.

Later that summer, 1881, the notorious "Flipper affair" rocked Fort Davis and brought Shafter into conflict with another officer. On his arrival at the post in March, one of Shafter's first acts had been to remove 2d Lt. Henry O. Flipper, Tenth Cavalry, the first black graduate of West Point, as acting assistant quartermaster. Shafter wanted an officer of his own regiment in the position—a fairly standard act—but it is possible that there were also racial motives involved. Although Flipper continued as acting commissary of subsistence, after the trouble started Shafter informed Flipper that as soon as a suitable replacement could be found he would also be removed as commissary of subsistence. Flipper believed that the new commander removed him for personal reasons. He became alarmed at the sudden change in command, and, when his civilian friends cautioned him to beware of the impulsive colonel, he made a sincere effort to avoid trouble, stay clear of Shafter, and get along with his fellow officers.[34]

Good relations with two officers proved impossible, however. One officer with whom Flipper clashed was 1st Lt. Louis Wilhelmi, a friend of Shafter who had been at West Point with Flipper. Because of ill-health Wilhelmi had failed at the academy and perhaps resented the presence of the talented black soldier. The other officer was Lt. Charles E. Nordstrom of his own Tenth Cavalry. Flipper, who was at Fort Davis before Nordstrom, had found a riding companion in Mollie Dwyer, a good friend, whose companionship he guarded. When Nordstrom arrived at the post, the relationship changed as Miss Dwyer found less time to go riding with Flipper but more time to spend with Nordstrom. Because the rivals for Dwyer's attention shared "the same set of double quarters" with "a common hall," the situation was awkward and vexatious. Flipper resented the tall Swede and dubbed him a "brute" and a "hyena."[35] Ordinarily, the nettled young officer would have had periodic field assignment to relieve him of the tension, but his duties at the post kept him at Fort Davis each time his Company A left for service in the field.

[33]Barry Scobee, *Old Fort Davis*, pp. 86–87.

[34]Theodore D. Harris, ed., *Negro Frontiersman: The Western Memoirs of Henry O. Flipper, First Negro Graduate of West Point*, pp. vii, 18–19.

[35]Ibid., pp. 19–20.

Henry Flipper. *Courtesy Fort Concho Museum*

Removed from a position of responsibility, harassed by the man with whom he shared quarters, and resentful of having lost his riding companion, Flipper concluded, when questions arose about the commissary funds, that he was the subject of a nefarious plot to ruin his military career. Years later he recalled that Shafter, Nordstrom, and Wilhelmi deliberately went out of their way to "persecute" and "lay traps" for him. The "traps," he wrote, were "cunningly laid and [although] never did a man walk the path of uprightness straighter than I did . . . I was sacrificed."[36]

Flipper may have been set up. However, there is little evidence of a plot. Granted that Nordstrom and Wilhelmi resented the black officer and that Shafter, as Robert M. Utley has said, was "afflicted with barely concealed racism," it was Flipper's mishandling of the post commissary funds that prompted his arrest and subsequent court-martial. First, rather than place the commissary funds in his office safe, Flipper kept them in a trunk in private quarters frequented by servants, one of whom, Lucy E. Smith, kept her clothes there. According to Flipper's statement at the trial, he had kept the funds in the trunk for several months before Shafter's arrival at Fort Davis.[37]

Second, Flipper assumed that a directive in May from Maj. Michael P. Small, chief commissary of subsistence for the Department of Texas, notifying all acting commissaries of his absence from headquarters in San Antonio for the remainder of the month and ordering the temporary cessation of cash transmittals, applied to all commissary funds. Thus, he stopped forwarding all weekly statements and checks as well as the cash. Flipper, who received no further communication from department headquarters, did not resume the transfer of funds until Shafter in July ordered him to send all commissary funds in his possession to Major Small.[38]

Next, when he prepared an inspection of the returns, Flipper discovered a deficiency in funds of $1,440.43. Reasoning that he could submit a check for the amount of the deficit and then deposit personal funds in the San Antonio National Bank to cover it, Flipper experienced no undue alarm. But when he was unable to raise the required cash, the plan failed. Moreover, he did not have a personal account at the bank.

Rather than admit to the missing funds, the illegal check, and the ill-advised plans for sending personal money to the bank, Flipper procrastinated and resorted to further duplicity. He made illegal entries

[36] Ibid.

[37] J. Norman Heard, *The Black Frontiersmen: Adventures of Negroes among American Indians, 1828–1918,* p. 117; Robert M. Utley, "'Pecos Bill' on the Texas Frontier," *American West* 6 (Jan., 1969): 6.

[38] Proceedings of a General Court-Martial which met at Fort Davis, Texas, pursuant to Special Orders No. 108, Headquarters, Dept. of Texas, Sept. 3, 1881, pp. 44–53, 402–406, 456; Records Relating to the Army Career of Henry Ossian Flipper, 1873–1883, Microcopy No. T1027, Roll 1, National Archives (hereafter Court-Martial Proceedings, Flipper Records, MC T1027, NA); Donald R. McClung, "Henry O. Flipper: First Negro Officer in the United States Army" (Master's thesis, East Texas State University, Commerce, 1970), pp. 81–82.

in the weekly accounts, reporting the funds "in transit," and hoped that Shafter at each Sunday morning inspection would cast no more than a cursory glance at the invoices submitted for his signature. The stratagem succeeded. Shafter, not suspecting his junior officer of wrongdoing, remained ignorant of Flipper's situation until August 10 when Major Small informed him that no funds had arrived in San Antonio.

Finally, Flipper resorted to lying. When questioned by Shafter about the missing funds, he said that he could offer no explanation other than that the money must have been lost in transit. Unsatisfied, Shafter relieved Flipper as acting commissary of subsistence and ordered all the commissary funds in Flipper's possession turned over to Lt. Frank H. Edmunds, First Infantry, who assumed Flipper's duties.[39]

An investigation that followed was revealing, and any conspiracy, if there was one, began during the investigation. Shafter, Wilhelmi, and Edmunds found more than $2,000.00 in commissary checks scattered on a desk in Flipper's quarters. They uncovered weekly statements of funds for May, June, and July in the trunk. They discovered clothes belonging to Lucy Smith in Flipper's room, and when she was searched, some $2,800.00 in checks were removed from her person. Arrested and temporarily confined to the guardhouse, Flipper admitted the worthlessness of the $1,440.43 check he had written to cover the deficit in commissary funds and that he had lied to Shafter.[40]

Arraigned on charges of embezzlement and conduct unbecoming an officer and gentleman, Flipper, beginning in September, faced a general court-martial. Despite revealing circumstantial evidence to the contrary, most people, including Shafter, believed the lieutenant was innocent of embezzlement. They knew that disorder among commissary funds at any post was not unusual, and they believed that in this case it was more a question of inexperience or carelessness than one of dishonesty.[41]

But from Shafter's point of view, Flipper had also lied to and deceived a superior officer, a gross breach of the military code of honor. Unwilling to forgive his subaltern, Shafter struck back with all the considerable weight of his position as post commander. Although his name headed a list of people who had lent money to the young officer

[39] Court-Martial Proceedings, pp. 44–53, 402–406, 456, Flipper Records, MC T1027, Roll 1, NA. Also see Bruce J. Dinges, "The Court-Martial of Lieutenant Henry O. Flipper: An Example of Black-White Relationships in the Army, 1881," *American West* 9 (Jan., 1972): 14; McClung, "Henry O. Flipper," pp. 86–89.

[40] Post Returns, Fort Davis, Aug., 1881–March, 1882, Roll 297, MC617, NA.

[41] William H. Leckie and Shirley A. Leckie, *Unlikely Warriors: General Benjamin H. Grierson and His Family,* p. 275.

to recover the missing funds and thus perhaps receive leniency from the court, the fickle Shafter filed the charges and specifications, including those relating to embezzlement, and collected the evidence to be used at the trial.

At the trial Flipper, who later said that he was the victim of a vicious plot concocted by Shafter, Nordstrom, and Wilhelmi, pleaded not guilty to all the charges and specifications.[42] Due to a delay in obtaining an attorney, the trial dragged on for three months, ending on December 8, 1881. The court acquitted Flipper of embezzlement but found him guilty of conduct unbecoming an officer and gentleman. In the spring Lt. Henry O. Flipper was sentenced to be dismissed from the United States Army, a sentence undeniably harsh.

Flipper did not steal government monies. Nordstrom was not involved in a plot; his name was hardly mentioned at the court-martial. If they had spread the checks around Flipper's quarters or otherwise conspired against him, Shafter and Wilhelmi would have needed the cooperation of Capt. Kinzie Bates, second in command to Shafter, of Frank Edmunds, and of Flipper's assistant and most important supporter at the trial, commissary Sgt. Carl Ross. Such a conspiracy was unlikely, and trial testimony and cross-examination made no mention of a plot. Who stole the funds? The most likely culprit was Lucy Smith, who had a key to Flipper's trunk.[43]

Although he was rightfully acquitted of theft, Flipper was guilty of a gross breach of honor. He put his name on official returns, knowing them to be false. When questioned about official business, he lied several times to Shafter. He deceived Shafter about a worthless check. These were dishonest acts that violated the trust others put in him as an officer and a gentleman.

Shafter played a major role in the affair. As the post commander, he was one of the chief prosecution witnesses, and his testimony that Flipper had lied was a key factor in the trial. But no records in the Shafter Personal File of the Adjutant General's Office, in the several collections of Shafter's papers, or in the court-martial testimony hint that he had conspired with Wilhelmi, Nordstrom, or anyone else. Moreover, participation in such a scheme would not have been characteristic of him. Although he badgered subordinate officers and was rough on them, he was not malicious. To the contrary, Shafter was an honest, thor-

[42]Court-Martial Proceedings, pp. 44–53, Flipper Records, MC T1027, NA; Dinges, "The Court-Martial of Lieutenant Henry O. Flipper," pp. 15–16.

[43]Barry C. Johnson, "Flipper's Dismissal: The Ruin of Lt. Henry O. Flipper, U.S.A.—First Coloured Graduate of West Point," in Barry C. Johnson, ed., HO, For the Great West, pp. 140–72, 225–26; San Antonio Light, Feb. 10, 1985.

oughly professional soldier, committed by the very nature of his calling to an aggressive attitude toward what he regarded as incompetency on the part of his officers and men.

In the months after the Flipper trial events at Fort Davis passed quietly. Indians avoided the area, and there was little cattle rustling in the isolated and empty country. With military conditions stable, the army determined to move Shafter to a more volatile frontier, and in April, 1882, Shafter received orders to proceed with his First Infantry Regiment to Arizona.[44] When he left Texas by train early the next month, Shafter could not know that in an official capacity he would not return again to the state that had been his home for fifteen years. In Texas he had fought against the powerful Indians of the plains and the formidable Apaches of the southwestern mountains. He had helped to secure peace along the troublesome Rio Grande border. Others already were, or soon would be, safely grazing thousands upon thousands of cattle, the economic lifeblood of Texas during the 1870's and 1880's, over the vast area where he had rendered dedicated military service for a decade and a half to make it possible. Despite his numerous imperfections and his lack of West Point training, his superiors in Texas — Mackenzie, Augur, and Ord — recognized Shafter as one of their most effective field officers.

[44]Post Returns, Fort Davis, April–May, 1882, Roll 297, MC617, NA.

CHAPTER NINE

The Arizona Years

A s he left Texas in 1882, William R. Shafter could not know that he was beginning a short interlude free from extended field operations. But as the long drama of Western Indian wars moved toward its inevitable close, the forty-eight-year-old colonel of infantry found himself in the far Southwest performing mainly garrison duty. Even so, the curtain had not yet dropped, and Shafter played important if brief and routine roles in two difficult and protracted Apache campaigns in Arizona's torrid mountain ranges.

The Arizona campaigns started suddenly. On April 18, 1882, a party of Chiricahua Apache refugees from the Janos River in Mexico rode onto the San Carlos Indian Reservation on the Gila River in southeastern Arizona and convinced about two hundred Indians there under Loco, their chief, to return with them to Mexico. The trek southward was marked by raids and depredations. Although troops from the posts in southern Arizona and New Mexico were sent in pursuit, the Indians, mounted on horses and well armed, escaped across the border.[1] With the addition of Chief Loco's people, the number of hostiles, as the army called them, swelled to over four hundred, a third of them men and boys able to bear arms, and increased the apprehension of ranchers in Arizona and New Mexico. Moreover, Indians remaining on the reservation, angry over the poor treatment they were getting, threatened to leave and join their relatives in Mexico.[2]

[1]William T. Sherman, "Report of the General of the Army," Nov. 6, 1882, in *Annual Report of the Secretary of War*, 1882, 42d Cong., 2d sess., H. Exec. Doc. 1, pt. 2, pp. 3–9; Jason Betzinez, *I Fought with Geronimo*, ed. Wilbur S. Nye, pp. 56–74.
[2]Britton Davis, *The Truth about Geronimo*, p. 81; Clarence C. Clendenen, *Blood on the Border: The United States Army and the Mexican Irregulars*, pp. 96–97; Dan L. Thrapp, *The Conquest of Apacheria*, pp. 235–37.

Faced with the unstable situation, Col. (Bvt. Maj. Gen.) Orlando B. Willcox, commanding the Department of Arizona, late in April asked for reinforcements to aid in subduing the defiant Apaches. Lt. Gen. Philip H. Sheridan, commanding the Division of the Missouri, acting upon orders from Gen. William T. Sherman, commander of the army, sent Col. Albert G. Brackett, Third Cavalry, with his regiment from Fort Russell near Cheyenne, Wyoming, to Fort Thomas, Arizona, on the southern edge of the San Carlos Indian Reservation. In addition Sheridan ordered Shafter and the First Infantry, except Company H at Fort Leavenworth, Kansas, to Fort Grant and several other posts in the southeastern part of the territory.[3]

Upon leaving Fort Davis on May 1, after fourteen eventful months at the post, Shafter and his regiment moved overland to Marfa, boarded the Southern Pacific Railroad, and headed west. Even as they rode toward Arizona, other American troops pursued and fought renegade Apaches on Mexican soil. Two days later, at Deming, New Mexico, Shafter detached Capt. Kinzie Bates with one company to proceed via Albuquerque to Holbrook, Arizona, on the Little Colorado River for guard and escort duty. Here also the battalion was reinforced by two companies that had arrived a few hours earlier from Leon Water Hole, Texas.

As the regiment moved westward by rail, Shafter dispersed his troops. He sent various companies to such scattered posts as Fort McDowell on the Verde River near its junction with the Salt; Fort Verde about sixty miles upstream from Fort McDowell; Fort Mojave on the Colorado River near modern-day Toprock; Fort Bowie near Apache Pass in the Chiricahua Mountains, almost midway between Willcox and the New Mexico line; Fort Apache on the White River in the panhandle of Navajo County; and Fort Huachuca near Sierra Vista at the foot of the Canelo Hills, not far from the Mexican border and astride the main Apache route to Mexico. Finally, with Company A, field staff, and band, Shafter marched twenty-five miles to arrive on May 5 at Fort Grant.[4]

[3]Orlando B. Willcox, Commanding the Dept. of Arizona, "Report of Bvt. Maj. Gen. O. B. Willcox," Aug. 31, 1882, in *Annual Report of the Secretary of War, 1882,* 47th Cong., 2d sess., H. Exec. Doc. 1, pt. 2, pp. 143–53; Philip Sheridan to R. C. Drum, Adj. Gen., Washington, April 30, 1882, 1926 AGO 1882 (filed with 1749 AGO 1882), Letters Received, Attorney General's Office, Record Group 393, National Archives (hereafter LR, AGO, RG 393, NA); James Weldon Smith, "Colonel Ranald Slidell Mackenzie and the Apache Problem, 1881–1883" (Master's thesis, Texas Tech University, Lubbock, 1973), pp. 51–52.

[4]U.S. Dept. of War, Returns from Regular Army Infantry Regiments, June, 1821–Dec., 1916, First Infantry, May, 1881, and June, 1882, Rolls 7 and 8, Microcopy No. 665, National Archives (hereafter Regimental Returns, MC665, NA).

Band at Fort Grant, Arizona. *Courtesy U.S. Signal Corps, National Archives*

Fort Grant, in the Aravaipa Valley, was originally established in 1865 as Camp Grant at a site some seventy miles northwest. In 1873 it was moved to the base of Graham Mountain, a location convenient to one of the routes often taken by Apaches who periodically fled the San Carlos Reservation fifty miles north of the post to raid in Mexico. The climate at Shafter's new post was perfect, wrote the wife of one officer, and life there was simple and healthful.[5]

As commanding officer of Fort Grant, Shafter had a pleasant Spanish-style home with a courtyard in the center. Built of adobe, with three rooms on each side of the courtyard, the house opened out on a wide porch and garden. At the back of the garden were the stables. With her daughter Mary away at school in Poughkeepsie, New York, Hattie Shafter spent much of her time outside on the porch sewing, reading, or visiting with friends. Often at night the Shafters started a bright fire in the hearth, but during the day a fire was unnecessary even in winter.[6]

During the first two months after his arrival at Fort Grant, Shafter was busy. Placed in charge of scouting operations in southeastern Arizona, on May 30 he took an inspection tour to Fort Bowie to familiar-

[5]Ellen McGowan Biddle, *Reminiscences of a Soldier's Wife,* pp. 203–205.
[6]Biddle, *Reminiscences of a Soldier's Wife,* pp. 203–205.

ize himself with the garrison and with the wildly rugged terrain in the vicinity in which he commanded scouting operations. At Fort Bowie, he inspected the military facilities with Capt. Leo O. Parker, commanding the post. Before returning to Fort Grant on June 2, Shafter ordered Parker to detach fifteen men to establish a camp in the Chiricahua Mountains near the present-day town of Paradise, from which the soldiers were to watch for Indians. On June 6, he left for ten days to examine a camp on the Gila River near the mouth of the San Simon River. Only eight days after his return from the Gila River camp, he visited Fort Huachuca, where he ordered his troops to maintain tight control of the mountain passes into Mexico, especially those through the Sulphur Spring and Santa Cruz valleys.[7]

In late June two additional small Apache outbreaks occured at San Carlos. Charged with intercepting the fleeing bands before they reached Mexico, Shafter moved quickly. He ordered several detachments of his infantry to guard water holes in his vicinity and telegraphed the officers at Forts Bowie and Huachuca to strengthen the patrols in the mountain passes. He wired Colonel Brackett at Fort Thomas to offer his assistance to the cavalry, but Brackett ignored the request. Then Shafter urged Colonel Willcox to permit him to draw a tight cordon of troops around the San Carlos Reservation and another along the Mexican border. But Willcox, who in 1881 had disobeyed Sherman's orders and thwarted other operations, inefficient and unreliable as usual, pretended to be busy with administrative details and did nothing.[8]

A week later, on July 6, as Willcox considered Shafter's strategy, a fourth outbreak took place. This time the Indians killed Colvig, chief of the agency police, and three of his men. Now Shafter offered the Indian agent at the reservation, J. C. Tiffany, his assistance and telegraphed Colonel Willcox for authority to ride at once upon San Carlos. Willcox again procrastinated and referred Shafter's request to Gen. Irvin McDowell, commanding the Division of the Pacific, his immediate superior. Meanwhile, the Indians who had left the reservation attacked settlers at McMillenville on the northwest boundary of the reservation and proceeded northeastward along the old Moqui

[7]U.S. Dept. of War, Returns from Regular Army Infantry Regiments, June, 1821– Dec., 1916, First Infantry, May–June, 1882, Roll 8, Microcopy No. 665, National Archives (hereafter Regimental Returns, MC665, NA).

[8]Willcox, "Report," Aug. 31, 1882, in Annual Report of the Secretary of War, 1882, 47th Cong., 2d sess., H. Exec. Doc. 1, pt. 2, pp. 143–53; Davis, *The Truth about Geronimo*, p. 9; Smith, "Colonel Ranald Slidell Mackenzie and the Apache Problem, 1881–1883," pp. 57–67. Also see Robert M. Utley, *Frontier Regulars: The United States Army and the Indian, 1866–1890*, pp. 371–77.

Trail toward General's Springs about forty miles east of Fort Verde.[9]

Before the Indians could be rounded up, Shafter left Arizona. He received orders to proceed to New York City to serve as superintendent of the army's recruiting service. Relinquishing command of Fort Grant, the First Infantry, and all scouting operations in his vicinity to Lt. Col. William H. Brown, on July 13, 1882, he departed for the East.[10] Although desirous to help establish peace in Arizona by returning the Apaches to the reservation, Shafter looked forward to his new assignment in New York, for it would place him near his daughter at Poughkeepsie. Knowing that the aggressive colonel would no longer bombard him with requests to hunt the Apaches, Colonel Willcox must have breathed a sigh of relief as Shafter took leave.

For over two years Shafter served as superintendent of the General Recruiting Service. The number of applicants for enlistment in the army was large throughout the twenty-six months, and during part of the time recruiting officers had instructions to select only the very best men for acceptance and enlistment. For a few months, "lest the strength of the army should be exceeded," it was necessary to confine recruiting almost entirely to reenlistments of soldiers with good records. Part of the time, because of a shortage of appropriations, Shafter was responsible for recruiting mounted troops as well as infantry.[11]

On October 1, 1884, relieved of his duties in New York, Shafter went with his family, both Hattie and Mary, to Galesburg. After a short stay there, he proceeded by rail to Fort Grant. The day following his arrival, November 9, he again took command of the post and regiment, noting that the officers and troops of his regiment were stationed at the posts to which he had assigned them in 1882 except for Company K, which, under its new captain, Douglas M. Scott, had been transferred to Fort Whipple Barracks northeast of Prescott. At Fort Grant, Shafter had one company of his regiment and four companies of cavalry.[12]

During Shafter's absence from Arizona, Brig. Gen. George C. Crook had replaced the egotistical and incompetent Willcox. By using a contingent of two hundred Apache scouts, pursuing the hostiles across the border into Mexico, and negotiating patiently, Crook had over-

[9]Willcox, "Report," Aug. 31, 1882, p. 150; Davis, *The Truth about Geronimo*, p. 9.
[10]Regimental Returns, First Infantry, July, 1882, Roll 8, MC665, NA; U.S. Dept. of War, Returns from United States Military Posts, 1800–1916, Fort Grant, July, 1882, Roll 415, Microcopy No. 617, National Archives (hereafter Post Returns, MC617, NA).
[11]Drum to Sheridan, Oct., 1884, in *Annual Report of the Secretary of War*, 1884, 48th Cong., 2d sess., H. Exec. Doc. 1, pt. 2, p. 76.
[12]Post Returns, Fort Grant, Nov., 1884, Roll 415, MC617, NA; Regimental Returns, First Infantry, Nov., 1884, Roll 8, MC665, NA.

taken the Apaches, including Geronimo and his band, and had returned them to the San Carlos Reservation. During the action, which placed a premium on hard-riding cavalry units, First Infantry troops had observed water holes, guarded mountain passes, and protected isolated ranches in Arizona.[13]

Upon his return to Fort Grant, Shafter led a quiet, routine garrison life.[14] The winter months passed slowly. Shafter remained at his post through December. With only a few monotonous military duties to perform, he left on January 18, 1885, for an eight-day hunting trip, his first for an extended time in six years. The following month, when he received word through General Crook that the Tenth Cavalry Regiment, commanded by Benjamin F. Grierson, Shafter's old nemesis from Texas, was to be transferred to Arizona, he ordered troops at Fort Bowie to trade places with those at Fort McDowell, but he made no other preparations for the arrival of the new regiment. When the Tenth Cavalry reached Arizona, Shafter, assuming command of part of the regiment, detailed five companies to Fort Grant and one company to Fort Bowie. Other companies of the Tenth, under Grierson, took station at Forts Whipple Barracks, Thomas, Apache, and Verde.[15]

The peaceful but monotonous life at Fort Grant did not last. On May 18, 1885, a party of 134 Chiricahua Apaches led by the gifted Geronimo, dissatisfied with their poor treatment and longing for the old freedom, slipped out of the San Carlos Reservation.[16] As soon as he had received information that the Indians were gone, Shafter detached two scouting parties to intercept them. Acting upon instructions from General Crook, he sent 183 officers and enlisted men to pursue westward in the vicinity of the San Pedro River. He ordered eleven others to scout eastward to the Peloncillo Mountains. At the same time he sent word to his troops at Forts Bowie and Huachuca to stand guard and to turn back the Indians. The orders were to little avail. The

[13]Charles F. Lummis, *General Crook and the Apache Wars*, ed. Turbese Lummis Fiske, pp. vi–vii, 1–10, 25–29, 65–66, 140–44; Clendenen, *Blood on the Border*, pp. 100–106; Utley, *Frontier Regulars*, pp. 377–78.

[14]George C. Crook, Commanding the Dept. of Arizona, "Report of Brigadier General Crook," Nov. 21, 1884, in *Annual Report of the Secretary of War*, 1884, 48th Cong., 2d sess., H. Exec. Doc. 1, pt. 2, p. 133.

[15]William C. Endicott, Secy. of War, *Annual Report of the Secretary of War*, 1885, 49th Cong., 1st sess., H. Exec. Doc. 1, pt. 2, p. 88; Post Returns, Fort Grant, Jan.–April, 1885, Roll 415, MC617, NA; William H. Leckie, *The Buffalo Soldiers: A Narrative of the Negro Cavalry in the West*, p. 239.

[16]Crook, "Report," Nov. 21, 1884, *Annual Report of the Secretary of War*, 1884, 48th Cong., 2d sess., H. Exec. Doc. 1, pt. 2, pp. 123–33, 169. Also see Utley, *Frontier Regulars*, pp. 377–86.

Apaches fled eastward into the mountains of the Black Range in New Mexico and escaped.[17]

In response General Crook organized a major assault against the Indians, now believed to be in the Sierra Madres, rugged mountains in northern Mexico. He ordered Capt. Emmet Crawford, Third Cavalry, with troops from his regiment and the Sixth Cavalry and Apache scouts, to march on June 11 from Deming, New Mexico, southwestward into Mexico. A month later he sent Capt. Wirt Davis, Fourth Cavalry, with troops of his regiment into Mexico farther west.[18] Between these major forces Crook had Shafter order Maj. Frederick Van Vliet, Tenth Cavalry, to proceed on the twenty-sixth south from Fort Grant to the head of the Sulphur Spring Valley with five companies of the Tenth Cavalry.

The Crawford and Davis columns scoured the Sierra Madres, checking any valley or depression that might hide the Indians. As they searched their trails met and crossed on several occasions, but neither party could overtake the Apaches. Although Crawford and Davis entered Mexico, Van Vliet scouted in the valley below Willcox but remained north of the border.

On July 30 Shafter ordered Capt. Thomas C. Lebo, his trusted officer from the Texas campaigns now attached to Van Vliet's command, with his company back to Fort Grant. Two days later he sent Lebo westward through Redfield Canyon near modern-day Redington and up the San Pedro River about thirty-five miles to where the Southern Pacific Railroad crosses it at Benson. From there Lebo with his Company H followed the railroad tracks northeastward thirty-five miles to Willcox. Here in mid-August, having seen no Indians, he rejoined Major Van Vliet.[19]

Impatient with the lack of success in capturing the Apaches, General Crook early in September called his officers to Fort Apache. For more than a week Crook, Shafter, Grierson, and other officers in the department discussed the nature of the campaign. When the strategy session closed, Crook, against Shafter's advice, adopted the same tactics he had used in the 1882–83 campaign: negotiate with the hostiles,

[17]Post Returns, Fort Grant, May–June, 1885, Roll 415, MC617, NA; Jack C. Lane, ed., *Chasing Geronimo: the Journal of Leonard Wood, May–September, 1886*, p. 8; Clendenen, *Blood on the Border*, pp. 106–107.

[18]Crook, "Report," April 10, 1886, in *Annual Report of the Secretary of War, 1886*, 49th Cong., 2d sess., H. Exec. Doc. 1, pt. 2, pp. 150–51.

[19]Post Returns, Fort Grant, Aug., 1885, Roll 415, MC617, NA; Regimental Returns, First Infantry, Aug., 1885, Roll 8, MC665, NA.

enlist the services of the Apache scouts, and use small detachments of hard-riding cavalry units.

Once Crook put his new plans into operation, Shafter had few responsibilities. As the fast, unimpeded cavalry units went after the Indians, Shafter's First Infantry, assigned to guard favorite passes and to establish a second line of defense paralleling the Southern Pacific Railroad, spent endless days and nights staring at water holes.[20] His work evolved again into a routine broken only by duties that took him away from the garrison or by the arrival at Fort Grant of unexpected visitors.

One group of visitors, who arrived on October 18, was a congressional subcommittee on Indian affairs investigating the Apache campaign. Because Crook was under heavy criticism from the press, citizens of Arizona, and Congress for his methods of pursuing the Apaches, the committee members wanted to obtain firsthand information on the campaign before making a report. They spent a day discussing the situation with Shafter, who talked about his responsibilities in the territory. The record of his testimony is mute, but he probably complained of his own inactivity and Crook's reliance on fast-moving cavalry units. Perhaps he complained as well about Crook's practice of negotiating with the enemy. Shafter did not agree with the plan.

A month after the subcommittee had left a second party of unexpected visitors entered the post. The group included one hundred recently recruited Apache scouts from San Carlos who stopped for the night. As they outnumbered federal troops at the post, their presence caused unnecessary alarm among soldier families. Shafter assured everyone that the Indians were peaceful, and early the next morning, after a night without incident, the recruits left to join Capt. Emmet Crawford in Mexico.[21]

The Apache campaign continued through the winter, but it did not go well. Time after time Geronimo and his followers in Mexico slipped away from Crawford and his Apache scouts. There was a serious lack of cooperation with Mexican troops, and then in January, 1886, Mexican troops accidently shot and killed Crawford. Near the end of March, after the Indians had surrendered and as they headed for the United States, an American rancher and bootlegger named Robert Tribolet

[20]Crook, "Report," Sept., 1886, in *Annual Report of the Secretary of War, 1886,* 49th Cong., 2d sess., H. Exec. Doc. 1, pt. 2, pp. 148–49; Lane, ed., *Wood Journal,* p. 26.
[21]Crook, "Report," Sept., 1886, in *Annual Report of the Secretary of War, 1886,* 49th Cong., 2d sess., H. Exec. Doc. 1, pt. 2, pp. 148–49; Post Returns, Fort Grant, Oct.–Nov., 1885, Roll 415, MC617, NA; Regimental Returns, First Infantry, Oct.–Nov., 1885, Roll 8, MC665, NA.

plied Geronimo and others with whiskey and told them that Crook intended to execute them when they reached the reservation. Geronimo and about thirty-five of his followers, including perhaps twenty-two warriors, unwilling to test the rancher's veracity, fled back into the Sierra Madres.[22]

Geronimo's escape led to an exchange of sharp telegrams between Crook and Gen. Philip Sheridan, who now was commanding general of the army, and to the appointment of a new commander in Arizona. The national press criticized Crook for negotiating with the hostiles, and Sheridan thought his use of Apache kinsmen as scouts was an unforgivable error. Moreover, Crook was disheartened by the death of Captain Crawford, one of his most trusted aides. Humiliated and angry, Crook asked to be relieved. Thus, on April 2, Brig. Gen. Nelson A. Miles took command of the Department of Arizona.[23]

Miles, an exceedingly ambitious officer who had not attended West Point, had a distinguished record in the Civil War and a wide experience in the wars against the Plains Indians. He discharged Crook's Apache scouts and moved to take the Indians by force. The methods, obvious thrusts at Crook's theory of diplomacy and belief that regular troops could not compete with the Apache in his own country, initiated a controversy on the capture, treatment, and disposition of the Apaches that has continued to the present day.

Although he did not become directly involved in the Miles-Crook dispute, Shafter, who preferred to use force against the hostiles, sided with Miles. He was one of the few officers who disagreed with Crook's statement that the Apaches could not be caught in twenty years, and he was irritated because Crook had not given him personal command of any of the scouts. One aspect of the controversy perhaps illustrates a problem of the Gilded Age army. Throughout the last half of the nineteenth century an unfriendly and sometimes bitter rivalry existed between West Point officers and those without formal military training. The problem no doubt was one cause of the Miles-Crook difficulties, and Shafter, like Miles, had not attended the military academy.[24]

[22]Clendenen, *Blood on the Border*, pp. 107–10; Post Returns, Fort Grant, Sept., 1885–April, 1886, Roll 415, MC617, NA; John Gregory Bourke, *On the Border with Crook*, pp. 465–80; Nelson A. Miles, *Personal Recollections and Observations of General Nelson A. Miles*, p. 472; Utley, *Frontier Regulars*, pp. 384–86.

[23]Philip H. Sheridan, Gen. of the Army, to Gen. George Crook, Fort Bowie, Ariz. Terr., March 31, 1886, reproduced in Miles, *Personal Recollections*, p. 472; Lane, ed., *Wood Journal*, pp. 8–9; Lummis, *General Crook and the Apache Wars*, pp. vi–viii.

[24]Lane, ed., *Wood Journal*, pp. 20–26; Utley, *Frontier Regulars*, p. 386; Clendenen, *Blood on the Border*, pp. 111–12.

Upon Miles's arrival in Arizona, Shafter was named to command the District of San Pedro. Comprising parts of the modern-day counties of Cochise, Pima, Pinal, Graham, and Santa Cruz in southeastern Arizona, the new district embraced nearly the same area over which, except for his absence in New York, he had commanded scouting operations since 1882. Among his first duties as commander of the district was to bring several detachments of the Tenth Cavalry to Fort Grant for a short rest before reassigning them to replace the discharged Apache scouts, ninety of whom stopped at Fort Grant enroute to Fort Apache near the end of April.

The Tenth Cavalry did not have to wait long to take up the pursuit. Geronimo on April 27 crossed the border into Shafter's area of operation and swept through the Santa Cruz Valley, killing a number of cowboys, a Mrs. Peck, and one of her children. Then, taking another of Mrs. Peck's daughters as captive, he turned and headed back to Mexico. The next day Captain Lebo, who was scouting with his company in the vicinity, got news of the raid and took up the chase. The pursuit continued for two hundred miles before Lebo brought his quarry to bay on a rocky slope in the Pinito Mountains thirty miles south of the border in Sonora. After a sharp skirmish the Indians escaped. Lebo and his troops followed the trail for four more days and then returned to Fort Grant. Capt. C. A. P. Hatfield, Fourth Cavalry, who had been with Shafter in Texas, took up the pursuit.[25]

Early in May, while the pursuit was underway, Shafter conferred with General Miles at Willcox in regard to strategy. The officers probably studied Crook's method of using a hard core of soldiers to support the scouts. In any event, shortly thereafter Miles ordered that in each company of cavalry, the lighter men, who could ride farther and faster, would handle the bulk of the pursuit details. They adopted the very method they had criticized Crook for using. They also discussed the establishment of a network of heliograph stations at the posts and on appropriate high peaks for the rapid transmission of messages and information.

Before the heliograph system was fully operative, however, Shafter left Arizona. He received orders on June 1 for his First Infantry to exchange stations with the Eighth Infantry in the Department of California. His troops, who had been in the arid, hot, and mountainous Southwest since 1880, welcomed the new assignment. Although he

[25]Crook, "Report," April 10, 1886, in *Annual Report of the Secretary of War, 1886,* 49th Cong., 2d sess., H. Exec. Doc. 1, pt. 2, pp. 147–55; Miles, *Personal Recollections,* p. 489; Leckie, *The Buffalo Soldiers,* p. 245; Utley, *Frontier Regulars,* p. 387.

would not be able to participate in the final conquest of the Apaches, Shafter too must have been happy with the new orders, for his meager responsibilities in Arizona had not gratified either his insatiable energy or his ambition to command troops in the field. In preparation for the move Shafter reduced the strength of his regiment by one hundred enlisted men to four hundred.[26]

While thus engaged, Shafter served for a week as a member of a general court-martial to try Lt. C. R. Ward, Tenth Cavalry, who had been with Shafter on the Staked Plains in 1875, for drunkenness and disorderly conduct. During Ward's trial, Shafter met Leonard Wood, who afterward served with Shafter in California and with the Rough Riders in Cuba. An army contract surgeon and recent graduate of Harvard Medical School who had come to Fort Grant to testify, Wood on the morning of June 3 called at Shafter's home. Shafter introduced the young doctor to his wife and daughter, who was "plump and jolly" like her father, and invited him to lunch.[27] Later the two men became close friends.

Less than a month after the trial ended, Shafter and his regiment on July 9, 1886, arrived in California. His new post was located on Angel Island in San Francisco Bay. Established as Camp Reynolds in 1863, Angel Island was a large and elaborate post when Shafter arrived there. Barracks and officers' quarters were two-story frame buildings, and the commanding officer's home was a large, comfortable house built of wood. Although conditions in the barracks would become crowded and noisy during the 1890's when infantry companies were recruited to their full strength, in 1886 the post was pleasant and peaceful.[28]

The quiet, unpretentious transfer to California in several respects presaged Colonel Shafter's service in the department. For the next twelve years, except for duty at Pine Ridge, South Dakota, in 1890–91 and in Los Angeles during the Pullman Strike, Shafter experienced little more than a tranquil, routine garrison life. During those years he added over thirty pounds to his already bulky frame and probably would have gained even more had he not spent time hunting in the California mountains, riding about the post, and swimming in the Pacific surf. Nonetheless, his general health remained good. On two occasions, the old leg injury sustained in 1875 on the Llano Estacado ulcerated to cause

[26]Post Returns, Fort Grant, May, 1886, Roll 415, MC617, NA; Clendenen, *Blood on the Border*, p. III; Miles, *Personal Recollections*, pp. 481–84; Regimental Returns, First Infantry, June, 1886, Roll 8, MC665, NA.

[27]Lane, ed., *Wood Journal*, p. 44; Calhoun Collins, *The McKittrick Ranch*, p. 19.
[28]Augustin G. Rudd, ed., *Histories of Army Posts*, pp. 75–76.

him difficulty, but he kept his gout under control, and medical stockings neutralized his otherwise painful varicose veins.[29]

With few military responsibilities to perform, Shafter increasingly turned to civilian activities. During 1887 and 1888 he began to attend Republican Party functions in San Francisco and to participate in the affairs of the Grand Army of the Republic. He became a popular after-dinner speaker. The few speeches that survive indicate that the Civil War was his favorite topic, but he spoke as well about the frontier army. Although an excellent storyteller, he seldom related personal incidents of his command. He spoke instead in general terms about the army's role in the Indian wars or the Civil War.[30]

For many officers of the Gilded Age army, the Civil War had been the most important event in their lives. They looked to it as a major conflict and rarely saw the western Indian campaigns as an example of a real war. Those officers who left memoirs of their years in the service devoted far more space to Civil War battles than to the Indian campaigns. Shafter, likewise, at least in his speeches, looked to the glorious days of the Civil War when soldiers faced a conventional foe in traditional battles.[31]

Fighting the western Indians was another matter. Indians used guerrilla-style hit-and-run raids, taking few casualties and fewer prisoners. To the army Indian fighting meant long days of marching through heat and dust or cold, wind, and snow; it meant endless days of staring at lonely water holes; it usually meant capturing women and children, if any Indians were taken. Such events did not stir the imagination of noncombatants or fulfill any image the soldiers had of army life. Most officers sympathized with the terrible plight of the western tribes, but such feeling made their employment as soldiers, as Paul Hutton writes, "more a necessary evil than a glorious enterprise."[32] In addition, they had little respect for their Indian enemy. Shafter, too, spoke of what he called "the savages of the plains," and he believed that Indians must give way to the more progressive white settlers.[33]

[29]Shafter to Adj. Gen., U.S. Army, Oct. 8, 1896, United States, William R. Shafter, Letters Received, Appointments, Commission, and Personal Branch, Adjutant General's Office, Record Group 94, National Archives (hereafter ACP File, AGO, RG94, NA).

[30]*Los Angeles Times*, Aug. 10, 1894. Also see Charles D. Rhodes, "William Rufus Shafter," *Michigan History Magazine* 16 (Fall, 1932): 371–83.

[31]For example, Shafter quoted in *Los Angeles Times*, Aug. 10, 1894.

[32]Paul Andrew Hutton, *Phil Sheridan and His Army*, p. 145.

[33]*Los Angeles Times*, Aug. 10, 1894; James Mooney, "The Ghost Dance Religion and the Sioux Outbreak of 1890," in *Fourteenth Annual Report of the Bureau of Ethnology, 1892–1893*, pt. 2, pp. 888–90.

One of the topics on which Shafter dwelt in his speeches was army reform. Although he had promoted such basic innovations as new weapons and streamlined equipment and approved of special schools for training in army tactics and military science, he could not be considered a reformer. Fearful that change meant largely a reduction in the size of the army, he was a conservative and an aging traditionalist who believed the army's very success against Indians proved its effectiveness and modernity. Like many older officers of his day, Shafter, instead of looking to the future, was captivated with the past and influenced by the long shadow of the Civil War. The purpose of the army, he believed, was helping destitute settlers, providing guard details, and keeping the peace. In a secondary role it was to engage in explorations, road building, and scientific study. In doing all of these things, Shafter suggested, the major role of the army in the West was to fight "savages" on isolated frontiers, but in the future its major function would be to fight "savages"—striking workers—in America's cities.[34]

In California each summer Shafter directed a military training camp. The 1889 camp was typical. Preparations started late in January. During February and March the diligent colonel communicated with representatives from several cities and with officials of the Department of California for a camp site. Early in May, when the site had been narrowed to a choice of three places, Shafter made an inspection, selecting a spot near Monterey.[35]

Monterey was a delightful place to spend the summer. Its white stucco buildings looking out across the Pacific, its fishing boats in the harbor, and its Spanish mood lent the camp an atmosphere of ease and comfort. After Shafter arranged for the officers to be housed in the Hotel del Monte, the encampment took on a festive air with fancy balls and splendid dinners. Welcoming the soldiers with enthusiasm, the hotel management provided full, efficient service, including musical entertainment each evening.

Shafter ordered troops from each of the three branches of the army to Monterey, including two companies of the Fourth Cavalry, two light batteries of the Fifth Artillery, and eight companies of the First Infantry. When the troops began to arrive, Shafter established on July 20 a camp at the edge of the city, and, after four more days of prepara-

[34]*Los Angeles Times*, Aug. 10, 1894.
[35]Gen. Oliver O. Howard, Commanding the Division of the Pacific, to Adj. Gen., U.S. Army, May 2, 1890, ACP File, AGO, RG94, NA; Regimental Returns, First Infantry, Jan.–May, 1889, Roll 8, MC665, NA; Post Returns, Fort Angel Island, May, 1889, Roll 30, MC617, NA.

tions, he began instruction. He placed Leonard Wood in charge of athletic activities with instructions to give special attention to the physical efficiency of the soldiers. As a part of the program, Wood held a "marathon" race around a seventeen-mile drive at the outskirts of Monterey and then won the race himself in just under three hours.[36]

The military exercises during the 1889 encampment included battalion and brigade drills, picket duty, night alarms, attack and defense maneuvers, map making, target practice, and, as far as possible, all else that pertains to field service in time of war. As a final exercise, the troops waged during mid-August what the enlisted men called the "Monkey War of Jack Rabbit Flat." Although not much of a campaign, the "war" simulated in many respects actual warfare insofar as conditions permitted Shafter to improvise it.[37]

The sham battles, rating as one of the high points in the city's social season, proved popular with the people of Monterey. When the hour of Shafter's 1889 battle approached, crowds by the hundreds poured into the encampment grounds, thronging the area in every direction. Quite a number of the more enthusiastic spectators climbed up trees to witness the war. They came from every direction in wagons, buggies, carriages, on foot, any way just to get there to enjoy the fight.[38]

At several of the summer camps, the California National Guard troops participated. Usually they observed the regular army maneuvers, but on occasion they took part in all the activities, including the war games. The encampments provided the guard with excellent opportunities for instruction.

Shafter conducted each summer camp with ability, energy, and thoroughness. Gen. Oliver O. Howard, who witnessed at least two, wrote in May, 1890: "I was particularly pleased with the completeness of his summer encampments. . . . his hearty cooperation with troops of the National Guard and the conduct of his men on duty in camp, and on pass, begot for him and his command very high commendation among the civilians of the Pacific coast." Gen. Nelson A. Miles, who commanded the Division of the Pacific and personally reviewed the camp in 1889, wrote that "the general bearing and conduct of both officers and soldiers during this encampment, as well as the excellent manner

[36]Shafter to Asst. Adj. Gen., Dept. of California, Sept. 13, 1889, in Report of Brig. Gen. Nelson A. Miles, Commanding the Division of the Pacific, LR, AGO, RG94, NA; Hermann Hagedorn, *Leonard Wood: A Biography*, 1:116–17.

[37]*Annual Report of the Secretary of War*, 1889, 51st Cong., 1st sess., H. Exec. Doc. 1, pt. 2, pp. 173–74; Hagedorn, *Leonard Wood*, 1:117.

[38]Hagedorn, *Leonard Wood*, pp. 116–17.

in which the different exercises were executed, indicated a high degree of efficiency and discipline in the command."[39]

Upon returning to Angel Island in September, 1889, Shafter routinely executed the duties at his post. The winter passed slowly. Because of his comparatively light responsibilities, he no doubt thought nostalgically about the past eight years in Arizona and California as a relatively unhappy finale in his military career. Nevertheless, those traits that had always characterized his leadership continued to dominate his command. His troops were well disciplined, his garrisons thoroughly policed, and his regiment ready for combat on a moment's notice. Largely for these reasons Shafter was again to have an opportunity to command troops in the field. He could hardly have anticipated his next assignment.

[39]Howard to Adj. Gen., U.S. Army, May 2, 1890, ACP File, AGO, RG94, NA; Gen. Nelson A. Miles, Commanding the Division of the Pacific, to Commanding General of the Army, Aug. 30, 1889, in *Annual Report of the Secretary of War*, 1890, 51st Cong., 2d sess., H. Exec. Doc. 1, pt. 2, pp. 155–56.

CHAPTER TEN

From Wounded Knee to the Pullman Strike

B ETWEEN 1886 and 1890 Col. William R. Shafter, impatient with his garrison command in the Department of California, yearned for military action that might place him in command of field troops. He got his wish. A series of Indian Bureau failures, terrible misunderstandings, and pathetic events took him in the winter of 1890–91 to Pine Ridge, South Dakota, scene of the army's last major Indian campaign.

Developments leading to the campaign were painful. Methodical extermination of the last remnants of the once-great buffalo herds in part forced the Plains Indians to abandon their roaming and to settle down on reservations where whites prodded them to become farmers and laborers. Few Indians had as yet acquired practical mechanical skills, they had little experience in farming, and the reservation lands were poorly suited for growing crops. White settlers' greed for land eliminated some reservations altogether and significantly cut the size of others. The Oklahoma land rush of April 22, 1889, for example, one of the most fantastic episodes in frontier history, saw almost two million acres of Indian land claimed by white settlers in one day. The same year federal authorities divided Sioux reservations in Dakota and took huge areas of land from the tribes. The Indians, short of land and deprived of usual ways of obtaining their own food, came to depend too much on government annuities that, because of graft, corruption, or mismanagement, arrived late and short in supply. By 1890 hunger among western Indians had become commonplace, disease prevalent, and malnutrition and exposure ordinary.

The age was a time of misery and misfortune. To relieve their woes, many Indians turned to a messiah named Wovoka, a thirty-five-year-old Paiute called Jack Wilson by whites who had adopted him when his father had died. Wovoka had received an inspiration in 1888 that God had directed him to preach love and peace among his people. He also preached that the earth was to be regenerated and returned to the Indians, including many of their dead brethren. The miracle would come to pass by repeated performances of a special ceremonial dance, and the more often it was performed, the quicker the coming of the millennium. The Indians in their suffering listened eagerly to Wovoka and his missionaries.[1]

Wovoka's Ghost Dance religion, as it was called, spread over much of the West. As the Indians danced, the excess of their emotions sent many of them into trances in which they saw visions of the new day and sang simple, chanting songs. Mrs. J. A. Finley, wife of the post trader at Pine Ridge, who described a Ghost Dance in which 480 Sioux men, women, and children, participated, said that it lasted from Friday noon until sundown on Sunday. During that time, she explained, none of the dancers touched food or water and scores succumbed to trances or exhaustion.[2] It was not a war dance, but the new Indian restlessness caused alarm among many white citizens in the vicinity of reservations. At Pine Ridge Indians wore "ghost shirts" believed to be impervious to bullets beneath their outer garments, which perhaps suggests the Sioux expected trouble.[3]

In early October, 1890, Daniel F. Royer of Alpena, South Dakota, whom the Sioux called Young Man Afraid of the Sioux, became the new agent at Pine Ridge. A political hack who had little experience with Indians, Royer misunderstood the Ghost Dance and its message. Before he had been at the agency a week, he lost the confidence of the Indians. Within two weeks of his arrival, he reported that half his thousand Sioux charges were dancing, and at the end of the month, believing the Ghost Dance had to be suppressed, he wrote that the situation was getting out of hand and that six or seven hundred troops

---

[1]Wilcomb E. Washburn, *The Indian in America*, pp. 192–93, 217–22; Arrell M. Gibson, *The American Indian: Prehistory to the Present*, pp. 476–81; T. J. Morgan, "Report of the Commissioner of Indian Affairs," in *Annual Report of the Secretary of the Interior*, 1891, 52d Cong., 1st sess., H. Exec. Doc. 1, pt. 5, 2:123–27; James Mooney, "The Ghost Dance Religion and the Sioux Outbreak of 1890," in *Fourteenth Annual Report of the Bureau of Ethnology, 1892–1893*, pt. 2, pp. 24–25, 30, 34, 73, 114–20. Also see Weston La Barre, *The Ghost Dance: Origins of a Religion*, pp. 227–30, 300, 304.

[2]Cited in Paul I. Wellman, *Death on the Prairie*, p. 186. Also see Robert M. Utley, *Frontier Regulars: The United States Army and the Indian, 1866–1890*, pp. 401–403.

[3]Washburn, *The Indian in America*, pp. 221–22.

were needed.[4] Two weeks later he wrote that to control the Indians one thousand troops were required.[5]

On November 13 Commissioner of Indian Affairs T. J. Morgan recommended on the basis of Royer's frantic reports that the Indians in South Dakota, especially at Pine Ridge, be turned over to the War Department. The same day, Pres. Benjamin Harrison directed Secretary of War Redfield Proctor to assume military responsibility and to prevent an outbreak. Four days later Proctor ordered Brig. Gen. John R. Brooke, commanding the Department of the Platte, to Pine Ridge where he arrived on November 20 with five companies of infantry, three companies of cavalry, and one Hotchkiss and one Gatling gun. At the same time he directed Gen. Nelson A. Miles, commanding the Division of the Missouri since September 4, 1890, to assume charge of all military operations in the vicinity of Pine Ridge.[6]

Several days later Indians in South Dakota began to leave their reservations in large numbers. Lt. Col. John Poland, Twenty-first Infantry, led two companies of the Ninth Cavalry and portions of the Eighth and Twenty-first infantries to the Rosebud Agency in modern-day Todd County. On November 20, the soldiers arrived and foolishly fired upon the Indians. Some eighteen hundred Brulés—men, women, and children —led by Two Strikes, then left the Rosebud. After destroying their property, the Indians fled to Pine Ridge, ninety miles to the west. When others joined them, the combined party headed northward, some to the Stronghold, a plateau between the Cheyenne and White rivers about forty miles from Pine Ridge, and some to the Badlands, a rough, broken country about ten miles beyond. During the next few weeks hundreds of additional Indians abandoned reservations in the state.[7]

In response, General Miles requested that additional troops be posted at the Sioux agencies and at other points farther removed. Upon hearing of the request, Shafter, by telegraph to the War Department, volun-

[4]Royer's letter quoted in Morgan, "Report," *Annual Report of the Secretary of the Interior,* 1891, 52d Cong., 1st sess., H. Exec. Doc. 1, pt. 5, 2:128; Mooney, "The Ghost Dance Religion and the Sioux Outbreak of 1890," pt. 2, pp. 848–50.

[5]D. F. Royer to Robert V. Belt, Acting Commissioner of Indian Affairs, Nov. 15, 1890, cited in Robert M. Utley, *The Last Days of the Sioux Nation,* p. 111. Also see L. W. Colby, "The Sioux Indian War of 1890–91," *Transactions and Reports of the Nebraska State Historical Society* 3 (1892): 180.

[6]Morgan, "Report," *Annual Report of the Secretary of the Interior,* 1891. 52d Cong., 1st sess., H. Exec. Doc. 1, pt. 5, p. 128; Mooney, "The Ghost Dance Religion and the Sioux Outbreak of 1890," pt. 2, p. 850.

[7]Mooney, "The Ghost Dance Religion and the Sioux Outbreak of 1890," pt. 2, pp. 848–69.

teered his command. Secretary of War Proctor accepted and communicated the information to Miles, who in turn ordered Shafter with his regiment to the cold and frozen plains. On December 4, 1890, with the field staff, band, Companies A, B, C, D, E, G, and H, and a hospital corps, almost four hundred men and officers, Shafter boarded an eastbound Central Pacific passenger train to Omaha, Nebraska, and from there proceeded westward to Valentine, Nebraska, on the Fremont, Elkhorn, and Missouri Valley Railroad. After deboarding, his command marched six miles to a camp near Fort Niobrara on the Niobrara River and three days later moved into the fort.[8]

Colonel Shafter again suffered from ill health. The entire time at Fort Niobrara he was confined to his room with a suppurating ulcer in the calf on his right leg, a recurrence of his old injury. He could not leave the room for meals. The recurring injury and other physical maladies, including gout, varicose veins, and excessive weight, suggested that he should have considered retirement. Although he had served the army well for nearly thirty years, he was now in the midst of a major campaign and nearly debilitated, but he never seriously considered leaving the service. Shafter retained command of the post and regiment, the officers going to his room for their orders.[9]

On December 15, three days after Shafter moved into Fort Niobrara, Sitting Bull, the old and influential Sioux leader, died. In a wretched attempt to arrest him at his camp on the Grand River in the Standing Rock Reservation, Indian police of his own band killed him. After the murder, thousands of frightened Indians all over the state left their reservations. Among the refugees was a band from the Cheyenne River

[8] Amos H. Martin to Sen. Matthew S. Quey, Pennsylvania, March 3, 1897, United States, William R. Shafter, Letters Received, Appointments, Commission, and Personal Branch, Adjutant General's Office, Record Group 94, National Archives (hereafter ACP File, AGO, RG94, NA); U.S. Dept. of War, Returns from Regular Army Infantry Regiments, June, 1821–Dec., 1916, First Infantry, Dec., 1890, Roll 9, Microcopy No. 665, National Archives (hereafter Regimental Returns, MC665, NA); U.S. Dept. of War, Returns from United States Military Posts, 1800–1916, Fort Angel Island, Dec., 1890, Roll 30, Microcopy No. 617, National Archives (hereafter Post Returns, MC617, NA).

[9] Col. G. H. Burton, Insp. Gen., Dept. of California, extract of report to Adj. Gen., U.S. Army, June 24, 1891, ACP File, AGO, RG94, NA; Regimental Returns, First Infantry, Dec., 1890, Roll 9, MC665, NA. Also see Shafter to Adj. Gen., U.S. Army, March 29, 1893; Shafter, endorsement to Report of Post Surgeon, Fort Angel Island, Calif., April 11, 1891; Nelson Miles to Adj. Gen., U.S. Army, March 25, 1893; and W. R. Hall and Leonard Wood to Whom It May Concern, March 28, 1893, all in ACP File, AGO, RG94, NA.

Reservation of more than three hundred Miniconjous, Brulés, and Hunkpapas, all under the leadership of Big Foot, a Miniconjou. Within hours, however, some of the Indians returned to their agencies. On December 18, a thousand Oglalas showed up at Pine Ridge, and six days later another band of 224 surrendered to the army at Fort Bennett on the Missouri about twenty miles above Pierre.

Meanwhile, General Miles on December 17 arrived at Rapid City, where he established his headquarters. Here he had three companies from the Fifth and Eighth cavalries. Because most of the Sioux had fled to the Badlands, Miles concentrated 3,500 troops in that vicinity, completely surrounding the Indians. At Pine Ridge, he placed eight companies of the Seventh and a battalion of the Ninth cavalries, a battalion of the Fifth Artillery, and eight companies of the Second and one company of the Eighth infantries. To the north and west, he stationed portions of the First, Second, and Ninth cavalries, and along the south fork of the Cheyenne River he detailed seven companies of the Seventeenth Infantry. To shut off communications between Indians of the Rosebud and Pine Ridge agencies and those farther north, he posted seven companies of the Seventh Infantry along the Cheyenne River. To the east, at Rosebud, he already had two companies of the Ninth Cavalry and detachments of the Eighth and Twenty-first infantries. To the south at Fort Niobrara and along the Fremont, Elkhorn, and Missouri Valley Railroad, Shafter commanded his seven companies of the First Infantry.[10]

Miles was in firm control. As the Indians returned to their reservations, he tightened his cordon of troops and prepared to round up any holdouts. To expedite operations, he shifted his troops slightly. He ordered Shafter to send two companies of his regiment to Rushville, Nebraska, twenty-eight miles south of Pine Ridge, and to proceed with five companies to Hermosa, South Dakota, sixteen miles due south of Rapid City. Shafter carried out these orders without difficulty, arriving on December 26 at his destination.

Because his ulcer had not improved, Shafter requested and received permission to go for a few days to Hot Springs, South Dakota, near the southern edge of the Black Hills, for treatment. Here he placed himself under the care of a physician at a sanitarium and bathed in the natural hot springs from which the city derived its name. Although the First Infantry was ordered to proceed to within twenty miles of

---

[10]Mooney, "The Ghost Dance Religion and the Sioux Outbreak of 1890," pt. 2, p. 850; Utley, *The Last Days of the Sioux Nation*, pp. 251–52.

Pine Ridge on the twenty-eighth, Shafter remained at Hot Springs until January 6, 1891, when he proceeded by rail to Rushville.[11] Consequently, neither Shafter nor his troops participated in the fighting at Wounded Knee.

A band of Brulés, Hunkpapas, and Miniconjous led by Big Foot, about 340 altogether, including men, women, and children, had been riding toward Pine Ridge on December 28 to surrender when Maj. S. M. Whiteside, Seventh Cavalry, arrested them and told them to encamp at Wounded Knee a few miles north of Pine Ridge. Col. James W. Forsyth, Seventh Cavalry, arrived with reinforcements late on the same day, assumed command, and planned to disarm the Indians on the following day.

During the morning of December 29, after some hesitation the Indians turned over a few old weapons. Forsyth, unsatisfied with the amount, instructed some of 470 men to search the tepees. While these orders were being carried out Yellow Bird, an old medicine man, harangued some of the men into beginning their death chants. One of the warriors suddenly drew a rifle from under his blanket and opened fire.

In seconds bedlam prevailed. Hand-to-hand fighting followed and Hotchkiss guns, which had been placed in position on a bluff overlooking the Indian camp, rained down fire upon all participants of battle. Both soldiers and Indians died. The Indian women and children attempted to escape, but troopers rode out and killed them. After a few minutes it was over. About 146 Indian men, women, and children lay dead and at least 50 more were wounded. Army losses were 26 men killed and 39 injured. The army hauled in Indian survivors who had not escaped to Pine Ridge.[12]

The Wounded Knee massacre changed the entire complexion of the Siouan campaign. Most of the Indians, including diehard remnants of the Ghost Dancers, had left both the Badlands and the Stronghold and were returning to their agencies on the day of the disaster. Upon learning of the slaughter of their kinsmen at Wounded Knee, they refused to surrender, and their ranks were swollen by new refugees from the reservations. By the first of January, 1891, some four thousand Indians, including close to five hundred Cheyennes, were in camp along White Clay Creek about fifteen miles northwest of the agency.

[11]Burton to Adj. Gen., U.S. Army, June 24, 1891, and Miles to Shafter, Dec. 28, 1890, both in ACP File, AGO, RG94, NA.

[12]Morgan, "Report," *Annual Report of the Secretary of the Interior,* 1891, 52d Cong., 1st sess., pt. 5, p. 130; Utley, *The Last Days of the Sioux Nation,* pp. 227–29; Mooney, "The Ghost Dance Religion and the Sioux Outbreak of 1890," pt. 2, pp. 855–71; Utley, *Frontier Regulars,* pp. 404–405.

The army at once increased its pressure. The troops, including five companies of Shafter's regiment temporarily under General Brooke's command, moved toward the White Clay Creek Valley in tight battle formation. At the same time negotiations with the chiefs commenced. Had the Sioux succeeded in breaking out of the valley, they would have suffered heavy casualties and the survivors would have been met by a second ring of soldiers. With 3,500 troops in the area and 2,000 more farther removed, there was no place for the Indians to go. After one party of fifty warriors was repulsed on the afternoon of January 1 when they attacked the wagons of the Sixth Cavalry, the Sioux realized that they were at the mercy of the soldiers. A few days later they began to drift back toward Pine Ridge.[13]

Shafter, meanwhile, had returned to duty. He rejoined a portion of his regiment at Rushville and on January 7 moved by wagon with Companies D and E to Pine Ridge where his five other companies had arrived from White Clay Creek a few days before. On the eighth he assumed command of all troops at Pine Ridge, including the seven companies of his regiment and most of the Seventh Cavalry, about seven hundred troops in all. Upon assuming command, Shafter replaced Daniel F. Royer as Indian agent with Capt. Francis R. Pierce, Company G, of his regiment, who in 1884 had served capably as agent to the Haulipas in Arizona.[14]

Although Shafter's dismissal of agent Royer may have had little effect, during the week afterward scores of Indians returned to Pine Ridge and continued on to their assigned reservations. Only two days after Shafter relieved Royer, the Sioux began to shift their entire camp in the direction of the agency. Each time they moved, the army drew its northwestern line tighter, and the troops at Pine Ridge apprehensively awaited the Indians' arrival.[15]

---

[13]Wellman, *Death on the Prairie*, pp. 235–40; Mooney, "The Ghost Dance Religion and the Sioux Outbreak of 1890," pt. 2, pp. 855–71, 873–86; Utley, *The Last Days of the Sioux Nation*, pp. 227–29, 252–60; William H. Leckie, *The Buffalo Soldiers: A Narrative of the Negro Cavalry in the West*, pp. 255–58; Utley, *Frontier Regulars*, pp. 408–409.

[14]Special Orders No. 12, Division of the Missouri, Jan. 8, 1891, ACP File, AGO, RG94, NA; Regimental Returns, First Infantry, Dec., 1890–Jan., 1891, Roll 9, MC665, NA; Miles to his wife, Jan. 11, 1891, reproduced in Virginia Weisel Johnson, *The Unregimented General: Nelson A. Miles*, pp. 296–97; Mooney, "The Ghost Dance Religion and the Sioux Outbreak of 1890," pt. 2, p. 887. General Miles, who on January 3 had moved his headquarters to Pine Ridge, was in overall command of the campaign.

[15]Special Orders No. 12, Division of the Missouri, Jan. 8, 1891, ACP File, AGO, RG94, NA; Utley, *Frontier Regulars*, p. 409.

The final surrender came on January 15. With nerves taut, guns ready, and lookouts alert, the troops at Pine Ridge were nervous and even fearful of the approaching Sioux. They witnessed an impressive sight. Capt. William E. Daugherty of the First Infantry recalled that the Indians, including Oglalas, Brulés, Hunkpapas, Miniconjous, and others, in excellent order, "moved in two columns up White Clay Creek, one on each side, about [4,000] people in all, with 7,000 horses, 500 wagons and about 250 travois." In the four-mile procession there was no sound but that of the bells tinkling on the horses, the clatter of hoofs on the frozen ground, the creaking of the wagons, and the scraping of travois poles. There was no incident. As they rode into Pine Ridge, the Sioux set up their tents and awaited Shafter's orders.[16]

The next day Shafter, Miles, and their staffs rode out to review the Indian camp. Satisfied with what he saw, Miles ordered Shafter to issue to the returnees rations, blankets, clothing, and other available needed supplies. Shafter immediately carried out the orders. With the intention of preparing his own regiment for an extended stay through a bitter cold South Dakota winter, he then examined his troops, assuring himself that they were adequately provisioned.

Not all difficulties had ended. A week earlier an Indian named Plenty Horses, a Brulé, had killed Lt. Edward W. Casey, Twenty-second Infantry, while the lieutenant reconnoitered the Brulé camp. Casey's death occasioned great excitement among some of the military and most citizens of the vicinity, who demanded the arrest and punishment of the Indian. A few days later Plenty Horses was apprehended.

About the same time some civilians attacked five peaceful Indians who were returning from a hunting trip in Montana. They killed Few Tails, one of the Indians, and seriously wounded Clown, his wife. One Feather, another of the Indians, got his wife and daughters into a wagon and sent them in flight while he warded off the attackers long enough to escape to Shafter's protection at Pine Ridge. Clown, on foot and suffering from two bullet wounds, somehow made it to safety two days later. Shafter reported the incident to leaders in Meade County where the killing took place, but the civilian authorities neither questioned nor arrested the attackers, who were known.[17]

Shafter would not accept such inaction. As an army officer and an uncompromising friend of the western settler, he disliked the Indians

[16]Capt. W. E. Daugherty, "The Recent Messiah Craze," *Journal of the Military Service Institute of the United States* 12 (1891): 577.
[17]Mooney, "The Ghost Dance Religion and the Sioux Outbreak of 1890," pt. 2, pp. 888–90; Utley, *The Last Days of the Sioux Nation*, pp. 262–67; Robert M. Utley, *The Indian Frontier of the American West*, p. 227.

Tepee village at Pine Ridge after the surrender, January, 1891. *Courtesy Library of Congress*

against whom he so often fought. But in this instance he sided with the Sioux, complaining that "so long as Indians are being arrested and held for killing armed men under condition of war, it seems to me that the white murderers of a part of a band of peaceful Indians should not be permitted to escape punishment."[18] As a result of his vigorous protest, the white suspects were arrested for the murder of Few Tails, tried, but acquitted.[19]

In a lesser problem some seventy-three Hunkpapas refused to go

[18]Mooney, "The Ghost Dance Religion and the Sioux Outbreak of 1890," pt. 2, pp. 888–90.
[19]Utley, *The Last Days of the Sioux Nation*, pp. 262–67. Plenty Horses was arraigned before a United States court but acquitted of murder on the ground that

Plenty Horses, a Sioux youth involved in the Ghost Dance troubles of 1890.
Courtesy Library of Congress

back to the Standing Rock Reservation where Sitting Bull had been killed, and some seven hundred restless and militant Brulés vowed not to return to Rosebud. Although Shafter recommended that they

---

the killing was an act of war and could not be considered murder in the legal sense of the word.

be forcibly returned, the army permitted the Indians to remain at Pine Ridge.

With peace restored the federal troops, preparatory to their being returned to their former stations, on January 24 staged an impressive grand review. Shafter led it. Behind him 3,500 soldiers marched in sharp cadence over the snow-clad fields to stirring music played by the First Infantry band. It had a profound effect upon the suspicious and angry Brulés, for after the soldiers had gone to their tents the Indians continued to stand like statues on the crests of the hills from which they had witnessed the parade.[20]

Two days later, on January 26, 1891, when Miles left for Washington, Shafter assumed overall command of the campaign. At Pine Ridge he had the First Infantry and a battalion each of the Sixth and Ninth cavalries. With the exception of small garrisons at Forts Meade, Bennett, and Sully, on the Missouri River across from Fort Bennett, all other troops had been sent to their respective posts. Shafter saw that the Indians received their rightful annuities and gifts, that they got proper winter clothing and shelter, and that they settled down to a normal reservation life. A month after he took charge, with peace ensured, he relinquished command to civilian authorities and departed with his regiment via Rushville for his home base at Angel Island, California, where he arrived on March 4.[21]

Shafter and his First Infantry Regiment had played a significant role in the Siouan Campaign. Upon arriving at Fort Niobrara, he had protected settlements in the vicinity of Valentine, Nebraska. He had guarded the Fremont, Elkhorn, and Missouri Valley Railroad to prevent the Indians from fleeing southward. As Miles had tightened his cordon of troops, Shafter had helped to defend western escape routes near Hermosa, South Dakota. At the height of the campaign, Miles had sent Shafter and his regiment to Pine Ridge, the seat of the trouble. Throughout the conflict, except for the week he had spent nursing his injured leg, he had efficiently performed his duties.

With the close of the Pine Ridge campaign, the long struggle against the Indians was essentially over. This made it possible for the army to abandon some of the small posts in the West and to concentrate units under regimental control. Consequently, there were pressures

---

[20]Charles G. Seymour, "The Sioux Rebellion: The Final Review," *Harper's Weekly* 35 (Feb. 7, 1891): 106; Nelson A. Miles, *Serving the Republic: Memoirs of the Civil War and Military Life of Nelson A. Miles*, pp. 245–56; William Harding Carter, *From Yorktown to Santiago with the Sixth United States Cavalry*, pp. 263–64.

[21]Special Orders No. 28, Division of the Missouri, Jan. 26, 1891, ACP File, AGO, RG94, NA; Regimental Returns, First Infantry, March, 1891, Roll 9, MC665, NA.

Some of Shafter's troops in a tent at Pine Ridge, January, 1891. *Courtesy U.S. Signal Corps, National Archives*

for reorganization of the army. In the early 1890's the army stripped Companies I and K of each infantry regiment of all personnel, and their enlisted men and officers filled out the remaining units. Companies I and K of Shafter's regiment existed thereafter in name only. Change occurred only slowly, however, and not until well after the Spanish-American War did any major alterations take place.

Shafter took little part in the struggle over reorganization. Years earlier, when he commanded black troops in Texas, he had urged integration of Negro soldiers with white units, but he did it more with a view to getting a command of a white regiment than to promoting racial equality or military effectiveness. Now as an older officer, hoping for promotion to brigadier general and commanding a white regiment, he was satisfied with the army's organization of twenty-five regiments of infantry, ten of cavalry, and five of artillery. His official reports in the 1890's suggest that Shafter believed the army was adequate for national defense and that its principal role would continue to be one of keeping the peace—serving as a constabulary force. Younger officers, not Shafter, led the struggle for reform, but Shafter seems not to have been alarmed by their warnings that the army was provincial and narrowly focused.[22]

The reformers, "armed progressives" as Peter Karsten calls them, wanted several changes. In one they suggested that the ten-company, one-battalion infantry regiment had become obsolete. The increased accuracy of firearms and the rapid development of the Gatling gun, they pointed out, had forced dispersion of troops to such an extent that no one man could adequately control ten companies in battle. With statistics on battle formations from European wars supporting his recommendations, Secretary of War Proctor in his annual report for 1890 urged the adoption of a plan whereby each regiment would consist of three battalions of four companies.[23]

While the modifications were being debated (but not adopted), Shafter was ordered to use his troops in a role unrelated to Indian fighting. The expanding industrial complex with its concomitant struggles between management and workers led to several bitter labor strikes in the late nineteenth century. One of the most famous of the conflicts was the Pullman Strike, which began near Chicago on May 11, 1894, when workers of the Pullman Palace Car Company struck over a reduction of wages and related matters.

Events associated with the Pullman Strike moved quickly. The American Railway Union, led by the dynamic Eugene V. Debs, on June 26 declared a sympathy strike against all railroads using Pullman cars. The work stoppage, although centering chiefly in Chicago, occurred along railroads all the way to the Pacific, and the next day not a train left Los Angeles, California, then a city of some 68,000 people.[24] Richard Olney, United States attorney general, on June 28 cabled the fed-

[22]See W. Bourke Corleren [?] to Pres. Grover Cleveland, Oct. 29, 1894, and Shafter to Adj. Gen., U.S. Army, April 20, 1893, both in ACP File, AGO, RG94, NA. Also see Shafter to Adj. Gen. of the Army, Aug. 20, 1899, in *Annual Report of the Secretary of War*, 1899, 56th Cong., 1st sess., H. Exec. Doc. 2, 1:74–76.

[23]Peter Karsten, "Armed Progressives: The Military Reorganizes for the American Century," in Peter Karsten, ed., *The Military in America: From the Colonial Era to the Present*, pp. 229–60; Redfield Proctor, Sec. of War, *Annual Report of the Secretary of War*, 1890, 51st Cong., 2d sess., H. Exec. Doc. 1, pt. 2, pp. 11–12, 44–47.

[24]*Los Angeles Times*, June 28 and 29, 1894. Also see Jerry M. Cooper, *The Army and Civil Disorder: Federal Military Intervention in Labor Disputes, 1877–1900*, pp. 144–57; Almont Lindsey, *The Pullman Strike: The Story of a Unique Experiment and a Great Labor Upheaval*, pp. 90–106, 248–52.

eral attorney at Los Angeles, George Denis, to see that trains carrying United States mails were not obstructed. When Denis had difficulty carrying out the instructions, Olney urged the use of federal troops, and on July 1 Pres. Grover Cleveland authorized Secretary of War Daniel S. Lamont to ensure the safe passage of mails in and out of the southern California city. The following day through Brig. Gen. Thomas H. Ruger, commanding the Department of California, William R. Shafter received orders to proceed with part of his regiment to Los Angeles.[25]

Taking five companies, not quite three hundred men and officers, Shafter on July 2 left Angel Island by rail for Los Angeles. En route, at Bakersfield in the upper end of the San Joaquin Valley, he was delayed for four hours by strikers who tampered with the train engines during a water stop. On the third he was at Mojave, halfway between Bakersfield and Los Angeles, and about five in the morning of July 4, with his command increased by the addition of another company of troops, he reached his destination. He stationed his men at the roundhouse and depots of the Southern Pacific and Santa Fe railroads.[26]

Shafter's timely arrival may have prevented bloodshed. Many area citizens in sympathy with the strikers believed that the laws of the United States were being used unfairly against working people. Consequently, during the first two days of July federal marshal Joseph H. Call had not been able to secure enough men to act as special deputies to protect the railroads. There was little Call could do to prevent acts of violence that included breaking windows, setting fires to buildings, and tearing up tracks.[27]

After Shafter reached Los Angeles, the violence stopped. On the fifth, both the Southern Pacific and the Santa Fe railroads were in full possession of all their depots, yards, and shops. Having restored the property, Shafter ordered the railroads to get the trains moving, and to see that there was no interruption, he dispatched several troops as escort rid-

[25]Olney to Denis, June 28, 1894, and Denis to Olney, June 29, 1894, in *Appendix to the Annual Report of the Attorney General*, 1896, 54th Cong., 2d sess., H. Exec. Doc. 9, pt. 2, pp. 17–18; Brig. Gen. Thomas H. Ruger, Report of the Dept. of California, to Maj. Gen. Commanding the Army, Sept., 1894, in *Annual Report of the Secretary of War*, 1894, 53d Cong., 3d sess., H. Exec. Doc. 1, pt. 2, p. 111.

[26]Shafter to Daniel S. Lamont, Sec. of War, July 5, 1894, in *Report of the Attorney General*, 1896, 54th Cong., 2d sess., H. Exec. Doc. 9, pt. 2, p. 28; Regimental Returns, First Infantry, July, 1894, Roll 9, MC665, NA; *Los Angeles Times*, July 5, 1894. Also see Lindsey, *The Pullman Strike*, pp. 248–50.

[27]Joseph H. Call, Spec. Asst. U.S. Atty., Los Angeles, to Olney, July 18, 1894, in *Report of the Attorney General*, 1896, 54th Cong., 2d sess., H. Exec. Doc. 9, pt. 2, pp. 34–35.

ers on outbound trains. Before the day was out, a Santa Fe train carrying a Pullman car left for San Diego and another at the Southern Pacific yard was preparing to leave for Santa Barbara. When he received a rumor that strikers planned to attack any train carrying Pullman sleepers, Shafter, convinced that he had enough men to handle the situation, welcomed the strikers to interfere. None did. Shafter thereupon wrote Secretary of War Lamont that beyond the rumors there was nothing to indicate that the strikers intended to use violence.[28]

Two days later the situation remained unchanged. There was no excitement or large congregation of men at either of the railroad yards. In case the strikers meant to stop trains at some other place along the line, Shafter sent escorts with the mail trains all the way to Needles on the Arizona border. The stratagem was carried out with good results. The strikers made no attempts to interfere.[29]

Within three days of his arrival in Los Angeles, Shafter had restored peace in the area. Officials in the Department of California therefore planned to send him with his regiment to Sacramento, an important terminus for the Southern Pacific and Central Pacific railroads, where serious disturbances were occurring. City officials in Los Angeles, alarmed over the rumors of Shafter's departure, telegraphed Attorney General Olney on July 7 that Shafter ought not be transferred and that the peace in southern California was due to his presence. Moreover, they insisted that his removal would cause a blockade of the rail lines.[30] Because Olney agreed, Shafter remained in Los Angeles for two more weeks.

By July 16 the strikers in Los Angeles had returned to work. Although damage to business, agriculture, and industry across the state had been great, in the Los Angeles area losses had been kept to a minimum. Mail had been held up for almost two weeks in northern California, but Shafter had kept the trains moving where he had jurisdiction. Throughout the state the work stoppage affected 11,537 railroad and other employees who lost about $1 million in wages; the railroad losses aggregated some $545,000. On July 24 Shafter, in preparation for returning them to their respective posts, moved his troops to Santa Monica.[31]

Before he started for Angel Island, businessmen of Los Angeles honored Shafter for the efficiency and promptness with which he had

[28]Shafter to Lamont, July 5, 1894, ibid., p. 28.
[29]Shafter to Lamont, July 7, 1894, ibid., p. 29.
[30]G. R. Peck, Atty., to Olney, July 7, 1894, and Denis to Olney, July 8, 1894, ibid., p. 29.
[31]Ira Brown Cross, *A History of the Labor Movement in California*, pp. 218–21; Regimental Returns, First Infantry, July–Aug., 1894, Roll 9, MC665, NA.

handled his troops and dealt with the public during the strike. The Chamber of Commerce staged a special banquet for "the gallant soldier" on Thursday evening, August 9, at Santa Monica. At the dinner, attended by leading citizens of Los Angeles and all the officers of the First Infantry, Federal District Judge R. M. Widney made an opening speech in which he condemned the strikers and compared J. Peter Altgeld of Illinois, whom Widney thought responsible for the Pullman Strike, to Benedict Arnold.

Shafter delivered the major address. In a speech that lasted nearly an hour, he reviewed the history of the United States Army. He talked briefly about the Civil War but devoted most of his remarks to the role of the army in the West. "For the first seventy-five years," he said, "the principal and constant duty of the army was to the protection of those hardy men, . . . who struck out into the wilds of Kentucky, Ohio, Michigan, Illinois, Minnesota, and later farther west." Because there was no longer an Indian frontier, he concluded, instead of "protecting the lonely settler from the savages of the Plains, [the army] had now to turn its attention to the savages of the great cities."[32]

The speech, one of Shafter's few surviving public addresses, revealed many of his prejudices. He held little respect for strikers of the American Railway Union or the Indians against whom he so often had campaigned. He sympathized with the workers because of the low wages they received and with the proud warriors of the Plains who were now reduced to reservation poverty, but as an aggressive, self-confident soldier he would brook no opposition to the authority of the United States Army in its goal to maintain peace, order, and stability either on the country's frontier or in its cities.

When he returned to Angel Island after the end of the Pullman Strike, Shafter experienced a routine army life. The years passed quietly but eventfully. In 1895 he received the Congressional Medal of Honor for "most distinguished gallantry in the battle of Fair Oaks, May 31, 1862," during the Civil War. Early in 1897 he bought a 60-acre farm in Kern County, California, about fifteen miles southwest of Bakersfield. The property adjoined a 2,300-acre ranch belonging to his daughter and her husband, William McKittrick, who also held options to lease about 5,000 acres more in Kern County and in Arizona. On May 3, 1897, Shafter accepted a long overdue commission as brigadier general.[33]

[32] *Los Angeles Times*, Aug. 10, 1894; Cooper, *The Army and Civil Disorder*, p. 156.
[33] Francis B. Heitman, *Historical Register and Dictionary of the United States Army*, 1:806; Calhoun Collins, *The McKittrick Ranch*, pp. 1, 5, 7; Indenture between Kern County Land Company and William R. Shafter, March 6, 1899, filed at Kern County Recorder's Office, Bakersfield, Calif.; *Bakersfield News Press*, Dec. 20, 1967.

Upon being promoted to a general rank, Shafter left the First Infantry Regiment. On May 5, 1897, while on leave at his farm, he accepted an assignment to command the Department of Columbia with headquarters at Vancouver Barracks, but while still vacationing at Bakersfield, he received a brief telegram from Secretary of War Russell A. Alger changing the assignment to the Department of California. He took the next train to San Francisco, arriving there late that same day.[34]

The following day, Shafter assumed command. With the department embracing a dozen posts in California and Nevada, he supervised the operations of three regiments—the First Infantry, Third Artillery, and Fourth Cavalry—totaling more than two thousand men and officers. His headquarters was at the Presidio in San Francisco, one of the largest garrisons in the country. Having been stationed in California for more than a decade, he was familiar with the department. Nonetheless, he spent the first weeks of his new assignment studying his responsibilities. Because he no longer conducted a summer camp of instruction, the only troops who left their garrison on active duty were a few companies that served in Sequoia and Yosemite national parks. Later, he made certain that work on the construction of strong coastal defenses at San Diego and San Francisco was continued. During the fall and winter, his duties were usual and routine.[35]

Early in 1898 Hattie Shafter died.[36] A soldier's bride who had lived near the battlefronts in the Civil War and who had without complaint shared her husband's hardships in the remote and troubled Southwest, she died only a few weeks too soon to know that her husband would command the largest force of United States troops that had ever left American soil.

[34] Alger to Shafter, May 14, 1897, and Shafter to Adj. Gen., U.S. Army, May 14, 1897, both in ACP File, AGO, RG94, NA.

[35] *Annual Report of the Secretary of War*, 1897, and Shafter, "Report of Brig. Gen. William R. Shafter, Commanding the Department of California," Sept. 23, 1897, 55th Cong., 2d sess., H. Exec. Doc. 2, 1:4, 185–87.

[36] Shafter to Adj. Gen., U.S. Army, Mar. 30, 1898, ACP File, AGO, RG94, NA.

CHAPTER ELEVEN

The Spanish-American War

URING the Spanish-American War in 1898 William R. Shafter directed the United States military campaign at Santiago de Cuba. His prominent role in the war, however, has been overshadowed by the romantic exploits of Theodore Roosevelt at San Juan Hill and the naval heroics of Com. George Dewey in the Philippine Islands. During his assignment in Cuba, although criticized by his troops, by newspaper correspondents, and by Republican politicians, Shafter carried out a swift and successful operation on enemy soil in the tropics in the most unhealthful season of the year. Although the campaign in Cuba, the main theater of army operations, was something of an anticlimax, it was an engagement that proved as important to Shafter as any of his much longer frontier campaigns.

The war had many causes. Expanding American financial investments and increasing colonial desires promoted United States interest in Cuba. Several times in the nineteenth century the Cuban people, unsatisfied with Spanish rule, had revolted against Spain, and in the 1890's they rebelled again. From the outset people in the United States supported the rebel cause, and American feeling against Spain mounted as newspapers, appealing to the American taste for sensationalism, vividly described the war and Cuban suffering. In mid-February, 1898, when the battleship *Maine*, in Havana to protect American lives, exploded and sank with a heavy loss of life, the American public pressured the federal government for military action. In response, Congress on April 25, hoping to set the people of Cuba free, declared war against Spain.[1]

---

[1] For a summary analysis of the war's causes see David F. Trask, *The War with Spain in 1898*, pp. 473-76. Trask gives a more detailed discussion on pages 1-59.

American plans to achieve the goal shifted. Pres. William McKinley, who had little desire for a war with Spain, did not have an ultimate objective until after the declaration of war. He was, in addition, unsure about the proper American role: whether United States troops should engage Spanish forces directly, provide only aid and equipment to Cuban rebels, or take other kinds of action. As late as March and early April there were no plans, if war came, to hold Cuba, the Philippines, Puerto Rico, or other territories that might be won.

In the War Department, headed by Russell A. Alger, bureau and agency officers had given some thought to fighting Spain, but the army was neither organized nor prepared to fight a modern war. Until war was declared or Congress appropriated funds, army strategists could do little more than think about the army's role. They could not contract for equipment, supplies, or accoutrements. They could not call men to arms, and they did not know what kind of war they would be directed to fight.[2] The army needed time and direction.

The Department of the Navy, headed by John D. Long, was by contrast relatively clear about its role. Naval authorities had worked on contingency plans for a war with Spain for some time. In addition, reform in the American navy over the past decade had produced a relatively modern force, and to fulfill its role, the navy needed fewer men and less time or money to get under way. The navy believed its function would be to destroy Spanish sea power, to harass Spanish commerce, and to blockade Spanish positions in the Caribbean Sea, particularly Cuba. Along these lines it prepared tentative strategy.

When war came, the navy moved quickly. On May 1, just six days after the war declaration, the Pacific navy under Com. George Dewey destroyed the Spanish far-eastern fleet in the Philippines. Late in June Rear Adm. William T. Sampson's forces bottled up a major Spanish fleet at Santiago de Cuba and on July 3 destroyed it when it made a suicidal attempt to run the American blockade.

The army's plans, therefore, changed as the nature of naval engagements evolved. Nelson A. Miles, commanding general of the army, originally pushed a plan to increase the size of the regular army and to use the troops in Cuba after a naval blockade had reduced the Spanish forces there to starvation. As regulars in Cuba destroyed any pockets of Spanish resistance, the National Guard units could handle coastal

[2]See T. Harry Williams, *The History of American Wars: From Colonial Times to World War I,* pp. 323–27; Russell F. Weigley, *History of the United States Army,* pp. 304–305; Trask, *War with Spain,* pp. 148–49, 154; Matthew Forney Steele, *American Campaigns,* 1:590–91, 595; and G. J. A. O'Toole, *The Spanish War: An American Epic—1898,* pp. 96–99, 117, 196–97.

defenses. Miles wanted to use 80,000 troops to strike at Havana, Cuba, the center of Spanish strength, in the fall of 1898, after the summer rainy season when yellow fever would not be a menace. Although much of the plan found favor with President McKinley and Secretary of War Alger, some War Department planners wanted an early engagement at Havana.[3]

Before plans became final, however, the National Guard, a powerful political lobby, intervened. Its representatives in Congress blocked passage of a bill to increase the size of the regular army to over 100,000. A substitute bill, increasing the army to approximately 65,000 but providing a strong role for volunteer units, passed and became law on April 22, three days before war was declared. McKinley promptly issued a call for 125,000 volunteers and later requested 75,000 more. Although regular troops provided the bulk of Shafter's forces in Cuba, the War Department, in anticipation of the bill's passage, had begun to establish training sites and assembly camps to receive the new troops. On April 21, pursuant to orders from the War Department, Shafter left San Francisco for New Orleans to take command of troops gathering there. He arrived on the twenty-fifth.[4]

By this time an army-navy board had recommended that a small army expedition proceed to Cuba. Believing that a naval blockade of the island would not in itself be sufficient, the board wanted the small force to land on the southern coast, from which American troops could supply Cuban insurgents. The board agreed with Miles that if a larger expedition were needed, it should not go to Cuba until the unhealthful summer season had ended.

As they hammered out the new plans, McKinley, Miles, Alger, and several others considered who should command the force to Cuba. They wanted someone to lead a reconnaissance of the island, to form a junction with the Cuban insurgents, to learn all he could about the situation on Cuba, and to come back in a few days with an idea as to where more United States soldiers could land. Putting his finger on Shafter's name, Miles said, "If you want a man with force and ability, to insure the success of such a task, there is the man to do it." Shafter also had the support of Adj. Gen. Henry C. Corbin, an old frontier comrade and

[3]Graham A. Cosmas, *An Army for Empire: The United States Army in the Spanish-American War*, pp. 80–82, 87, 98–100, 104–107, 177–81.

[4]Williams, *History of American Wars*, pp. 323–24; Weigley, *History of the United States Army*, pp. 297–98; Henry C. Corbin, Adj. Gen., U.S. Army, to Shafter, April 21, 1898, United States, William R. Shafter, Letters Received, Appointments, Commission, and Personal Branch, Adjutant General's Office, Record Group 94, National Archives (hereafter ACP File, AGO, RG94, NA).

close friend, and Alger, who like Shafter was from Michigan. Because all three men considered him a level-headed and able field officer, Shafter became their choice to lead the first command to Cuba.[5]

Shafter in 1898 seemed a wholly illogical choice. He was nearly sixty-three years old and weighed about three hundred pounds. In describing him, John F. Weston, a commissary officer, said Shafter "couldn't walk two miles in an hour, just beastly obese." A newsman said that he looked "like three men rolled into one — or, a quip said, a floating tent."[6] Shafter also suffered from painful varicose veins, severe gout, and other maladies that made him physically unsuited for reconnaissance in tropical Cuba.[7] Moreover, on horseback — or in the Maine buckboard he often used, which sagged under his great weight — and wearing a tight-fitting uniform topped by a pith helmet, he appeared an embarrassingly comic figure who did not inspire vigor in his troops.[8]

Shafter's selection was largely political. Army habits, developed through years of Indian fighting, favored senior officers. McKinley could have choosen any number of younger men, many of whom had West Point training, or he could have named Miles to lead the expedition. Certainly the publicity-seeking Miles, who had presidential ambitions, wanted to lead the campaign or a larger one to Havana or Puerto Rico. But the Republican McKinley and his chief political advisor, Mark Hanna, suspected that the dashing and dramatic Miles was a Democrat. More concerned that the war might create political heroes than with the selection of a competent commander, they turned to Shafter, who represented a threat to neither McKinley nor Miles. Shafter harbored no political ambitions, and the army considered him a vigorous, aggressive, and forceful old soldier.[9]

[5]Charles D. Rhodes, "William Rufus Shafter," *Michigan History Magazine* 16 (Fall, 1932): 378; Cosmas, *An Army for Empire*, p. 193; Miles quoted in Margaret Leech, *In the Days of McKinley*, p. 202.

[6]Weston quoted in Cosmas, *An Army for Empire*, p. 193; newsman quoted in Trask, *War with Spain*, p. 180. Also see Charles Johnson Post, *The Little War of Private Post*, pp. 212, 231; Cosmas, *An Army for Empire*, pp. 193–94; and Williams, *History of American Wars*, p. 335.

[7]Shafter to Adj. Gen., U.S. Army, April 11, 1891, and March 29, 1893, and Brig. Gen. James W. Forsyth to Adj. Gen., U.S. Army, June 30, 1896, all in ACP File, AGO, RG94, NA.

[8]Post, *The Little War of Private Post*, pp. 112, 231, 290.

[9]See, for example, J. C. Breckinridge to Adj. Gen., U.S. Army, May 1, 1896, John L. Mitchell to Secy. of War, Oct. 31, 1894, and J. N. Dean to Secy. of War, Oct. 20, 1894, all in ACP File, AGO, RG94, NA. Also see Joseph Wheeler, *The Santiago Campaign*, pp. 6, 196–97; Cosmas, *An Army for Empire*, pp. 193–94; and Post, *The Little War of Private Post*, pp. 112, 212–14, 290.

With its choice made, the War Department summoned Shafter to Washington. On April 27 he lumbered into the White House to pay his respects to the president. It was a courtesy call en route to disaster. After receiving official word that he would lead the reconnaissance expedition to Cuba, Shafter, rather than returning to New Orleans, proceeded to Tampa, Florida. He arrived on April 29 only to hear that, because of the possible appearance of a Spanish fleet in Cuban waters, the expedition had been postponed. Nonetheless, he established his headquarters in the Tampa Bay Hotel and began preparations for a Cuban campaign.[10]

Preparations for a Cuban campaign were not hampered by financial problems. Congress, in contrast to its tight army appropriations of the Gilded Age, provided substantial funds. The first money, $50 million, came in March from surplus funds in the United States Treasury. Congress authorized an additional $100 million by passage of a War Revenue Act designed to obtain money through taxes, and the American public oversubscribed a bond issue allowing $200 million more. Some of the money could not be spent before the war ended, and it was returned to the Treasury.[11]

Using the money to secure adequate supplies was a nightmare of confusion. Although the navy experienced few serious shortages, the suddenly enlarged army endured a crisis of supply from mobilization to the end of the Cuban campaign. The War Department was caught by surprise at the rapid increase, and without a special agency or staff to handle procurement, its bureau chiefs, unaccustomed to the need for close cooperation, preferred to function in their own agencies. In addition, writes T. Harry Williams, Secretary of War Alger "was a mediocre administrator who took little initiative in supervising his department."[12] The shortages and confusion extended to everything but rifles.[13]

[10]John D. Miley, *In Cuba with Shafter*, p. 12; Leech, *In the Days of McKinley*, p. 202; William J. Schellings, "The Advent of the Spanish-American War in Florida, 1898," *Florida Historical Quarterly* 39 (April, 1961): 312–14.

[11]Williams, *History of American Wars*, p. 325; Weigley, *History of the United States Army*, p. 299; Cosmas, *An Army for Empire*, pp. 139–65.

[12]Williams, *History of American Wars*, p. 326. Also see Cosmas, *An Army for Empire*, pp. 58, 67. For a discussion of War Department bureaus, see Cosmas, pp. 16–19; Trask, *War with Spain*, pp. 146–48; Russell A. Alger, *The Spanish-American War*, pp. 13–14; and Leech, *In the Days of McKinley*, p. 102.

[13]Russell F. Weigley calls the War Department obtuse but writes that "though the press conveyed an impression of thorough ineptitude in the supply departments, the procurement of supplies actually seems to have gone fairly well for the circumstances." There was no scandal associated with the large purchases that were

Confusion existed as well at the army assembly points. The War Department eventually selected fifteen campsites for the gathering and training of troops. The most important of these were Chickamauga Park, Georgia, and Tampa, Florida. All sites experienced problems of supply and food distribution. Uniforms were sometimes unavailable and housing inadequate. Horse- or mule-drawn wagons to transport supplies were also scarce, and it was not until near the end of the war that the army could provide as many as four wagons to each regiment. Most of the National Guard troops arriving at the camps carried Springfield rifles, single-shot breechloaders that fired black powder and thus gave away positions to the enemy. The Springfields often were worn out and dangerous, sometimes exploding in the user's face. The army had discarded them in favor of the bolt action, 30-caliber, five-shot Krag-Jörgensen that used smokeless ammunition. National Guard units usually lacked extra clothing and accoutrements. Graham A. Cosmas writes that "many of the uniforms, cartridge belts, knapsacks, and other items in their possession were near disintegration from age." Few of the units had enough tentage or other camp equipage. That none of the assembly camps at first had adequate warehouses or railroad sidings added to the chaos.[14]

Confusion in Tampa mirrored the confusion at other assembly points. A city of 26,000 in 1898, Tampa was soon overrun with soldiers, both regular army and National Guard. Some of the Guard regiments had no cooks, utensils, or camp stoves, and they were unable to prepare meals when rations were issued in bulk. Meals became a matter of eating hardtack, cooking bacon over campfires, and boiling coffee in tin cans. Unsanitary conditions produced sickness, and the doctors lacked medicines and medical supplies. Hot, sandy campgrounds made life miserable, and at night hordes of mosquitoes invaded the camps.[15]

Shafter had little control over the conditions. The War Department had selected Tampa because of its proximity to Cuba but had given

---

needed, and although the army went to the tropics in heavy woolen uniforms, the War Department, except for wagon shortages, overcame most of its difficulties of supply in a relatively short time. Weigley, *History of the United States Army*, p. 300. Also see U.S. Senate, *Report of the Commission Appointed by the President to Investigate the Conduct of the War Department in the War with Spain* (hereafter *Investigation*), 1:138–41, 5:2184–85, 6:2643, 2692–95, 2702, and 7:3140, 3763; Cosmas, *An Army for Empire*, pp. 155–56.

[14]Cosmas, *An Army for Empire*, pp. 12, 167. Also see *Investigation*, 1:522, 525, 533–34, 536, 538–39, 4:1237–38, and 6:2610, 3103.

[15]Frank Freidel, *The Splendid Little War*, pp. 33–36; Schellings, "The Advent of the Spanish-American War in Florida, 1898," pp. 320–26; Theodore Roosevelt, *The Rough Riders*, p. 41; Post, *The Little War of Private Post*, pp. 46–47, 59, 61, 68–69.

little thought to other logistical problems. Tampa was inadequately connected to the industrial North by rail lines, only a single track connected it with Port Tampa several miles away, and there were not sufficient facilities for storage of supplies, equipment, and food as they arrived. The War Department's conviction that Tampa was a good place was, according to T. Harry Williams, "one of the most incredible miscalculations of the war."[16] Moreover, the freight cars were not marked as to their contents, often had to be backed up on sidings ten miles from the camps, and some of the food in them spoiled. Quartermaster and commissary officers worked long hours for proper distribution of supplies, but Col. Leonard Wood of the famous Rough Riders "found everything confused and in a most frightful mix" when he arrived in Tampa.[17]

To end the "frightful mix," Shafter streamlined his supply organization. There was at first a depot quartermaster and a chief quartermaster. The resulting lack of harmony in management and methods caused Shafter to place everything pertaining to the quartermaster department under one head. Thus Lt. Col. (brigadier general of volunteers) Charles F. Humphrey took charge on May 2. Col. John F. Weston, assistant commissary of subsistence, answered to Humphrey and became chief commissary of the expedition to Cuba. The move helped, but it was not enough. Before he could take other workable steps Shafter was relieved of command. He and James F. Wade on May 9 both accepted promotion to major general of volunteers. Because he was the senior officer in time of service, although by only a few weeks, Wade assumed charge at Tampa. But he had no more luck in establishing order than Shafter, and the muddle continued. Not until May 20 when Wade left for Jacksonville, Florida, did Shafter again assume leadership.[18]

The federal government in the meantime had decided to enlarge Shafter's command. After Commodore Dewey's electrifying naval vic-

[16]Williams, *History of American Wars*, p. 334. Also see Trask, *War with Spain*, pp. 131–86; O'Toole, *The Spanish War*, p. 229.

[17]Cited in Trask, *War with Spain*, p. 184.

[18]Miley, *In Cuba with Shafter*, pp. 6–8. When Shafter took command from Wade at Tampa on April 29, he and Wade both were brigadier generals, but Shafter was the senior officer by date of appointment. Because both men were named major general on the same date, May 4, 1898, Wade, who had entered the army in 1861 a few weeks before Shafter, became the senior officer by date of service. Wade was the son of Benjamin F. Wade, president pro tempore of the Senate during Pres. Andrew Johnson's impeachment trial. Wade commanded the Third Corps. Ibid., pp. 7–8; Francis B. Heitman, *Historical Register and Dictionary of the United States Army*, 1:856. Also see Cosmas, *An Army for Empire*, p. 133 n.41; and Trask, *War with Spain*, p. 151.

tory on May 1 at Manila in the Philippines, a joint army-navy board determined that the reconnaissance expedition was no longer necessary. The Spanish navy was much weaker than American authorities had thought. A large invading force to strike at Havana, they now reasoned, was the proper army strategy. Because the troops at Tampa, chaotic though the situation was, were better prepared than those at Mobile or New Orleans or any of the other assembly points, Shafter was to lead the invasion force. While Shafter welcomed the larger command, the news brought thousands of additional troops flocking to Tampa, overwhelming the army receptionists who were swamped in confusion.

As Shafter labored to bring order out of chaos, a Spanish naval fleet commanded by Adm. Pascual Cervera and in need of coal for its ships slipped into Cuba's Santiago harbor on May 19. Cervera's move was a mistake, for there was little coal there. A week afterward the United States Navy blockaded the place and a few days later dispatched a small force to establish a naval base at Guantanamo Bay. After minor action, the first on Cuban soil involving Americans, marines took the site. The naval action at Santiago harbor again changed the direction of the war. Strategists in Washington planned now to have Shafter's force help the navy destroy the Spanish fleet by capturing Santiago de Cuba.[19]

In 1898 Santiago de Cuba was a city of 45,000 inhabitants on the island's southeastern coast. The capital of the rugged, thinly populated eastern province, it was Cuba's third largest city in size and importance. There were no road or railway connections with Havana five hundred miles to the west, but it enjoyed one of the island's best harbors, a bay deep and narrow at the head of which lay the city. Approximately 10,000 Spanish troops garrisoned the city and about that many more guarded towns and plantations scattered through the eastern province. As Graham A. Cosmas notes, with Shafter's force not yet ready to strike at Havana, "Santiago de Cuba offered a worthwhile and vulnerable target" that could provide an early foothold in Cuba.[20] McKinley's advisors determined that a force of about 20,000 to 25,000 Americans would land east or west of the harbor, knock out the Spanish forts guarding the entrance, and prepare the way for the destruction of Cervera's fleet. After the foothold had been gained, Shafter's force, reinforced by troops from various assembly camps, would take

[19]Cosmas, An Army for Empire, pp. 177–81.
[20]Ibid., pp. 177–78; Steele, American Campaigns, 1:594–95, 597–98. Also see U.S. Dept. of War, Adj. Gen.'s Office, Correspondence Relating to the War with Spain and Conditions Growing Out of Same . . . April 15, 1898, to July 30, 1902 (hereafter Correspondence), 1:14–15.

Puerto Rico. The Havana campaign would be postponed until the fall, when another expedition would sail from Mobile or New Orleans.

Shafter on May 31 received word to ready his command of about 25,000 troops for departure. Almost immediately he discovered problems. The transports, chartered by the Quartermaster's Department from private shippers who handled only a coastal trade, were small, dirty, rundown, and too few in number. Most had neither bunks for the troops nor stalls for the horses and mules. Shafter discovered on June 1 that the transports could carry only 15,000 to 18,000 troops, not the 25,000 the War Department wanted him to take. He began loading the supplies and equipment and announced that he could sail in three days. He was wrong. General Miles, who had arrived from Washington, reported on June 3 that loading problems were serious and delay was certain. Much of the trouble related to difficulties over which no one had control: the single railway track between Tampa and the port of departure created a massive bottleneck, and some of the unmarked freight cars loaded with necessary supplies now were sidetracked twenty-five miles away. The wharf at Port Tampa was a narrow place in which to work, and only four ships could dock at one time. The loading became an all but impassable traffic jam.[21]

To speed the process, Shafter directed the loading himself. He worked first from the veranda of the Tampa Bay Hotel and later from the wharf, where he sat on two cracker boxes to work at a desk improvised from a packing case. He labored around the clock to place coal, water, food, forage, artillery, and ammunition on the transports. In the absence of loading machinery, he ordered most of the supplies to be carried aboard on the backs of stevedores who walked up and down steep gangplanks lugging their loads until they were exhausted. He asked carpenters to work long hours in the holds of the ships to build tiers of bunks for the soldiers and stalls for the animals. Nonetheless, Shafter, overwhelmed by the enormous logistical problems, could not resolve the loading bottleneck. When it came time to load the troops, therefore, he resorted to a favorite frontier tactic: trust subordinate officers to demonstrate initiative.[22]

[21] Miley, In Cuba with Shafter, pp. 10, 22–23; Williams, History of American Wars, p. 334; Post, The Little War of Private Post, pp. 77, 80–81; Wheeler, The Santiago Campaign, pp. 6–7; O'Toole, The Spanish War, pp. 239–42; Weigley, History of the United States Army, p. 302.

[22] Miles to Shafter, May 29, and May 30, 1898, and Shafter to Miles, May 31, 1898, all in William R. Shafter Papers, Stanford University Library, Stanford, Calif., photocopy in Southwest Collection, Texas Tech University, Lubbock (hereafter Shafter Papers). Copies of these letters, or telegrams, may also be found in Miley, In Cuba

The plan worked. On the morning of June 8, the transports were loaded and ready to sail. Indeed, some had already started when orders from Alger, indicating that a Spanish fleet might be waiting to destroy the ships, instructed Shafter to remain in Tampa until further notice. Shafter recalled those transports that had started and used the extra time to inspect the loaded vessels. He transferred a few troops to other vessels and placed on board additional medical supplies. The troops remained on board but practiced a landing drill that Charles Johnson Post thought "nothing but a disguised opportunity for a swim."[23] The ships were hot, and Shafter ordered that the animals be removed to land. Satisfied that all was ready, he waited for approval to sail.

A few days later approval arrived, and Shafter, after reloading the animals, sailed on June 14 for Cuba. His command, the Fifth Army Corps, one of eight the army had created for the war, was organized into three divisions, each with three brigades, and each brigade with three regiments. Shafter's corps contained two infantry divisions under Brig. Gen. J. Ford Kent, a colonel who had received a wartime promotion, and Brig. Gen. Henry W. Lawton, who had been with Shafter in Arizona during the Geronimo campaign, and a dismounted cavalry division under Maj. Gen. Joseph W. Wheeler, a veteran of the Confederate Army.[24] There was in addition an independent brigade under Brig. Gen. John C. Bates. The units consisted of eighteen regular and two volunteer infantry regiments, ten regular and two volunteer cavalry regiments, a battalion of engineers, a detachment of the signal corps, a balloon detail, and four light artillery batteries. Altogether there were nearly seventeen thousand men and officers. The field weapons included eight field mortars, four siege guns, four seven-inch howitzers, four Gatling guns, a pneumatic dynamite gun, and a Hotchkiss revolving cannon.[25]

Thirty-two transports carried the troops, animals, equipment, and supplies, and the navy provided additional fleet tenders and several escort vessels. On board there were eighty-nine newsmen and a dozen observers from foreign armies, mostly European. Shafter used his time

with Shafter, pp. 16–19; and in Nelson A. Miles, *Serving the Republic: Memoirs of the Civil War and Military Life of Nelson A. Miles*, pp. 275–76.

[23]Post, *The Little War of Private Post*, pp. 91–92; Miley, *In Cuba with Shafter*, pp. 15–18; Freidel, *The Splendid Little War*, pp. 65–69.

[24]Because he could not transport as large a force as he wanted, Shafter's cavalry division had only two full brigades. See Wheeler, *The Santiago Campaign*, p. 15; and Steele, *American Campaigns*, 1:596.

[25]Miles to Shafter, May 30, 1898, Shafter Papers; Miley, *In Cuba with Shafter*, pp. 17–18; Freidel, *The Splendid Little War*, pp. 68–69.

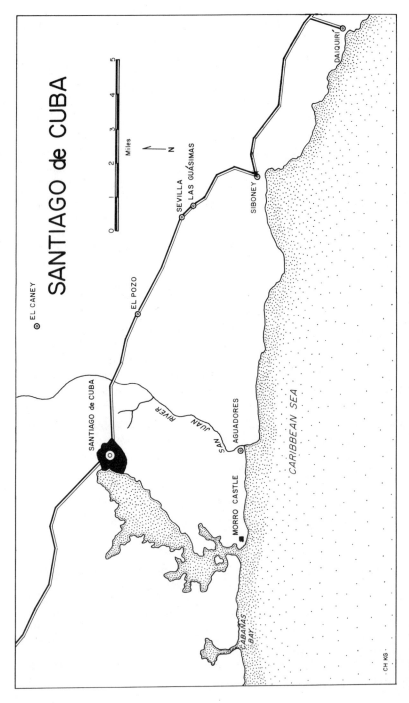

SANTIAGO de CUBA

EL CANEY

EL POZO

SEVILLA

LAS GUÁSIMAS

SIBONEY

DAIQUIRI

SANTIAGO de CUBA

SAN JUAN RIVER

AGUADORES

MORRO CASTLE

CABAÑAS BAY

CARIBBEAN SEA

Miles

N

· CH KG ·

en route to prepare for the invasion. He pored over histories of earlier campaigns in the West Indies, studying with special attention an unsuccessful attack on Santiago de Cuba in 1741 and Edward Hale's *The Capture of Havana in 1762 by Forces of George III.* He conferred with Cuban insurgent officers and a refugee from Santiago de Cuba. During the voyage the seas, except on the nineteenth, were calm.

Not so calm, however, were relations between the army and navy. Rear Adm. William T. Sampson, commanding the American naval squadron blockading Santiago harbor, dispatched a messenger to Shafter on board the *Seguranca,* the flagship of the expedition. The messenger, Capt. Henry C. Taylor, requested that Shafter allow the faster ships to proceed ahead and thus reach Santiago de Cuba earlier than the others. Concerned over splitting his forces, Shafter refused but offered to try increasing the speed. The plan did not work, and the voyage was delayed by the slower vessels. Shafter's response to Sampson's request reflected the first in a series of difficulties between himself and Admiral Sampson. Except for the loss of one small lighter, a vessel needed for landing troops, the passage to Cuba was completed without other serious difficulty.[26]

After six days at sea, Shafter early in the morning on June 20 reached a point off the mouth of Santiago harbor. Sampson came aboard the *Seguranca,* and the vessel steamed slowly along the coast on both sides of the mouth of the harbor for Shafter to gain some idea of the nature of the shoreline. "The beauty of the place," wrote John D. Miley, "can hardly be exaggerated."[27] For twenty miles on either side of the harbor the coast was rugged and mountainous. A ridge, varying in height from 150 to 200 feet and covered with luxuriant growth, rose abruptly out of the sea in most places, but at other points it stood back from the water's edge 300 to 400 yards. It was broken here and there by ravines or canyons through which flowed short streams, the largest being the San Juan River about three miles east of the harbor. There were several small communities east of the harbor, including Aguadores at the mouth of the San Juan, Siboney eleven miles from the harbor, and Daiquiri six miles beyond. West of the harbor were such small places as Cabañas two miles from the harbor and Guaicabon two miles farther. Back from the coast was a thick tropical jungle interrupted by the streams and two short rail lines. Roads, often no more than narrow jungle trails, crisscrossed the area.

After the reconnaissance Shafter, Sampson, and some members of

[26]Miley, *In Cuba with Shafter,* pp. 41–42.
[27]Ibid., p. 53.

their respective staffs went ashore at Aserraderos, a tiny village about twenty miles west of Santiago harbor, to confer with insurgent leaders. They met with Gen. Calixto García and Gen. Jesús Rabí. García informed them as to the approximate number of Spanish troops at Santiago de Cuba and at the small communities along the coast and through the interior. They also discussed the choice of landing spots. Sampson wanted Shafter to land at Cabañas just west of the harbor and to use the base to storm the Spanish positions guarding the entrance. Shafter and García considered a landing there impractical. A fort called Castle Morro, perched on a hill rising sharply from the sea to a height of 230 feet, was too difficult a position, they concluded, to take without heavy artillery. Shafter with García's concurrence decided to land at Siboney and Daiquiri.[28]

The disagreement over landing sites added to the growing antagonism between Sampson and Shafter. They could not cooperate. Too often Shafter thought in terms of a frontier command where he alone held authority and did not, or could not, share responsibility for success or failure of an expedition. Conditioned by such narrow thinking and piqued by the difficulties with Sampson, Shafter refused to recognize the equal role the navy shared in the war. His position wrecked chances for a smooth campaign, but Shafter was not alone at fault. Sampson, too, possessed a short temper as well as a desire to claim the major honors for success in war. He did not provide full support to the army or fair recognition to his subaltern Com. Winfield S. Schley, who directed the destruction of Admiral Cervera's fleet. That Shafter and Sampson should have cooperated better is clear, but their differences reflected the disagreements in Washington between secretaries Alger and Long. Army-navy disharmony was a scandal, and President McKinley should have demanded greater cooperation. There was a good record of combined operations in the Civil War, but after some thirty years of separate existence an easy partnership in 1898 was perhaps impossible. Certainly it did not exist either in Washington or in Cuba.[29]

In Cuba General Shafter planned to debark his troops on the morning of the twenty-first, but rain, rough seas, and squally weather delayed the operation until the following day. While waiting for improved weather, Shafter met with division and brigade commanders and held further discussions with Admiral Sampson's chief of staff, Capt.

[28] Ibid., pp. 54–56; Steele, *American Campaigns*, 1:598; General Orders No. 18, Fifth Army Corps, June 20, 1898, ACP File, AGO, RG94, NA; Alger, *The Spanish-American War*, pp. 84–91.
[29] Cosmas, *An Army of Empire*, pp. 206–208; Williams, *The History of American Wars*, pp. 327–28.

French E. Chadwick. He determined that Lt. Col. Charles F. Humphrey on the part of the army and Capt. Caspar F. Goodrich on the part of the navy would direct the debarkation.

On the morning of June 22, after a feint west of Santiago harbor to throw the Spanish off guard and a heavy naval shelling of the coast behind Daiquiri to draw out any Spaniards who might be in the neighborhood, troops began to move ashore. The area was undefended. The harbor at Daiquiri contained a wooden wharf about twenty-five feet wide and forty feet long and a large pier that was used for loading iron ore from mines a few miles back from the coast. Although the iron ore pier was too high for use during debarkation, most of the men with the supplies disembarked on the wooden wharf. Landing officials brought a few of the smaller transports with a draught of not more than eight or ten feet up to the wharf, but the bulk of the troops leaving transports went ashore in small boats. There was a sandy beach about three hundred yards long, and back of it spread open ground that the army utilized as temporary camps for the men and corrals for the animals.

The landing did not go well. It was a slow and time-consuming process that without the navy's assistance would have lapsed into total confusion. Even so there was little order or system, and the small wharf and shortage of lighters added to the disarray. Only six thousand troops landed the first day. Many of these, rather than wait for a beachhead to be secured, began an immediate march under their division commanders, but Shafter's orders, toward Santiago de Cuba. Some of the horses and mules, which were pushed overboard from side hatches on the transports, became disoriented, headed toward open sea instead of toward shore, and drowned in the surf. Two soldiers of the all-black Tenth Cavalry drowned when they fell into the water while attempting to climb onto the wharf from their surf-tossed landing boat. After debarkation commenced at Siboney, unloading continued to drag out, with four full days needed to get all the troops ashore. Several more days were needed to complete the removal of supplies and equipment. The problems and delays caught Shafter, who remained aboard the *Seguranca* to oversee debarkation, by surprise.[30]

In addition, the impolitic Shafter angered many of the newspaper correspondents. As he prepared for debarkation, Shafter studied Cuba's unfamiliar shore fringed with jungle that might hold an ambush. He determined that each precious space in the steam launches, in the small

---

[30] *New York Times*, June 24, 1898; Marvin Fletcher, *The Black Soldier and Officer in the United States Army, 1891–1917*, p. 35; Miley, *In Cuba with Shafter*, p. 69.

boats, and on the lighter landing craft should be occupied by a soldier. Accordingly, he ordered that reporters would remain aboard ship until the landing at Daiquiri had been accomplished. Because most felt it their duty to go ashore with the first waves of troops and to report any fight that occurred, the correspondents were upset.

Richard Harding Davis, the most famous war correspondent of his generation, thought Shafter had made a mistake. A vivid writer who could recognize the picturesque as well as the news value of situations, Davis had thousands of readers. He was brilliant, if at times overdramatic. A jaunty fellow, he decided to explain to the general that he was wrong. Davis found Shafter on the deck of the *Seguranca* with several other officers and correspondents looking out over the guard rail at the unfriendly shore and gave him advice on how newsmen should be treated. Shafter listened impatiently, and then he said, "No reporters will go ashore until we have the beach under control."

"I am no ordinary reporter," Davis answered.

"I do not care a damn what you are," Shafter barked, "I'll treat you all alike."

Shafter's abrupt treatment shocked Davis, and the general's attitude toward other newspapermen turned them against him. "From the moment of the issuing of that order," wrote one of Shafter's aides, "pencils began to be sharpened for Gen. Shafter—and they have not yet lost their point."[31]

After the incident Shafter became the subject of blistering denunciations. The correspondents, who initially had focused their attacks on the War Department for discomfort and shortages of equipment in the assembly camps, cabled home criticism of Shafter's tactics, supply management, and personal conduct. Sometimes they were fed their information by disaffected army officers who either had not received one of the few choice assignments in the war or made a habit of leaking information that was derogatory.[32]

Shafter turned to a more important matter, the capture of Santiago de Cuba. His plan was simple enough: a quick drive toward the city by the most direct route, which meant along a tiny jungle road leading through Siboney. On June 23, Brig. Gen. Henry Lawton reached Siboney and captured it without difficulty. He established a perimeter defense

[31]Freidel, *The Splendid Little War*, pp. 85–86; General Orders No. 18, Fifth Army Corps, June 20, 1898, ACP File, AGO, RG94, NA. Also see Miley, *In Cuba with Shafter*, pp. 60–71; Charles H. Brown, *The Correspondents' War: Journalists in the Spanish-American War*, pp. 304–305; and Gerald Langford, *The Richard Harding Davis Years: A Biography of a Mother and Son*, p. 197.

[32]Miley, *In Cuba with Shafter*, pp. 60–71.

behind the beach to enable debarkation operations to move to that area. When this was done, Siboney became Shafter's base for the campaign. Shafter purposed for Lawton's division to take a strong position a short distance beyond Siboney. He wanted Brig. Gen. J. Ford Kent with his division to camp at Siboney, Brig. Gen. John C. Bates with his brigade to support Lawton, and Maj. Gen. Joseph W. Wheeler with his division to bivouack in the rear along the Daiquiri-Siboney road. He planned to hold his troops in these positions until he got his equipment and supplies ashore and reinforcements arrived from Camp Alger in Falls Church, Virginia.

General Wheeler, the senior officer on shore, changed those plans. While Lawton prepared a defensive line, Wheeler, without Shafter's authority, pushed his dismounted cavalry division toward Santiago de Cuba. At Las Guásimas, a village about two miles northwest of Siboney, on June 24 he ran into the rear guard of a retiring Spanish force, nearly two thousand troops, and suffered some casualties. Because the Spanish had no intention of making a stand beyond Santiago de Cuba's outer defenses, he took Las Guásimas, a position the Spaniards could have defended with strength, without any serious delay. The victory boosted American morale, and it reinforced Shafter's determination for a land victory in the interior away from Sampson's naval forces along the coast.[33]

Shafter devoted the next few days to landing operations and to strengthening his position. His signal corps established a telephone line from Daiquiri to the front. Later, as troops moved forward, the line followed and enabled Shafter to talk at all times to the division commanders and supply officers. A few days afterward his troops found a coastwise cable. They cut it and carried the end to Siboney, connecting the place to Playa del Este, a little village at the mouth of Guantanamo Bay, the terminus of the ocean cable. Thus, by telephone messages to Siboney, Shafter's headquarters was in direct communication with the War Department.[34]

Although communication was not a problem, Shafter's troops endured several other difficulties. Scattered rain showers fell between June 23 and June 30. Then in the week afterward it rained nearly every day in the afternoon for about three hours, and one night during that

[33] Trask, *War with Spain*, pp. 217–24; Wheeler, *The Santiago Campaign*, pp. 16–38; Charles E. Heller and William A. Stafft, eds., *America's First Battles, 1776–1965*, p. 121. When the Spanish troops, after two hours of fighting, began to retire, "Wheeler, the ex-Confederate," writes David F. Trask in quoting an observer, "yelled, 'We've got the damn Yankees on the run!'" (p. 221).

[34] Cosmas, *An Army for Empire*, pp. 188–89, 202–203.

time "a most terrific tropical thunderstorm" hit. The soldiers had few dry clothes. In addition, the first troops off the transports had carried food for only three days. After they had consumed the immediate rations, a problem of supply developed, for the wagons had not yet been unloaded and the pack mules could not carry loads large enough along the jungle trails to provision the advance troops adequately. Even after supply officers got the wagons into use, there were difficulties. Flooded roads and swollen streams became nearly impossible to cross. Teamsters, packers, and supply officers all wrangled with one another resulting in further confusion and delay. The problem of supply was never really solved, and refugees from Santiago de Cuba added to the logistical nightmare.[35]

Despite all this, Shafter determined to move on to Santiago de Cuba before Spaniards reinforced the city. On June 30, having solidified his beachhead, he rode forward with members of his staff to El Pozo, a junction on high ground within two and one-half miles of Santiago de Cuba, from where, using field glasses, he enjoyed an excellent view of his objective. The city's two most important outer defenses were located along a series of ridges known collectively as the San Juan Heights and in the village of El Caney about four miles to the north. To prevent the city from being reinforced and to cut its water supply, Shafter decided to attack El Caney early on July 1 and to follow in two hours with a frontal assault on the San Juan positions. Although the action required him to divide his forces, probably a mistake, Shafter believed that the village would fall quickly, allowing his troops at E' Caney to join those storming San Juan.[36]

Disorganized fighting followed. Shafter, nearly prostrated by gout and the hot, humid weather, proved unable to direct the battles, and inadequate staff work and poor communication contributed to the lack of direction. General Lawton, assigned to take El Caney, moved out on schedule, but poor roads and difficult terrain prevented him from beginning the assault on time. General Kent, who commanded the force assigned to take the San Juan ridges, after waiting more than the allotted two hours for the El Caney fight to get under way, began his attack. It proved a poorly coordinated effort, however, and within a short time units of Kent's command became badly confused. One contributing factor was the heavy artillery fire that a signal corps balloon brought

[35]Miley, *In Cuba with Shafter*, pp. 81, 86; Post, *The Little War of Private Post*, pp. 288–89.

[36]Freidel, *The Splendid Little War*, pp. 77–78; Miley, *In Cuba with Shafter*, pp. 52–72; William R. Shafter, "The Capture of Santiago de Cuba," *Century* 57 (Feb., 1899): 612–25.

Black troops in Cuba, 1898. *Original in National Archives, print courtesy Southwest Collection, Texas Tech University*

upon the troops as it was being towed along the advancing front line. Subordinate officers rose to the occasion, however, restored order, and stormed the Spanish positions with a variety of troops, including the black Ninth and Tenth Cavalry regiments, who had served with Shafter in the Southwest, and the Rough Riders, a volunteer unit commanded by Leonard Wood and future president Theodore Roosevelt. The Spanish fell back toward Santiago de Cuba.

The attack on El Caney, meanwhile, made little headway. Some five hundred Spanish troops in a strong position protected by barbed wire resisted stubbornly until late in the afternoon when, for lack of ammunition and the increasing effectiveness of United States artillery, they retired. With the fall of El Caney all the outer defenses of Santiago de Cuba were in American hands. The fighting was costly, however. Shafter's command suffered over 1,100 casualties, including 237 men and officers killed. Although it was not an excessive total in relation to the number of men engaged, the result appalled many officers, and they blamed Shafter for the casualties. The Spanish losses were greater. Most of the defenders of El Caney were dead or wounded, including the field commander, Brig. Gen. Joaquín Vera de Rey. About 2,000 Spaniards were wounded, many fatally, while retreating from the San Juan positions, and nearly thirty wagonloads of prisoners were taken.[37]

Shafter now faced the problem of what to do next. Despite his victory, he did not enjoy an enviable position. Before him lay the enemy's well-organized second line of defense and behind that the more formidable inner defenses, strongly protected by barbed wire. He was sick, suffering with gout and debilitated by an attack of malaria, and many of the general officers, especially Joseph Wheeler, were ailing. His troops, exposed to enemy fire they could not return effectively, huddled in hot, steaming trenches, their health and safety threatened by rain, malaria, yellow fever, and possible hurricanes. Knowing that an attempt to storm the city without sufficient artillery to blast through the barbed wire and the entrenched enemy positions would be suicidal, he proposed to withdraw to higher ground about four miles from the city. The War Department vetoed this move, however. He next tried to persuade the navy to run the channel into Santiago harbor and attack the city from the bay, but neither Admiral Sampson nor his superiors in the Navy Department in Washington dared to risk such a venture. Sampson believed he could not safely enter the harbor until the army captured Morro Castle and its sister fort across the harbor's mouth. He did not want to venture into the harbor until it had been cleared of mines, a task that could not be undertaken, he argued, until the forts were taken. Shafter and Sampson, unable to cooperate, wrangled in conferences without coming to a decision. When discussions broke off, Shafter asked Alger for fifteen thousand reinforcements to attack Santiago de Cuba and began to position his artillery for battle.[38]

Fortunately for Shafter, the enemy had serious problems. In San-

[37] Annual Report of the Secretary of War, 1898, 55th Cong., 3d sess., H. Exec. Doc. 2, 1:4–5; Freidel, The Splendid Little War, pp. 119–232; Miley, In Cuba with Shafter, pp. 82–128; Cosmas, An Army for Empire, pp. 205–15.

[38] Shafter to Alger, July 3, 1898, Alger to Shafter, July 3, 1898, and Shafter to Alger, July 4, 1898, all in Shafter Papers; Shafter, "The Capture of Santiago de Cuba," pp. 615–26; Wheeler, The Santiago Campaign, pp. 286–87; Trask, War with Spain, pp. 248–56. For the difficulties between Shafter and Sampson, see the long series of letters in William T. Sampson to Secy. of Navy, July 15, 1898, Aug. 1, 1898, and Aug. 4, 1898, all in Annual Reports of the Navy Department, 1898, 55th Cong., 3d sess., H. Doc. 3, pp. 607–14, 615–28, 630–32.

tiago de Cuba ammunition and food were low, and the Spaniards had little chance of getting more of either. Near-famine conditions prevailed, seriously affecting the health and morale of both the troops and inhabitants. Civilian refugees fled from the city to American lines, further complicating Shafter's difficulties of supply. Despite a relatively strong defensive position, Spanish leaders believed that the fall of the city was inevitable. They retained one hope. Since the city had been made a military target largely because Admiral Cervera had taken refuge in its harbor, the departure of the fleet for some other Cuban port probably would induce both the United States Navy and Army to follow in pursuit. Accordingly, while Shafter and Sampson attempted to work out proper strategy, Admiral Cervera on the morning of July 3 headed his fleet from the narrows of the bay for the open sea, hoping to reach the port of Cienfuegos almost 350 miles up the coast. A dramatic running battle ensued in which Americans, under Com. Winfield S. Schley, destroyed the entire Spanish fleet. The decisive naval victory ended whatever hope the Spanish still had for holding out successfully in Santiago de Cuba.[39]

Now Shafter, anxious to avoid more loss of life, opened negotiations with the enemy. On July 4, he sent a message to Gen. José Toral, commander of the Spanish troops in Santiago de Cuba, stating that the Spanish fleet had been destroyed and that Cervera was a captive aboard the armored American yacht *Gloucester,* and calling upon him to surrender. Acting upon orders from Gov.-Gen. Ramón Blanco y Arenas at Havana, Toral refused. Shafter thereupon strengthened his position along the San Juan Heights by deepening the trenches and positioning cannon and Gatling guns to sweep the enemy lines. Because road conditions between Siboney and Santiago de Cuba remained muddy and treacherous, he could bring forward only eight of the light mortars to supplement sixteen field guns already in place. While fortifying this line, he gradually extended his positions to entrap the Spaniards completely.[40]

Shafter and Sampson, meanwhile, exchanged several messages on the possibility of a joint army-navy assault, but little was accomplished.

---

[39]Trask, *War with Spain,* pp. 257, 269; French E. Chadwick, *The Relations of the United States and Spain: The Spanish-American War,* 2:114–15; Cosmas, *An Army for Empire,* pp. 225–26. Also see Williams, *History of American Wars,* p. 339. Trask gives a good, short analysis of the naval battle (pp. 261–69).

[40]Shafter to Toral, July 4, 1898, Toral to Shafter, July 4, 1898, and July 8, 1898, and Alger to Shafter, July 9, 1898, all in Shafter Papers; Chadwick, *Relations of the United States and Spain,* 2:193–94; Shafter "The Capture of Santiago de Cuba," pp. 615–16; Miley, *In Cuba with Shafter,* pp. 129–64; Trask, *War with Spain,* pp. 286–88.

Shafter again requested that Sampson run the harbor entrance, and Sampson continued to insist that such action would risk the loss of his vessels by submarine mines. He wanted Shafter to attack the harbor's fortifications. Because of Cervera's departure, however, the risk to naval vessels was reduced, possibly enough to justify an attack. Sampson, with the Navy Department's full support, refused the requests but offered to bombard Santiago de Cuba to induce surrender. As the two commanders exchanged their firm but polite messages, Shafter continued to press for a negotiated peace. Given the troubles of his army, Shafter's decision to besiege Santiago de Cuba and to parley with Toral made sense from a strictly military point of view. Sampson asked that he be included in the talks, but Shafter, unwilling to share full credit for the surrender, put Sampson off. Shafter's churlish attitude toward the navy did not win him many friends.[41]

General Toral, when he rejected Shafter's original request to surrender, had indicated an interest in further parleys. Bargaining continued, but for four days little happened. Then on July 8 Toral asked for terms that would allow his men to keep their arms, and Shafter the next day recommended that Washington accept. Alger replied that surrender must be unconditional, but in return the United States would agree to provide free transportation of Toral's troops to Spain. When Toral rejected the offer, light fighting occurred on July 10 and 11, including Sampson's ineffective bombardment of the city. On the twelfth, Gen. Nelson Miles arrived to support Shafter, and in a face-to-face meeting at noon on July 13 the two American officers gave Toral until 12:00 noon the following day to accept their terms. The next morning Toral surrendered. Soon thereafter Miles departed for Puerto Rico, leaving final arrangements in Shafter's charge. To draw up an appropriate statement, capitulation talks occurred during the next few days among Toral's three representatives—two Spanish officers and William Mason, a British consular official—and Shafter's representatives—Joseph Wheeler, Henry Lawton, and Lt. John D. Miley, Shafter's aide-de-camp. Newspapermen, naval personnel, and many of Shafter's officers, fearing that Toral was using the conferences as a delay tactic, urged an immediate attack. Shafter, with the concurrence of almost no one, believed that Toral was acting in good faith and refused to be stampeded.[42]

[41]See the long series of letters in Samson to Secy. of Navy, July 15, Aug. 1, and Aug. 4, 1898, in *Annual Reports of the Navy Department*, 1898, 55th Cong., 3d sess., H. Doc. 3, pp. 607–14, 615–28, 630–32.

[42]Virginia Weisel Johnson, *The Unregimented General: A Biography of Nelson A. Miles*, pp. 327–33; Newton F. Tolman, *The Search for General Miles*, pp. 205–208; Miley, *In Cuba with Shafter*, pp. 129–82; Shafter, "The Capture of Santiago de Cuba,"

Generals Joseph Wheeler, William Shafter, and Nelson Miles at Santiago de Cuba. *Photograph by Dinwiddie, courtesy Library of Congress*

Shafter's good judgment was rewarded. Early in the morning of July 16, 1898, Toral wrote to Shafter that the Madrid government had accepted the surrender terms. During a supper-hour conference that evening, the opposing generals set 9:30 A.M. on July 17 for the formal surrender ceremony.[43]

The surrender came off on schedule. To witness the ceremony, Shafter drew up all the troops in a line along the tops of the trenches.

---

pp. 625–29; Trask, *War with Spain*, pp. 289, 294, 298–306; Shafter to Corbin, July 10, 1898, and July 11, 1898, *Correspondence*, 1:123, 125; Shafter to Alger, July 12, 1898, *Correspondence* 1:132; Corbin to Shafter, July 8, 1898, *Correspondence*, 1:120; Chadwick, *Relations of the United States and Spain*, 2:223, 225; Leech, *In the Days of McKinley*, pp. 264–66; Post, *The Little War of Private Post*, p. 290.

[43]Trask, *War with Spain*, pp. 309, 311–19; Miley, *In Cuba with Shafter*, pp. 129–82.

Escorted by his senior officers and one hundred horsemen, he rode out between the lines to the huge ceiba tree that had sheltered the commissioners during their meeting, where he met General Toral, accompanied by his staff and one hundred smartly dressed infantrymen. The two sides exchanged salutes, and Toral formally surrendered the eastern district of Cuba, including Santiago de Cuba. As a first gesture, Shafter presented Toral with the sword and spurs of the Spanish hero Joaquín Vera de Rey, who had died in the defense of El Caney. Then the two leaders and their entourage traveled to the Governor's Palace in the city, where two hours earlier Toral had lowered the Spanish flag. At twelve o'clock the Americans fired twenty-one guns while bands played the national anthems of Spain and of the United States. Two companies of United States infantry presented arms; then Shafter's two aides, Capt. William H. McKittrick, his son-in-law, and Lt. Miley, and General Wheeler's aide, his son, Lt. Joseph Wheeler, Jr., raised the American flag on the roof of the palace.[44]

During the flag-raising Sylvester Scovil, an aggressive American reporter, was also on the roof to photograph the scene. Because he thought Scovil spoiled the tableau, Shafter shouted to his aide-de-camp, "Miley, tell that man to get off there." When Scovil refused to leave, the volatile Shafter, exploding in instant anger, roared toward the roof top, "Throw him off!"

As the soldiers hesitated to obey, Scovil rushed down and indignantly charged at Shafter, intending to strike him. Infantrymen grabbed Scovil and moved him through the crowd to a niche in a wall where a statue had stood. They hoisted him to the statue's place, kept him there until the flag-raising was over, and then escorted him to the guardhouse, where he remained for a short time before being deported to the United States.[45]

At the time of the surrender, the Spaniards had no idea of the forlorn condition of the American army. Shafter suffered from ill health, one foot so swollen from gout that he rode with it in a gunny sack. The soldiers, miserable in their heavy woolen uniforms designed for fighting Indians on the Northern Plains, could defeat Spaniards despite inadequate ammunition, but they could not keep well while lying unsheltered in muddy trenches under a tropical sun and in drenching rains. And no one yet knew a defense against yellow fever, that deadly

[44] Shafter, "The Capture of Santiago de Cuba," pp. 620–30.
[45] Stewart H. Holbrook, *Lost Men of American History*, p. 293. Also see Leech, *In the Days of McKinley*, pp. 269–70; and Brown, *The Correspondents' War*, pp. 402–404.

plague which a century earlier on a nearby island had destroyed Napoleon Bonaparte's army and with it his dream of an empire in North America. Fortunately, Shafter withdrew to Siboney most of the seriously ill.[46]

During the next two weeks more and more soldiers became ill from malaria or yellow fever, and by the end of the month four thousand troopers were sick. Initially, there had been little alarm. Shafter had been confident that his army, by moving its camps to high, clean ground, could shake off the fever. But moving such large numbers of troops with dispatch was logistically impossible. Transportation facilities broke down. The disease worsened. On August 1, terribly worried about the situation, Shafter asked the War Department for permission to send Wheeler's dismounted cavalry division home. The next day he reported that an epidemic of yellow fever seemed imminent and that his Fifth Corps should be started northward as quickly as possible. On the third he informed a council of his general staff and chief surgeons that, to save hundreds from yellow fever and possibly death, he planned to recommend to Washington that all troops he could spare be returned home. His subordinates concurred and at his request drafted a tough letter in which they reiterated the main points of Shafter's ideas. Shafter on August 4 forwarded the document as supporting evidence for his own dispatch.[47]

The document read:

> To Major-General William R. Shafter, Commanding United States Forces in Cuba.
> We, the undersigned General Officers, commanding various Brigades, Divisions, etc., of the United States Army of Occupation in Cuba, are of the unanimous opinion that this army must at once be taken out of the Island of Cuba, and sent to some point on the northern sea-coast of the United States; that this can be done without danger to the people of the United States; that there is no epidemic of yellow fever in the army at present, only a few sporadic cases; that the army is disabled by malarial fever to such an extent that its efficiency is destroyed, and it is in a condition to be practically entirely destroyed by the epidemic of yellow fever sure to come in the near future.

[46] *Investigation,* 1:171–98, 275–79, and 2:374–79; Cosmas, *An Army for Empire,* pp. 254–56.

[47] Shafter to Alger, Aug., 1898, Russell A. Alger Papers, 1862–1907, William L. Clements Library, University of Michigan, Ann Arbor; Alger, *The Spanish-American War,* pp. 219–25; Shafter, "The Capture of Santiago de Cuba," pp. 629–30; Roosevelt, *The Rough Riders,* pp. 133–35.

We know from reports from competent officers, and from personal observations, that the army is unable to move to the interior, and that there are no facilities for such a move if attempted, and will not be until too late; moreover, the best medical authorities in the island say that with our present equipment we could not live in the interior during the rainy season, without losses from malarial fever, almost as deadly as from yellow fever. This army must be moved at once, or it will perish as an army. It can be safely moved now. Persons responsible for preventing such a move will be responsible for the unnecessary loss of many thousands of lives. Our opinions are the result of careful personal observation, and are also based upon the unanimous opinion of our medical officers who are with the army, and understand the situation absolutely.[48]

The letter was signed by Wheeler, Lawton, Kent, Bates, Wood, Roosevelt, and five other ranking officers.

The "round robin," as the subordinate officers' letter became known, caused a furor. It appeared on the front pages of America's newspapers before Washington authorities were prepared to release reports on the condition of the Fifth Corps. President McKinley and Alger, who were delaying the removal of troops until a debarkation center was ready, considered the letter a criticism of their leadership. Some newspapermen, who perhaps learned of the letter from Shafter himself, interpreted the round robin as a criticism of the commander, and they blamed Shafter for the medical difficulties. The dramatic revelation of the miserable conditions in Cuba led to a public demand for an explanation. Moreover, the round robin was indiscreet. It should not have been sent while diplomatic negotiations with Spain over the general course of the war were being held. It may not have saved lives, as intended, but it did infuriate McKinley and embarrass the country, laying bare its inability to hold territory won in Cuba.[49]

In response to the letter's publication, McKinley and Alger, rather than shipping additional medical aid to Shafter and keeping his troops on the island a week longer until construction of a rest camp could be finished, ordered Shafter to start his men north at once. A few days later, on August 7, the first homebound troops left Santiago de Cuba. Others followed as rapidly as they could be embarked, and within three weeks the entire corps, replaced by other units, had left Cuba. On Au-

[48]Miley, *In Cuba with Shafter*, pp. 220–23.
[49]See Trask, *War with Spain*, p. 432; Cosmas, *An Army for Empire*, pp. 258–59; Hermann Hagedorn, *Leonard Wood: A Biography*, 1:201. Also see *New York Times*, Aug. 5, 1898, and Aug. 6, 1898.

gust 25 Shafter and his staff, among the last to go, boarded a transport and sailed for the United States.[50]

The Santiago campaign was over. For speed and results, the capture of Santiago de Cuba had been remarkable. Shafter and his Fifth Corps in less than four weeks had established American sovereignty over the eastern region of Cuba and had taken over twenty thousand prisoners, an army larger than his own. In an effort to escape his operations one of the enemy's most important battle fleets had suffered destruction, thereby rendering Spain helpless to resist further American attacks on her colonies and adding leverage to the Spanish-American negotiations to end the war.

There is a tradition that Shafter blundered his way to victory in the Spanish-American War.[51] He had his troubles, the most serious being his inexperience in organizing and maneuvering large formations. He failed to bring order at Tampa, neglected to draw clear lines of responsibility for staff officers and troop commanders, and too often overlooked important details. Indeed, his leadership may not have been decisive to the success of the expedition. Nonetheless, despite his shortcomings he moved an army of some 16,000 men a distance of 1,200 miles by water, landed on an enemy shore in open boats, in ten days drove the enemy back to his last line of entrenchments in front of Santiago de Cuba, and in fifteen days more compelled surrender of the city, the district, and an army of 24,000 men. The entire campaign, moreover, was carried on in the most unhealthful season of the year. In this connection in 1898 Pres. William McKinley remarked at a peace celebration in Omaha, Nebraska, that General Shafter "embarked his command and set sail, well knowing that there were deficiencies in his equipment. But instead of waiting for what he wanted, he took what he could get, and brought back what he went for."[52]

Shafter's troops gained a quick and decisive victory, as much by their own good luck and Spanish misfortune and ineptitude, however, as by Shafter's leadership. But Shafter was not as completely hapless as

---

[50]Cosmas, An Army for Empire, pp. 251–64; Roosevelt, The Rough Riders, pp. 134–35; Alger, The Spanish-American War, pp. 265–75.

[51]E. V. Westrate, Those Fatal Generals, p. 264; Wheeler, The Santiago Campaign, pp. 196–97; Chadwick, Relations of the United States and Spain, 2:6; Cosmas, An Army for Empire, pp. 193–94; Post, The Little War of Private Post, pp. 213–14.

[52]McKinley quote from Rhodes, "William Rufus Shafter," p. 381; New York Times, Nov. 14, 1906; Brooklyn (New York) Daily Eagle, Nov. 18, 1898, ACP Fil e, AGO, RG94, NA; San Francisco Call, Nov. 13, 1906; San Francisco Chronicle, Nov. 13, 1906; Cosmas, An Army for Empire, p. 194; Post, The Little War of Private Post, pp. 213–14, 231, 290; Wheeler, The Santiago Campaign, pp. 196–97.

many of his contemporaries and some scholars have suggested. The impression in the summer of 1898 was that Shafter was "criminally incompetent."[53] The opinion made its way into subsequent histories of the war, and, although Shafter now receives more balanced criticism, it largely continues to the present. While a younger, more energetic, less belligerent officer, such as James H. Wilson or Wesley Merritt, for example, might have done better, tropical diseases, rain-filled trenches, uncooperative United States naval commanders, superior numbers of Spanish troops, and second-guessing officials in Washington could have made the Cuban command as difficult for another general as it was for Shafter.

Shafter had little control of the situation at Tampa, and in fact for part of the time that he was in Florida he was not even in charge. The orders he received showed little consistency. Originally he was to prepare for a small reconnaissance of Cuba. At the last minute he received orders for a large invasion, not at nearby Havana, the first choice for a major land campaign, but at Santiago de Cuba, some 1,200 miles from the point of embarkation. His ships, his supplies, and his equipment were neither collected nor organized for the distant operation he was ordered to carry out.

Debarkation at Daiquiri and Siboney was hampered by the lack of lighters and launches, landing craft that, because he was originally to lead a small force to Cuba, were unavailable in sufficient numbers when he left Tampa. Shafter and his army paid dearly for the shortage, a deficiency over which he had little control.

Once the troops had landed, a quick, forceful, and concerted strike at Santiago de Cuba might, as some critics have suggested, have enabled American soldiers to overrun the Spanish forces and enter the city in triumph.[54] Such an attack was out of the question, however. The roads were mere trails through heavy jungle. Men and supplies could not be moved forward rapidly. The artillery and heavy guns could not be adequately called into use. In addition to the logistical problems, there was danger in attacking without making a careful study of the terrain and of the Spanish positions. Shafter's decisions to delay and to solidify his beachhead were completely justified, although the enemy admittedly used the time to reinforce its position in front of Santiago de Cuba. Later Shafter admitted that "the character of the

---

[53]Theodore Roosevelt to Henry Cabot Lodge, July 5, 1898, in Etting E. Morrison, ed., *The Letters of Theodore Roosevelt*, 2:849.
[54]Steele, *American Campaigns*, 1:594–98.

[Spanish] works is such that to take them by assault would be a sacrifice of life."[55]

Clearly Shafter should have cooperated more closely with Sampson. But in Washington the cabinet meetings, too often characterized by bitter exchanges between secretaries James Long and Russell Alger, revealed the unlikelihood of conducting joint operations. Nor was the much-acclaimed Sampson without fault. At times he seems to have hoped that the army would disintegrate in the hot, muddy trenches before Santiago de Cuba. His attitude regarding the peace negotiations, where he demanded a substantive role, also suggests his unwillingness to support an equal responsibility for the army. Sampson and Shafter, two headstrong and egotistical commanders, both drew criticism for their actions and must share the blame for poor interservice cooperation.

Shafter's strategy at San Juan Hill and El Caney is questionable. He did not need to divide his force. But his reconnaissance team reported and Gen. Henry Lawton strongly agreed that El Caney would fall quickly. When the tiny village did not, Shafter's plans crumbled. The debilitated general, unable to offer new strategy, witnessed his subordinate officers and his hard-charging troops save the day. Shafter must be faulted for his lack of direction, but he issued orders based upon the best, although as it turned out incorrect, information and advice available. As time passed heavy rains, impassable roads, supply difficulties, and spreading yellow fever hampered efforts to strike firmly at Santiago de Cuba.

Shafter's initial reaction to the victories at San Juan Hill and El Caney was uncharacteristic. The American general went into a deep fit of discouragement, asking to retreat and for reinforcements. Alarmed by increasing tropical illnesses among his men, for the first time in his long military career he did not know what to do, and he procrastinated.

Admiral Cervera's departure from Santiago harbor, however, quickly brightened Shafter's outlook. With the Spanish fleet gone, Shafter determined to lay siege to Santiago de Cuba. It was a wise decision, for his troops were badly fed, transportation was slow, supplies were scarce, yellow fever had struck, and the hospital corps proved utterly inadequate. Only two weeks later, during which time there was, at Shafter's insistence, very little fighting, the Spanish command formally surrendered.

The surrender of Santiago de Cuba ended the only appreciable land

---

[55]Quoted in Trask, *War with Spain*, p. 307.

campaign of the Spanish-American War. "The whole war," writes one historian, "was ended so quickly it was difficult to realize it had even begun."[56] Between May 1 and mid-July two Spanish fleets had been completely destroyed and a sizable Spanish army on the eastern end of Cuba had been captured. However easy it is to discredit Shafter, the land victory in no small measure caused Spain to concede not only Santiago de Cuba, but also the entire eastern district of the island.

Shafter was neither lionized nor made a hero. Perhaps he did not deserve to be. But despite all his faults, he had won a significant and rapid victory with minimal loss of life. Amid the war's scandals, the deadly tropical diseases, the wretched conditions in the trenches before Santiago de Cuba, and the newspaper correspondents' endless complaints, Shafter's detractors forget how quickly the Cuban campaign, and shortly afterward the war, ended.

As he turned to postwar concerns, Shafter looked to an easier command in a climate more congenial to his hefty bulk and debilitating illnesses. No doubt he yearned for northern California and his old cronies among the conservative and friendly business community in San Francisco. But first there was the matter of disbanding the Fifth Army Corps.

[56] E. V. Westrate, *Those Fatal Generals*, p. 264. Also see *New York Times*, Oct. 4, 1898; Casper Whitney, "The Santiago Campaign," *Harper's Magazine* 97 (Oct., 1898): 795–818; and Frederick Remington, "With the Fifth Corps," *Harper's Magazine* 97 (Nov., 1898): 962–75.

CHAPTER TWELVE

The Final Years

ROM THE END of the war in Cuba until his retirement three years later, William R. Shafter led a quiet army life. He toured the country to attend peace celebrations and commanded the geographic Department of the East briefly before reassignment took him to the Pacific coast and the Department of California. He wrote a little for national publications and commented about foreign wars, but he spent as much time as he could on leave to hunt or to relax on his small ranch, or farm, in southern California. Military duties associated with his commands he delegated, when he could, to others. He had not become lazily contented; to the contrary, even as he approached retirement he longed for opportunity again to lead American troops in the field. This time he was disappointed.

At the end of August, 1898, as he sailed north from Cuba, Shafter headed toward Long Island, New York, site of the army's rest camp. When reports of yellow fever affecting American troops had reached the United States, fear had spread through coastal communities that returning soldiers might infect their inhabitants. Few citizens wanted the diseased soldiers in their communities. Selection of the debarkation area as a result had occasioned controversy for the War Department, and Shafter as commander of the Fifth Army Corps had received some of it. He ignored the criticism as best he could and turned his attention to his returning army.

The army had chosen as a rehabilitation center for returning soldiers Camp Wikoff near Montauk Point on Long Island. It was not ready when President McKinley and Secretary of War Alger ordered the troops from Cuba. Thus, when the first group of transports arrived at Montauk on August 14, there were problems. Many of the troopers, who were landed a few miles from Camp Wikoff, could barely drag themselves over the intervening distance. The single railroad track serving Montauk Point at the eastern end of Long Island proved unable to handle adequate supplies on schedule. Until additional wells could be dug, the army hauled water by tank cars from the western end of the island. The medical corps was sadly understaffed and inadequately supplied. Under the direction of Maj. Gen. Joseph Wheeler, however, a creditable camp soon took shape. Situated on rolling dunes covered with scrub oaks and pines, the center aided men in recovering from tropical fevers, wounds, and other maladies suffered in Cuba.[1]

At noon on September 1, Shafter assumed command of Camp Wikoff. By then the conditions had improved. The medical corps had enlarged its hospital facilities and had brought in scores of contract surgeons and about three hundred nurses. Running water was available to each company, and private relief agencies were furnishing enough rich food that many soldiers did not bother to draw their regular army rations. During the next few days Shafter labored to muster the volunteers out of service or furlough those able to leave. Soldiers in the regular army who were well enough transferred to interior army posts. Before he had completed his demobilization work, however, Shafter temporarily relinquished command of the Fifth Corps and Camp Wikoff to Brig. Gen. John C. Bates and left Montauk Point on September 10 to command the Department of the East.[2]

The following day, September 11, 1898, Shafter assumed his new command with headquarters on Governor's Island in New York Harbor. The island, with an area of 173 acres, was rich in history and conservative in atmosphere, but Shafter, a much-sought speaker for celebrations honoring the end of the war with Spain, spent very little time in New York. On the twenty-first, he went to Kalamazoo, Michigan, to attend a three-day reunion of the Nineteenth Michigan Volunteer Regiment, his Civil War outfit, and on the twenty-fourth he traveled to Topeka, Kansas, to participate in a reunion of the Grand Army of the Republic. During the next month he traveled to Los Angeles to

[1]U.S. Dept. of War, Returns from United States Military Posts, 1800–1916, Camp Wikoff, Aug.–Oct., 1898, Roll 1433, Microcopy No. 617, National Archives (hereafter Post Returns, MC617, NA); Joseph Wheeler, *The Santiago Campaign*, pp. 204–21; U.S. Senate, *Report of the Commission Appointed by the President to Investigate the Conduct of the War Department in the War with Spain* (hereafter *Investigation*), 3:400–21, and 4:1473–87; Theodore Roosevelt, *The Rough Riders*, p. 140.

[2]Post Returns, Camp Wikoff, Aug.–Oct., 1898, Roll 1433, MC617, NA; Graham A. Cosmas, *An Army for Empire: The United States Army in the Spanish-American War*, pp. 260–64; Jacquelin Overton, *Long Island's Story*, pp. 297–301; John D. Miley, *In Cuba with Shafter*, p. 228; Frank Freidel, *The Splendid Little War*, pp. 299–300; *Investigation*, 3:608–67.

address its Chamber of Commerce and again to Michigan for a week. On October 15, he appeared with President McKinley in Omaha for the Nebraska Peace Jubilee. Four days later he stopped in Chicago for another peace jubilee, and near the end of the month he went for a day to Philadelphia to attend its peace celebration.[3]

Meanwhile, although retaining command of the Department of the East, on September 16 Shafter had again assumed personal charge of the Fifth Corps and Camp Wikoff. He transferred the soldiers as rapidly as possible. By September 23 only seven regiments remained, and a week later, on October 3, he disbanded the Fifth Army Corps. By the end of the month Camp Wikoff was empty. Although the subject of much criticism, some of it deserved, Camp Wikoff provided a good temporary rest spot for approximately 21,000 soldiers.[4]

Shafter was unhappy in the East. In December, therefore, after having attended another peace jubilee with President McKinley in Atlanta, he asked for and received a transfer to California. In mid-January, 1899, he assumed command of the Department of California and on the nineteenth also took charge of the Department of Columbia. Except for maintaining a very large camp of recruits who were being trained for fighting in the Philippines, his duties in his new assignment were routine. No summer training camps were held, no emergency action was necessary, and the only significant movement of troops found a few detachments of infantry on duty in Sequoia and Yosemite National parks each summer to prevent environmental damage by the visitors.[5]

Although there were many soldiers in California training for service in the Philippines, where the United States was attempting to

[3]Shafter to Corbin, Sept. 17, Oct. 5, and Oct. 23, 1898, and Corbin to Shafter, Oct. 14, 1898, all in United States, William R. Shafter, Letters Received, Appointments, Commission, and Personal Branch, Adjutant General's Office, Record Group 94, National Archives (hereafter ACP File, AGO, RG94, NA).

[4]Post Returns, Camp Wikoff, Aug.–Oct., 1898, Roll 1433, MC617, NA; Freidel, *The Splendid Little War*, pp. 299–300; *Brooklyn* (New York) *Daily Eagle*, Nov. 12, 1898, clipping in ACP File, AGO, RG94, NA; *New York Daily Tribune*, Nov. 22, 1898.

[5]Shafter to Corbin, and Corbin to Shafter, Dec. 28, 1898, and Cadet Taylor, Surveyor of Customs, Omaha, Neb., to Corbin, Sept. 11, 1899, all in ACP File, AGO, RG94, NA; Margaret Leech, *In the Days of McKinley*, pp. 348–49; "Report of Maj. Gen. William R. Shafter, Commanding the Department of Columbia," Aug. 15, 1899, and "Report of Maj. Gen. William R. Shafter, Commanding the Department of California," Aug. 20, 1899, *Annual Report of Sec. of War*, 1899, 56th Cong., 1st sess., H. Exec. Doc. 2, 1:74–79; "Report of Maj. Gen. William R. Shafter, Commanding the Department of Columbia," Aug. 31, 1900, and "Report of Maj. Gen. William R. Shafter, U.S. Volunteers, Commanding the Department of Columbia," Sept. 14, 1900, *Annual Report of Sec. of War*, 1900, 56th Cong., 2d sess., H. Exec. Doc. 2, 1 (pt. 3): 239–42.

suppress a revolution, Shafter largely separated himself from the activity. He visited a few of the camps, but his reports to the secretary of war make it clear that he delegated responsibility for their health, supplies, equipment, and training to the medical corps, the quartermaster department, and other agencies of his command.[6]

Shafter took greater responsibility in providing for soldiers returning from duty in the Philippines. He set up a rest camp on the grounds of the Presidio military reservation in San Francisco. He provided Sibley tents with floors and stoves, baths with hot and cold showers, and a large mess hall supplied with dining room tables and an efficient kitchen with ample range and cooking utensils. A convalescent ward was well provisioned and effectively run. Cadet Taylor, who visited the camp in the summer of 1899, wrote, "I never saw a more complete camp from any point of view. . . . I wish to compliment Major Gen. William R. Shafter for the excellent arrangements . . . nothing was left undone." Shafter regularly inspected the camp, which was next to his department headquarters, visiting with the soldiers and assuring himself that food, provisions, and housing were as good as they could be. Despite his attention to the camp for Philippine veterans, for the next two years, until his retirement on July 1, 1901, at age 66, Shafter enjoyed a quiet and uneventful command.[7]

Upon retirement, Shafter, now a wealthy and well-known private citizen, settled on his ranch near Bakersfield. Here, on sixty acres he had a one-story house and an enclosed barn with an aisleway and box stalls. He planted most of his ranch to prunes, apricots, grapes, alfalfa, and corn. Because her home was only a mile away, he visited often with his daughter and her husband, William McKittrick. In fact, a four-inch pipe that carried water from a well on Shafter's place to the headquarters of his son-in-law's ranch necessitated frequent visits.

After leaving the army, Shafter, who already weighed some three hundred pounds, "put on weight like a Berkshire in a corn field." As a result, he did not hunt much after settling at Bakersfield, because it was difficult for him to get around. He placed extra springs in his already extra-sized buckboard, and he would get some of the neigh-

[6]See "Report of Maj. Gen. William R. Shafter, Commanding the Department of California," Sept. 14, 1900, in *Annual Report of Sec. of War*, 1900, 56th Cong., 2d sess., H. Exec. Doc. 2, 1 (pt. 3): 239–41. Also see "Report of Maj. Gen. Samuel B. M. Young, Commanding Depts. of California and Columbia," Aug. 16, 1901, *Annual Report of Sec. of War*, 1901, 57th Cong., 1st sess., H. Exec. Doc. 2, 1 (pt. 4): 138–39.

[7]Cadet Taylor to Adj. Gen. Henry C. Corbin, Sept. 11, 1899, ACP File, AGO, RG94, NA; Francis B. Heitman, *Historical Register and Dictionary of the United States Army*, 1:876.

bors' children to go along to open gates. The young people at first were afraid of the big man with a booming voice, but his kindness and generous pay for services soon was rewarded by love and adoration for their famous hero.[8]

During retirement, Shafter continued to participate in various patriotic and political organizations. He remained an active member of the Loyal Legion of the United States, the Spanish War Veterans, Sons of the Revolution, and the Union League, and at one time served as commander of the Department of California and Nevada in the Grand Army of the Republic. He continued to correspond regularly with his old army pals, especially Henry C. Corbin, the United States adjutant general, Henry Plumber, a personal aide at the Presidio who had been with Shafter in Cuba, and Alger, who had returned to Michigan.[9]

In 1905, Shafter enjoyed a lengthy visit from his brother, James. Uncle Jim, as everyone called him, was fat and boisterous like brother William, verbose, lazy, and kind. In early February, 1906, the brothers traveled to El Paso, Texas, from where they went on a month-long hunt to Mexico. There is no record of the results, but while in El Paso Shafter stirred up a brief tempest along the border when he told reporters that he would like to lead an expedition to China to protect American lives. After the hunt Uncle Jim moved into a small one-room house on the McKittrick ranch where he lived until after World War I when he went to Oakland to spend his remaining years with his daughter.[10]

On Tuesday, November 6, 1906, while returning from voting, Shafter contracted a severe chill. Dr. T. W. Mitchell, the family physician, was summoned, but Shafter failed to improve, and Mitchell called in Dr. A. Schafer for consultation. The doctors discovered an intestinal obstruction and determined that the chill had been an acute attack of pneumonia. When no improvement occurred during the next two days, the physicians called in Dr. I. W. Thorne of San Francisco, and early the following Sunday morning, after Shafter rallied slightly, Dr. M. H. Herzstein of San Francisco arrived for consultation. Herzstein concluded that surgery was the only possible remedy for the intestinal obstruction but that, due to the pneumonia, an operation would be fatal. Nothing was done, and the following day, Monday, November 12, at 12:45 P.M., Shafter died at the McKittrick Ranch, were he had spent

[8]Calhoun Collins, *The McKittrick Ranch*, pp. 33–35.

[9]Edward H. Plumber to Mrs. Mary McKittrick, Jan. 18, 1918, William R. Shafter Collection, University Archives and Regional History Collections, Western Michigan University, Kalamazoo.

[10]Collins, *The McKittrick Ranch*, pp. 29–32; O. C. Knowles, El Paso, to War Dept., Feb. 25, 1906, enclosing an undated newspaper clipping, ACP File, AGO, RG94, NA.

his last six years. His body was taken to the Presidio at San Francisco and two days later buried next to his wife's grave in the post ceme-tery.[11] In the years afterward, Mary Shafter McKittrick often visited her father's grave. One would like to know whether she remembered him as a gentle, loving father or as a coarse, tough-minded field com-mander.

Certainly William R. Shafter possessed a complicated personality. He exhibited several characteristics typical of late-nineteenth-century military commanders: he enjoyed some college training, served with distinction in the Civil War, and directed troops during the Indian wars in the West. Interested in national politics, he accepted Republican political ideals without reserve. For several years he wore a beard but eventually replaced it with a large walrus mustache. Moreover, his re-spectable middle-class family, from the northern and eastern sections of the United States, was of British stock.

Atypically, Shafter throughout his career remained one of the army's most cruelly maligned field commanders. Uninformed citizens, arro-gant newspaper correspondents, whining men of his command, and his fellow officers, all of whom perhaps believed that at one time he had treated them in a cavalier manner, assassinated his character and reputation. Although his disdain for what Americans have come to call "interpersonal relations" helps to explain some of his trouble, the truth is that many who believed they knew him well never penetrated past the gruff, and even grim, front he presented to soldiers and civil-ians alike. He could be courteous and affable.

Intellectually, Shafter was at once naive and sophisticated. As a youth he read widely in literature. As an adult he preferred to obtain information from conversation — lots of it — rather than from study, and he relied more upon intuition than upon hard thinking in solving difficult problems, what he himself characterized as "playing it by ear." Although not a particularly original thinker, he demonstrated great capacity for learning and for thinking in broad terms, and he had a flexibility that freed him for experiment in command.[12]

---

[11]Dr. T. W. Mitchell, memo to [?], Nov. 19, 1906, ACP File, AGO, RG94, NA; *New York Times*, Nov. 13, 1906, and Nov. 14, 1906; *San Francisco Chronicle*, Nov. 13, 1906; *San Francisco Call*, Nov. 13, 1906; Barry C. Johnson, ed., *HO, For the Great West*, p. 194; Charles D. Rhodes, "William Rufus Shafter," *Michigan History Magazine* 16 (Fall, 1932): 381; *Brooklyn* (New York) *Daily Eagle*, Nov. 18, 1898, clipping in ACP File, AGO, RG94, NA; Cosmas, *An Army for Empire*, p. 194.

[12]Unsigned and undated letter to Mary Shafter McKittrick (Shafter's daughter), William R. Shafter Collection, Michigan Historical Collections, University of Michi-gan, Ann Arbor.

The techniques of command vary, of course, with the personality of the commander. While some men prefer to lead by suggestion or example or other methods, Shafter chose to drive his subordinates by bombast and by threats, and he believed that profanity was the most convincing medium of communication. Although his mannerisms achieved spectacular results, they did not win affection among his officers or men. Good-humored, even jolly, in his intimate personal relationships, he was likely to give short, blunt answers to his subalterns, he would never allow his orders to be challenged, and he always demanded the same dogged determination from his men that he himself gave to field maneuvers.[13]

An overview of his relationship with his men and officers and with civilians who questioned his authority reveals Shafter as a commander of forceful personality, unyielding determination, and aggressive leadership. An intractable martinet, he did not hesitate to use the influence of his position to achieve sharp discipline, and at critical moments he exerted extraordinary and ruthless power.

As a result, scouting with Shafter was no easy task. At one stretch during the 1875 Llano Estacado campaign, Shafter in ten days marched his men nearly three hundred miles. Because they were seldom in camp for more than one night, the men, in addition to marching thirty miles a day, had to pack their tents and other field equipment each morning and unpack it again each night. The subsequent wear and tear on both men and animals prompted Capt. Theodore Baldwin of the Tenth Cavalry to remark in a letter to his wife, "I do not think you would like to scout with Colonel Shafter."[14]

Baldwin's comment was understated. In the field Shafter demonstrated an unsurpassed ability to get the utmost out of his soldiers. During the torturous expedition many of Shafter's men had returned from the first crossing of the Plains without shirts or shoes, most were missing some article of clothing, and all were exhausted. Nonetheless, only two weeks later Shafter started back across the Plains again, and hardly had he completed the second crossing when a third was commenced.

Even more arduous was Shafter's 1876 expedition to the mouth of the Pecos River. Three times during the long five-month summer campaign, Shafter marched his troops across the torrid Coahuila deserts

---

[13]James Parker, *The Old Army: Memories, 1872–1918,* pp. 100–109.

[14]Theodore Baldwin to his wife, ca. August 18, 1875, in L. F. Sheffy, ed., "Letters and Reminiscences of General Theodore A. Baldwin: Scouting after Indians on the Plains of West Texas," *Panhandle-Plains Historical Review* II (1938): 19.

of Mexico. In each instance the troops rode in over one-hundred-degree heat, and on one occasion they went sixty-five miles through the parching desert without water.

Stern and demanding in the field, Shafter was equally exacting at the posts he commanded. He kept the acquisition of alcoholic beverages to a minimum, his posts were clean and well policed, he demanded sharp military discipline, and he always showed an intimate knowledge of what was going on about the post. One morning in the summer of 1878, Charles Crane, the son of a president of Baylor University and a young lieutenant only a few months out of West Point, reported to Shafter for orders as officer of the day. Shafter pointed to some soldiers standing and sitting near a pile of mesquite cord wood. "Don't disturb those men. They are gambling," he told Crane. "And don't allow any civilians to join the game or even to look on." Designed to avoid conflict among the men, the instructions were carried out with good results.[15]

As a field officer, Shafter spent many years commanding isolated frontier garrisons. Here, the food was usually inferior to that provided at other posts; often there were few of the staples. Facilities for recreation were few, and while off-post recreation of a sort was available in the sordid little towns that blossomed around the posts, usually trouble awaited troopers there. Consequently, boredom, loneliness, and mental depression among his troops were significant problems with which Shafter had to deal.[16]

Such conditions could have demoralized any regiment, yet morale in Shafter's commands in the West remained high. In Shafter's black regiments, desertion, the curse of the frontier army, dwindled steadily in the 1870's, and at times it was the lowest of any unit in the West. Instances of acute alcoholism, too, were far fewer in Shafter's Negro commands than in their white counterparts, prompting one military historian to conclude that in relation to the seriousness of alcoholism, "perhaps much depended on the morale of a company or regiment."[17]

Clearly, as a military commander, Shafter was tough and aggressive. Outspoken and contentious by nature, he found it difficult to be diplomatic. Although he could on occasion charm people, he really

[15]Charles J. Crane, *The Experiences of a Colonel of Infantry*, p. 85.

[16]William H. Leckie, *The Buffalo Soldiers: A Narrative of the Negro Cavalry in the West*, pp. 10, 14–15, 21–22, 259.

[17]Don Rickey, *Forty Miles a Day on Beans and Hay: The Enlisted Soldier Fighting the Indian Wars*, pp. 159–60.

preferred to shock them. He was self-confident, abrupt, and unyielding; he knew what he wanted, and he seldom changed his mind. During the years that he served on the western military frontier, Shafter gave the impression of being a large, forceful, indomitable man. Impartial, resourceful, and courageous, he possessed initiative, looked out for the welfare of his men and animals, and was utterly unafraid of responsibility. He proved to be a bold and energetic leader of unquestioned ability. His troops at all times were well disciplined and thoroughly trained. His success, like that of Andrew Jackson's, was due more to his toughness, resolution, and relentless energy than to military genius.

During the years he served in the segregated black infantry regiments, Shafter, using discipline based on fear and respect, transformed his ill-educated and often illiterate charges, of whose ability he always thought highly, into a ready, proficient, and crack army command. He became one of the first officers to advocate integration in the army, albeit for personal reasons. He vociferously defended his black soldiers when he believed they were not being treated properly, protecting them not because they were black, but because they were his. Judged by the standards of his own age, he was more advanced than most of his contemporaries.

During the Spanish-American War, Shafter admittedly had many difficulties. Nonetheless, he showed good judgment in giving his general staff wide freedom of action, and he kept the loss of American lives at a minimum. Conventional military wisdom argues that an army attack when its forces are larger in number than the enemy. Shafter, under pressure from superiors at home and the press in the field, struck with a smaller force, but he gained his important objective, displaying patience during surrender negotiations and trust in the enemy's good faith when others pushed to renew a battle that could have proved difficult, wasteful, and unproductive.

Traditional interpretations suggest that Shafter muddled through the final negotiations. Perhaps he did. But judged by results, Shafter's capture of Santiago de Cuba in just over three weeks was obtained with a quickness seldom matched in American warfare and even today little appreciated.

Shafter was a complicated individual, a combination of drifting-fog softness and rock-wall hardness. Although he was profane, coarse, and severe, beneath his rough exterior and thundering voice he was, in many ways, kind, sensitive, and sentimental. Most of his officers learned to like him, and although he rarely enjoyed their affection, his troops usually remembered him as a brave and relentless soldier. Through four decades William R. Shafter, or Pecos Bill as he was so often called in the West, served the United States Army as a successful field officer on the frontier and in the Spanish-American War.

Bibliography

MANUSCRIPT MATERIALS

Alger, Russell A. Papers, 1862–1907. William L. Clements Library, University of Michigan, Ann Arbor.

Brockway, Daniel D. Papers. Michigan Historical Collections, University of Michigan, Ann Arbor.

Corbin, Henry Clark. Papers. Library of Congress, Washington, D.C.

Crimmins, Martin Labor. Papers. Archives, University of Texas, Austin.

Daniels, Oliver. Papers. Transcript of interview with Wayne C. Mann, Director, University Archives and Regional History Collections, Western Michigan University, Kalamazoo, April, 1964.

Grierson, Benjamin. Letters to his Wife, June–July, 1875. Illinois State Historical Library, Springfield, Illinois. Microfilm copies, Southwest Collection, Texas Tech University, Lubbock.

———. Papers. Southwest Collection, Texas Tech University, Lubbock.

Griffin, Eli. Collection. Michigan Historical Collections, University of Michigan, Ann Arbor.

Habel, Mrs. Katherine. Collection. University Archives and Regional History Collections, Western Michigan University, Kalamazoo.

Hager Family. Collection. Michigan Historical Collections, University of Michigan, Ann Arbor.

Harvey, Dorothy and Joseph. Collection. University Archives and Regional History Collections, Western Michigan University, Kalamazoo.

Hodgman, Samuel Chase. Letters. University Archives and Regional History Collections, Western Michigan University, Kalamazoo.

Indenture between Kern County Land Company and William R. Shafter, March 6, 1899. Filed at Kern County Recorder's Office, Bakersfield, California.

Montgomery, B. F. Papers. Rutherford B. Hayes Memorial Library, Fremont, Ohio.

Patton, John. Papers, 1888–1905. Michigan Historical Collections, University of Michigan, Ann Arbor.

Presidio Mining Co. v. Alice Bullis, Court Transcript No. 5909 (now filed as M11633), filed in Texas Supreme Court at Austin, May, 1886.

Shafter, William R. Collection. Michigan Historical Collections, University of Michigan, Ann Arbor.

———. Collection. University Archives and Regional History Collections, Western Michigan University, Kalamazoo.

———. Papers. Stanford University Library, Stanford, California. Photocopy, 1861–1898, Southwest Collection, Texas Tech University, Lubbock.

United States. "Map of the Country Scouted by Colonels Mackenzie and Shafter, Capt. R. P. Wilson and Others in the Years 1874 and 1875." Drawn by Alex. L. Lucas. Adjutant General's Office (2832 AGO 1876). Record Group 94. National Archives, Washington, D.C.

———. William R. Shafter. Letters Received, Appointments, Commission, and Personal Branch, Adjutant General's Office. Record Group 94. National Archives, Washington, D.C.

U.S. Department of the Interior. Records of the Indian Bureau. Letters Received, Office of Indian Affairs. Record Group 75. National Archives, Washington, D.C.

U.S. Department of War. Affairs on the Rio Grande and Texas Frontier, 1875–81. Letters Received (1653 AGO 1878), Adjutant General's Office. Record Group 94, National Archives, Washington, D.C.

———. Papers Relation to the . . . Geronimo Uprising. Letters Received (4061 AGO 1883), Adjutant General's Office. Record Group 94, National Archives, Washington, D.C.

———. Papers Relating to the . . . Indian Outbreaks at San Carlos. Letters Received (1066 AGO 1883), Adjutant General's Office. Record Group 94, National Archives, Washington, D.C.

———. Post Medical Reports. Old Records Division of the Adjutant General's Office, National Archives, Washington, D.C., for:

Camp Peña Colorado, Texas, March, 1880–February, 1893, Book 95;
Fort Brown, Texas, July, 1868–September, 1906, Books 731-732-734;
Fort Clark, Texas, 1852–73, Vol. 907;
Fort Concho, Texas, December, 1867–June, 1891, Books 401-403-404-407;
Fort Davis, Texas, October, 1854–May, 1891, Books 7-9-12;
Fort Duncan, Texas, 1849–October, 1883, Books 86-87;
Fort Jefferson, Texas, January, 1869–May, 1871, Book 110;
Fort McKavett, Texas, 1852–June, 1883, Books 192-193-195;
Fort Ringgold Barracks, Texas, July, 1868–July, 1906, Books 725-726-727;
Fort San Antonio, Texas, 1866–71, Books 280-8;
Fort Stockton, Texas, 1869–82, Books 363-363.

———. Records Relating to the Army Career of Henry Ossian Flipper, 1873–83. Microcopy No. T 1027, Roll 1. National Archives, Washington, D.C.

————. Records of United States Army Commands. Letters Sent, Department of Texas. Record Group 93, National Archives, Washington, D.C.

————. Records of United States Army Comands. Letters Sent, Fort Davis. Record Group 98, National Archives, Washington, D.C.

————. Records of United States Army Mobile Commands. Letters Sent, First Infantry, 1891–96. Record Group 391, National Archives, Washington, D.C.

————. Records of United States Army Mobile Commands. Letters Sent, Twenty-Fourth Infantry, 1874–80. Record Group 391, National Archives, Washington, D.C.

————. Records of the Department of the Missouri. Letters Received, Adjutant General's Office. Record Group 393, National Archives, Washington, D.C.

————. Records of the Department of Texas. Letters Received, Adjutant General's Office. Record Group 393, National Archives, Washington, D.C.

————. Records of the Division of the Missouri. Special File, Victorio Papers, 1880. Record Group 98, National Archives, Washington, D.C.

————. Returns from Regular Army Infantry Regiments, June, 1821–December, 1916. Microcopy No. 665, National Archives, Washington, D.C., for:
First Infantry, June, 1879–March, 1897, Rolls 7, 8, 9;
Twenty-Fourth Infantry, August, 1869–June, 1879, Rolls 245, 246;
Forty-first Infantry, December, 1866–December, 1869, Roll 296.

————. Returns from United States Military Posts, 1800–1916. Microcopy No. 617, National Archives, Washington, D.C., for:
Camp Wikoff, New York, August, 1898–October, 1898, Roll 1433.
Fort Angel Island, California, July, 1886–October, 1896, Rolls 30, 31;
Fort Baton Rouge, Louisiana, December, 1866–June, 1867, Roll 86;
Fort Brown, Texas, August, 1872–June, 1875, Roll 152;
Fort Clark, Texas, March, 1868–April, 1879, Rolls 214, 215;
Fort Davis, Texas, May, 1871–May, 1882, Rolls 297, 298;
Fort Duncan, Texas, March, 1868–June, 1879, Rolls 336, 337;
Fort Grant, Arizona Territory, May, 1882–July, 1886, Roll 415;
Fort McKavett, Texas, March, 1869–February, 1881, Rolls 689, 690;
Fort Nashville, Tennessee, April, 1864–May, 1866, Roll 832;
Fort Randall, Dakota Territory, June, 1879–June, 1880, Rolls 989,990;
Fort Ringgold Barracks, Texas, July, 1867–March, 1868, Roll 1020;
Fort San Antonio, Texas, June, 1873–December, 1882, Roll 1084;
Vandale, Earl. Collection. Archives, University of Texas, Austin.
Webb, G. Creighton. Papers, 1898–1941. New York State Historical Association, New York.
Weissert, Charles A. Collection. Michigan Historical Collections, University of Michigan, Ann Arbor.

GOVERNMENT DOCUMENTS AND PUBLICATIONS

Crook, George. *Resume of Operations against Apache Indians, 1882 to 1886.* Washington, D.C.: 1886.

Heitman, Francis B. *Historical Register and Dictionary of the United States Army.* 2 vols. Washington, D.C.: GPO, 1903.

Infantry Equipment 1874. Ordnance Memoranda No. 19. Proceedings of the Board of Officers Convened under Special Orders No. 120, A.G.O., 1874. Washington, D.C.: 1875.

McClellan, George B. *Report of the Organization and Campaigns of the Army of the Potomac,* New York: Sheldon & Co., 1864.

Marcy, Randolph B. *Exploration of the Red River of Louisiana in 1852.* 32d Cong., 2d sess., 1854. S. Exec. Doc. 54.

Michigan, Adjutant General's Office. *Michigan in the War.* Rev. ed. Comp. Jno. Robertson, Adjutant General. Lansing: W. S. George Co., 1888.

———. *Record of Service of Michigan Volunteers in the Civil War, 1861–1865.* 46 vols. Kalamazoo: Ihling Bros. & Everard, 1905.

Mooney, James. "The Ghost Dance Religion and the Sioux Outbreak of 1890." *Fourteenth Annual Report of the Bureau of Ethnology, 1892–1893,* pt. 2. Washington, D.C.: PO, 1896.

Presidio Mining Co. v. Alice Bullis. 68 *Tex.* 581 (1887).

Rudd, Augustin G., ed. *Histories of Army Posts.* Washington, D.C.: Government Printing Office, 1924.

U.S. Attorney General. *Appendix to the Annual Report of the Attorney General, 1896.* 54th Cong., 2d sess., H. Exec. Doc. 9, pt. 2.

U.S. Congress, House. *Liquidating the Liability of the United States for Massacre of Sioux Indian Men, Women, and Children at Wounded Knee.* 76th Cong., 3d sess., 1939. H. Rept. 2317.

———. *Mexican Border Troubles.* 45th Cong., 1st sess., 1878. H. Exec. Doc. 13.

———. *Report and Accompanying Documents of the Committee on Foreign Affairs on the Relations of the United States with Mexico.* 45th Cong., 2d sess., 1878. H. Rept. 701.

———. *Sioux Indians, Wounded Knee Massacre.* Hearings before the House Sub-Committee on Indian Affairs, March 7, and May 12, 1938. 75th Cong., 3d sess., 1938, H. Rept. 2535.

———. *Special Committee of the House of Representatives to Investigate Texas Frontier Troubles.* 44th Cong., 1st sess., 1876. H. Rept. 343.

———. *Testimony Taken by Committee on Military Affairs in Relation to Texas Border Troubles.* 45th Cong., 2d sess., 1879. H. Misc. Doc. 64.

U.S. Congress. Senate. *The Disposal of a Portion of Fort Randall Military Reservation.* 52d Cong., 1st sess., 1891. S. Rept. 912.

———. *Report of the Commission Appointed by the President to Investigate the Conduct of the War Department in the War with Spain.* 8 vols. 56th Cong., 1st sess., 1901. S. Doc. 221.

————. *Report of the Joint Committee on the Conduct of the War.* 3 pts. 37th Cong., 1865. 3d sess., S. Rept. 142.

————. Strike Commission. *Report on the Chicago Strike, June–July 1894.* 53d Cong., 3d sess., 1894. S. Exec. Doc. 7.

U.S. Department of the Interior. *Annual Report of the Secretary of the Interior.* 52d Cong., 1st sess., 1891. H. Exec. Doc. 1, pt. 5.

U. S. Department of the Navy. *Annual Reports of the Navy Department, 1898.* 55th Cong., 3d sess., H. Doc. 3.

U.S. Department of War. *Annual Reports of the Secretary of War, 1866–1901.*

————. Adjutant General's Office. *Correspondence Relating to the War with Spain and Conditions Growing out of same . . . April 15, 1898 to July 30, 1902.* 2 vols. Washington, D.C.: GPO, 1902.

Utley, Robert M. "Special Report on Fort Davis, Texas," Mimeographed report for the National Survey of Historic Sites and Buildings. Santa Fe, N.Mex.: U.S. Department of the Interior, 1960.

Villegas, D. Cosio. *Cuestiones internacionales de México: Una bibliogrfía.* Mexico City: Secretaria de Relaciones Exteriores, 1966.

The War of the Rebellion: A Compilation of the Official Records of the Union and Confederate Armies. 130 vols. Washington, D.C.: GPO, 1891–98.

NEWSPAPERS

Army and Navy Journal, 1882–85, 1898.
Daily Capital (Pierre, S.Dak.), 1890–91.
Daily Ranchero (Brownsville, Tex.), 1868–69.
Daily State Gazette (Austin, Tex.), 1873–76.
Galveston Daily News, 1873–76.
Los Angeles Times, 1894.
New Press (Bakersfield, Calif.), 1967–68.
New York Times, 1890–91, 1898–1906.
New York Daily Tribune, 1867–68, 1898.
Press & Dakotan (Yankton, S.Dak.), 1890–91.
San Antonio Express-News, 1978–80.
San Antonio Light, 1984–85.
San Francisco Call, 1906.
San Francisco Chronicle, 1906.

THESES AND DISSERTATIONS

Boggs, Hershel J. "A History of Fort Concho." Master's thesis, University of Texas, Austin, 1940.

Gregg, John E. "The History of Presidio County, Texas." Master's thesis, University of Texas, Austin, 1933.

Hutcheson, Barry Wade. "The Trans-Pecos: A Historical Survey and Guide to Historic Sites." Master's thesis, Texas Tech University, Lubbock, 1969.

Jacobs, Kenneth R. "A History of the Ponca Indians to 1882." Ph.D. diss., Texas Tech University, Lubbock, 1977.

McClung, Donald R. "Henry O. Flipper: First Negro Officer in the United States Army, 1878–1882." Master's thesis, East Texas State University, Commerce, 1970.

Marcum, Richard T. "Fort Brown Texas: The History of a Border Post." Ph.D. diss., Texas Tech University, Lubbock, 1964.

Rockefeller, Alfred, Jr. "The Sioux Troubles of 1890–91." Ph.D. diss., Northwestern University, Evanston, Ill., 1949.

Sandlin, Betty J. "The Texas Reconstruction Constitutional Convention of 1868–1869." Ph.D. diss., Texas Tech University, Lubbock, 1971.

Smith, James Weldon. "Colonel Ranald Slidell Mackenzie and the Apache Problem, 1881–1883." Master's thesis, Texas Tech University, Lubbock, 1973.

Stone, Jerome. "A History of Fort Grant." Master's thesis, University of Arizona, Tucson, 1941.

Temple, Frank M. "Colonel B. H. Grierson's Texas Commands." Master's thesis, Texas Tech University, Lubbock, 1959.

Terrell, Peggy Joyce. "Colonel R. S. Mackenzie's Campaign against the Southern Plains Indians, 1865–1875." Master's thesis, Texas Tech University, Lubbock, 1953.

Thompson, Erwin. "The Negro Regiments of the U.S. Regular Army, 1866–1900." Master's thesis, University of California, Davis, 1964.

BOOKS

Alger, Russell A. *The Spanish-American War*. New York: Harper & Bros., 1901.

Armes, George Augustus. *Ups and Downs of an Army Officer*. Washington, D.C.: n.p., 1900.

Ashburn, Percy M. *A History of the Medical Department of the United States Army*. Boston: Houghton Mifflin Co., 1929.

Bald, F. Clever, *Michigan in Four Centuries*. New York: Harper & Bros., 1954.

Barrows, Chester L. *William M. Evarts: Lawyer, Diplomat, Statesman*. Chapel Hill: University of North Carolina Press, 1941.

Betzinez, Jason. *I Fought with Geronimo*. Ed. Wilbur S. Nye. Harrisburg, Pa.: Stackpole Co., 1959.

Biddle, Ellen McGowan. *Reminiscences of a Soldier's Wife*. Philadelphia: J. B. Lippincott Co., 1907.

Bigelow, J. *Reminiscences of the Santiago Campaign*. New York: Harper & Bros., 1899.

Bourke, John Gregory. *On the Border with Crook.* New York: Charles Scribner's Sons, 1891.

Bradley, George S. *The Star Corps; or, Notes of an Army Chaplain, during Sherman's Famous "March to the Sea."* Milwaukee: Jermain & Brightman, 1865.

Brandes, Ray. *Frontier Military Posts of Arizona.* Globe, Ariz.: O. S. King, 1960.

Brant, Jefferson E. *History of the Eighty-fifth Indiana Volunteer Infantry.* Bloomington, Ind.: Croven Bros., 1902.

Brown, Charles H. *The Correspondents' War: Journalists in the Spanish-American War.* New York: Charles Scribner's Sons, 1967.

Callahan, James M. *American Foreign Policy in Mexican Relations.* New York: The Macmillan Company, 1932.

Carlson, Paul H. *Texas Woollybacks: The Range Sheep and Goat Industry.* College Station: Texas A&M University Press, 1982.

Carter, Robert Goldthwaite. *The Mackenzie Raid into Mexico.* Washington, D.C.: Gibson Bros., 1919.

—————. *On the Border with Mackenzie: or, Winning West Texas from the Comanches.* Washington, D.C.: Eynon Printing Co., 1935.

Carter, William Harding. *From Yorktown to Santiago with the Sixth United States Cavalry.* Baltimore, Md.: Lord Baltimore Press, Friedenwald Co., 1900.

Cashin, Hershel V., *et al. Under Fire with the Tenth Cavalry.* Chicago: American Publishing House, [1900].

Catton, Bruce. *Mr. Lincoln's Army.* Garden City, N.Y.: Doubleday & Co., 1951.

—————. *This Hallowed Ground: The Story of the Union Side of the Civil War.* Garden City, N.Y.: Doubleday & Co., 1956.

Chadwick, French E. *The Relations of the United States and Spain: The Spanish-American War.* 2 vols. New York: Charles Scribner's Sons, 1911.

Clendenen, Clarence C. *Blood on the Border: The United States Army and the Mexican Irregulars.* New York: Macmillan Co., 1969.

Collins, Calhoun. *The McKittrick Ranch.* Bakersfield, Calif.: Kern County Historical Society and Kern County Museum, 1958.

Cook, John R. *The Border and the Buffalo.* Topeka, Kans.: Crane & Co., 1907.

Cooper, Jerry M. *The Army and Civil Disorder: Federal Military Intervention in Labor Disputes, 1877–1900.* Westport, Conn.: Greenwood Press, 1980.

Cornish, Dudley T. *The Sable Arm: Negro Troops in the Union Army, 1861–1865.* New York: Longmans, Green, 1956.

Corwin, Hugh D. *The Kiowa Indians: Their History and Life Stories.* Lawton, Okla.: n.p., 1958.

Cosmas, Graham A. *An Army for Empire: The United States Army in the Spanish-American War.* Columbia: University of Missouri Press, 1971.

Council on Foreign Relations. *Catalogue of the Foreign Relations Library.* 9 vols. Boston: G. K. Hall & Co., 1969.

Cox, Jacob D. *The March to the Sea, Franklin and Nashville.* New York: Charles Scribner's Sons, 1882.

Crane, Charles J. *The Experiences of a Colonel of Infantry.* New York: The Knickerbocker Press, 1923.

Cresap, Barnarr. *Appomattox Commander: The Story of General E. O. C. Ord.* New York: A. S. Barnes & Co., 1981.

Crook, George. *General George Crook: His Autobiography.* Ed. Martin F. Schmitt. Norman: University of Oklahoma Press, 1960.

Cross, Ira Brown. *A History of the Labor Movement in California.* Berkeley: University of California Press, 1935.

Davis, Britton. *The Truth about Geronimo.* Ed. M. M. Quaife. New Haven: Yale University Press, 1929.

Dictionary of American Biography. 22 vols. New York: Charles Scribner's Sons, 1958.

Dowdey, Clifford. *The Seven Days.* Boston: Little, Brown & Co., 1964.

Durant, Samuel W. *History of Kalamazoo County, Michigan.* Philadelphia: Everts & Abbott, 1880.

Evans, General Clement A., ed. *Confederate Military History.* 12 vols. New York: Thomas Yoseloff, 1962.

Faulk, Odie B. *The Geronimo Campaign.* New York: Oxford University Press, 1969.

Fletcher, Marvin. *The Black Soldier and Officer in the United States Army, 1891–1917.* Columbia: University of Missouri Press, 1974.

Forbes, Jack D. *Apaches, Navaho, and Spaniard.* Norman: University of Oklahoma Press, 1960.

Forsyth, George A. *Thrilling Days in Army Life.* New York: Harper & Bros., 1900.

Fowler, Arlen L. *The Black Infantry in the West, 1861–1891.* Westport, Conn.: Greenwood Publishing Corporation, 1971.

Frazer, Robert W. *Forts of the West.* Norman: University of Oklahoma Press, 1967.

Freidel, Frank. *The Splendid Little War.* Boston: Little, Brown & Co., 1958.

Fuller, George Newman. *Economic and Social Beginnings of Michigan.* Lansing: Wynkeep Hallenbeck Crawford, Co., 1916.

Gibson, Arrell M. *The American Indian: Prehistory to the Present.* Lexington, Mass.: D. C. Heath & Co., 1980.

————. *The Kickapoos: Lords of the Middle Border.* Norman: University of Oklahoma Press, 1963.

Ginger, Ray. *The Bending Cross: A Biography of Eugene Victor Debs.* New Brunswick, N.J.: Rutgers University Press, 1949.

Glass, E. L. N., ed. *The History of the Tenth Cavalry, 1866–1921.* Tucson: Acme Printing Co., 1921.

Grant, Bruce. *American Forts, Yesterday and Today.* New York: E. P. Dutton & Co., 1965.

Greeley, Horace. *An Overland Journey from New York to San Francisco in the Summer of 1859.* New York: C. M. Saxton, Barker & Co., 1860.

Gregg, Robert D. *The Influence of Border Troubles on Relations between the United States and Mexico, 1876–1910.* Johns Hopkins University Studies in Historical and Political Science. Baltimore: Johns Hopkins Press, 1937.

Hagedorn, Hermann. *Leonard Wood: A Biography.* 2 vols. New York: Harper & Bros., 1931.

Haley, J. Evetts. *Charles Goodnight: Cowman and Plainsman.* Boston: Houghton Mifflin Co., 1936.

———. *Fort Concho and the Texas Frontier.* San Angelo, Tex.: San Angelo Standard-Times, 1952.

Harrington, Fred Harvey. *Fighting Politician: Major-General N. P. Banks.* Philadelphia: University of Pennsylvania Press, 1948.

Harris, Theodore D., ed. *Negro Frontiersman: The Western Memoirs of Henry O. Flipper, First Negro Graduate of West Point.* El Paso: Texas Western College Press, 1963.

Hart, Herbert M. *Old Forts of the Far West.* New York: Bonanza Books, 1965.

Hassler, Warren W., Jr. *Commanders of the Army of the Potomac.* Baton Rouge: Louisiana State University Press, 1962.

Healy, David F. *The United States in Cuba, 1898–1902.* Madison: University of Wisconsin Press, 1963.

Heard, J. Norman. *The Black Frontiersman: Adventures of Negroes among American Indians, 1828–1918.* New York: The John Day Co., 1969.

Hein, Otto L. *Memories of Long Ago, by an Old Army Officer.* New York: G. P. Putnam's Sons, 1925.

Heller, Charles E., and William A. Stafft, eds. *America's First Battles, 1776–1965.* Lawrence: University Press of Kansas, 1986.

Higginson, Thomas W. *Army Life in a Black Regiment.* East Lansing: Michigan State University Press, 1960.

Historical and Pictorial Review, 24th Infantry Regiment. Baton Rouge, La.: Army and Navy Publishing Co., 1941.

Holbrook, Stewart H. *Lost Men of American History.* New York: The Macmillan Co., 1947.

Horn, Stanley F. *The Decisive Battle of Nashville.* Baton Rouge: Louisiana State University Press, 1956.

Hughes, William J. *Rebellious Ranger: Rip Ford and the Old Southwest.* Norman: University of Oklahoma Press, 1964.

Hutton, Paul Andrew. *Phil Sheridan and His Army.* Lincoln: University of Nebraska Press, 1985.

James, Henry. *Richard Olney and His Public Service.* Boston: Houghton Mifflin Co., 1923.

Jeffrey, William H. *Richmond Prisons, 1861–1862*. St. Johnsburg, Vt.: Caledonia County Publishing Company for the Republican Press, 1893.

Johnson, Barry C., ed. *HO, For the Great West*. London: Eatome Ltd., 1980.

Johnson, Robert Underwood, and Clarence Clough Buel. *Battles and Leaders of the Civil War*. 4 vols. New York: Thomas Yoseloff, 1956.

Johnson, Virginia Weisel. *The Unregimented General: A Biography of Nelson A. Miles*. Boston: Houghton Mifflin Co., 1962.

Karsten, Peter, ed. *The Military in America: From the Colonial Era to the Present*. New York: The Free Press, 1980.

Katz, William Loren. *The Black West*. Garden City, N.Y.: Doubleday & Co., 1971.

Keller, Allan. *Morgan's Raid*. Indianapolis: The Bobbs-Merrill Co., 1961.

LaBarre, Weston. *The Ghost Dance: Origins of a Religion*. New York: Doubleday & Co., 1970.

Lamers, William M. *The Edge of Glory: a Biography of General William S. Rosecrans, U.S.A.* New York: Harcourt, Brace & World, 1961.

Lane, Jack C., ed. *Chasing Geronimo: The Journal of Leonard Wood, May–September, 1886*. Albuquerque: University of New Mexico Press, 1970.

Langford, Gerald. *The Richard Harding Davis Years: A Biography of a Mother and Son*. New York: Holt, Rinehart & Winston, 1961.

Leckie, William H. *The Buffalo Soldiers: A Narrative of the Negro Cavalry in the West*. Norman: University of Oklahoma Press, 1967.

———. *The Military Conquest of the Southern Plains*. Norman: University of Oklahoma Press, 1963.

Leckie, William H., and Shirley A. Leckie. *Unlikely Warriors: General Benjamin H. Grierson and His Family*. Norman: University of Oklahoma Press, 1984.

Leech, Margaret. *In the Days of McKinley*. New York: Harper & Bros., 1959.

Lincoln, Charles P. *Engagement at Thompson's Station, Tennessee*. War Paper No. 14, Military Order of the Loyal Legion of the United States, District of Columbia Commandery, read November 1, 1893. Washington, D.C.: n.p., n.d.

Lindsey, Almont. *The Pullman Strike: The Story of a Unique Experiment and a Great Labor Upheaval*. Chicago: University of Chicago Press, 1942.

Lummis, Charles F. *General Crook and the Apache Wars*. Ed. Turbese Lummis Fiske. Flagstaff, Ariz.: Northland Press, 1966.

McBride, John R. *History of the Thirty-third Indiana Veteran Infantry*. Indianapolis: Wm. B. Burford, 1900.

McClellan, George B. *McClellan's Own Story: The War for the Union*. New York: Charles L. Webster &Co., 1887.

McConnell, H. H. *Five Years a Cavalryman; or, Sketches of Regular Life on the Texas Frontier, Twenty Odd Years Ago*. Jacksboro, Tex.: J. N. Rogers & Co., 1889.

McMurry, Richard M. *John Bell Hood and the War for Southern Independence*. Lexington: University Press of Kentucky, 1952.

Mason, Philip, and Paul J. Pentecost. *From Bull Run to Appomattox: Michigan's Role in the Civil War.* Detroit, Mich.: Wayne State University Press, 1961.

May, George S., ed., *Michigan Civil War History: An Annotated Bibliography.* Detroit, Mich.: Wayne State University Press, 1961.

Miles, Nelson A. *Personal Recollections and Observations of General Nelson A. Miles.* Chicago: The Werner Co., 1896.

————. *Serving the Republic: Memoirs of the Civil War and Military Life of Nelson A. Miles.* New York: Harper & Bros., 1911.

Miley, John D. *In Cuba with Shafter.* New York: Charles Scribner's Sons, 1899.

Millis, Walter. *The Martial Spirit.* Boston: Houghton Mifflin Co., 1931.

Mills, C. Wright. *The Power Elite.* New York: Oxford University Press, 1956.

Morgan, H. Wayne. *William McKinley and His America.* Syracuse, N.Y.: Syracuse University Press, 1963.

Morgan, Wallace M. *History of Kern County, California.* Los Angeles: Historic Record Co., 1914.

Morrison, Etting E., ed. *The Letters of Theodore Roosevelt.* 8 vols. Cambridge: Harvard University Press, 1951.

Muller, William G. *The Twenty-Fourth Infantry, Past and Present.* N.p., 1928.

Murrah, David J. *C. C. Slaughter: Rancher, Banker, Baptist.* Austin: University of Texas Press, 1981.

National Cyclopaedia of American Biography. 20 vols. New York: James T. White & Co., 1898–1926.

Nevins, Allan. *The War for the Union.* 2 vols. New York: Charles Scribner's Sons, 1959.

Nye, W. S. *Carbine and Lance: The Story of Old Fort Sill.* Norman: University of Oklahoma Press, 1938.

O'Connor, Richard. *Thomas: Rock of Chickamauga.* New York: Prentice-Hall, 1948.

O'Connor, Robert F., ed. *Texas Myths.* College Station: Texas A&M University Press, 1986.

Ogle, Ralph Hedrick. *Federal Control of the Western Apaches, 1848–1886.* Albuquerque: University of New Mexico Press, 1970.

O'Toole, G. J. A. *The Spanish War: An American Epic—1898.* New York: W. W. Norton & Co., 1984.

Overton, Jacqueline. *Long Island's Story.* Garden City, N.Y.: Doubleday Doran & Co., 1929.

Paris, Comte de. *History of the Civil War in America.* 4 vols. Philadelphia: Porter & Coates, 1875.

Parker, James. *The Old Army: Memories, 1872–1918.* Philadelphia: Dorrence & Co., 1929.

Patch, Joseph D. *The Battle of Ball's Bluff.* Fitzhugh Turner. Leesburg, Va.: Potomac Press, 1958.

Post, Charles Johnson. *The Little War of Private Post.* Boston: Little, Brown & Co., 1934.

Prucha, Francis Paul. *A Guide to the Military Posts of the United States.* Madison: State Historical Society of Wisconsin, 1964.

Quarles, Benjamin. *The Negro in the Civil War.* Boston: Little, Brown & Co., 1953.

Raht, Carlysle Graham. *The Romance of Davis Mountains and the Big Bend Country.* El Paso, Tex.: Rahtbooks Co., 1919.

Randall, James G. *The Civil War and Reconstruction.* New York: D. C. Heath Co., 1951.

Rice, Franklin G. *Diary of Nineteenth Michigan Volunteer Infantry during Their Three Years Service in the War of Rebellion.* Big Rapids, Mich.: n.p., n.d.

Richardson, Rupert Norval. *The Comanche Barrier to South Plains Settlement.* Glendale, Calif.: Arthur H. Clark Co., 1933.

———. *The Frontier of Northwest Texas, 1846 to 1876.* Glendale, Calif.: Arthur H. Clark Co., 1963.

Richter, William L. *The Army in Texas during Reconstruction.* College Station: Texas A&M University Press, 1987.

Rickey, Don, Jr. *Forty Miles a Day on Beans and Hay: The Enlisted Soldier Fighting the Indian Wars.* Norman: University of Oklahoma Press, 1963.

Rippy, J. Fred. *The United States and Mexico.* Rev. ed. New York: F. S. Crofts & Co., 1931.

Rister, Carl Coke. *Border Command: General Phil Sheridan in the West.* Norman: University of Oklahoma Press, 1944.

———. *Fort Griffin on the Texas Frontier.* Norman: University of Oklahoma Press, 1956.

———. *The Southwestern Frontier, 1865–1881.* Cleveland, Ohio: Arthur H. Clark Co., 1928.

Roosevelt, Theodore. *The Rough Riders.* New York: New American Library, 1961.

Sargent, Herbert H. *The Campaign of Santiago de Cuba.* 3 vols. Chicago: A. C. McClurg & Co., 1907.

Schofield, John M. *Forty-six Years in the Army.* New York: Century Co., 1897.

Scobee, Barry. *Fort Davis Texas, 1953–1960.* Fort Davis, Tex.: The Author, 1963.

———. *Old Fort Davis.* San Antonio, Tex.: Naylor Company, 1947.

Sefton, James E. *The United States Army and Reconstruction.* Baton Rouge: Louisiana State University Press, 1967.

Sheridan, Philip H. *Personal Memoirs of P. H. Sheridan.* 2 vols. New York: Charles L. Webster & Co., 1888.

Singletary, Otis A. *Negro Militia and Reconstruction.* Austin: University of Texas Press, 1957.

Smallwood, James. *Time of Hope, Time of Despair.* Westport, Conn.: Greenwood Press, 1981.

Smith, Edmund B. *Governor's Island: Its Military History under Three Flags.* New York: Valentine's Manual, 1923.

Sonnichsen, C. L. *The Mescalero Apaches.* Norman: University of Oklahoma Press, 1958.

Steele, Matthew Forney. *American Campaigns.* 2 vols. Washington, D.C.: U.S. Infantry Association, 1935.

Taylor, Paul Schuster. *An American-Mexican Frontier: Nueces County, Texas.* Chapel Hill: University of North Carolina Press, 1934.

Thomas, Wilbur. *General George H. Thomas: The Indomitable Warrior.* New York: Exposition Press, 1964.

Thrapp, Dan L. *The Conquest of Apacheria.* Norman: University of Oklahoma Press, 1967.

———. *General Crook and the Sierra Madre Adventure.* Norman: University of Oklahoma Press, 1972.

Tivy, Joseph A. *Souvenir of the Seventh, Containing a Brief History of It.* Detroit, Mich.: n.p., 1893.

Tolman, Newton F. *The Search for General Miles.* New York: G. P. Putnam's Sons, 1968.

Toulouse, Joseph H., and James R. Toulouse. *Pioneer Posts of Texas.* San Antonio, Tex.: Naylor Company, 1936.

Trask, David F. *The War with Spain in 1898.* New York: Macmillan Publishing Co., 1981.

Trelease, Allen W. *White Terror: The Ku Klux Klan Conspiracy and Southern Reconstruction.* New York: Harper & Row, 1971.

Udden, J. A. *The Geology of the Shafter Silver Mine District, Presidio County, Texas.* Austin: University of Texas Mineral Survey 1, Bulletin No. 8, June, 1904.

Utley, Robert M. *Fort Davis National Historic Site, Texas.* National Park Service Historical Handbook Series No. 38. Washington, D.C.: GPO, 1965.

———. *Frontier Regulars: The United States Army and the Indian, 1866–1890.* New York: Macmillan Co., 1973.

———. *The Indian Frontier of the American West.* Albuquerque: University of New Mexico Press, 1984.

———. *The Last Days of the Sioux Nation.* New Haven: Yale University Press, 1963.

Villegas, D. Cosio. *The United States versus Porfirio Díaz.* Trans. Nettie Lee Benson. Lincoln: University of Nebraska Press, 1963.

Wallace, Ernest. *Ranald S. Mackenzie on the Texas Frontier.* Lubbock, Tex.: West Texas Museum Association, 1964.

———, ed. *Ranald S. Mackenzie's Official Correspondence Relating to Texas, 1871–1873.* Lubbock, Tex.: West Texas Museum Association, 1967.

———, ed. *Ranald S. Mackenzie's Official Correspondence Relating to Texas, 1873–1879.* Lubbock, Tex.: West Texas Museum Association, 1968.

Wallace, Ernest, and E. Adamson Hoebel. *Comanches: Lords of the South Plains.* Norman: University of Oklahoma Press, 1952.

Washburn, Wilcomb E. *The Indian in America.* New York: Harper & Row, 1975.

Webb, Alexander S. *The Peninsula: McClellan's Campaign of 1862.* New York: Charles Scribner's Sons, 1887.

Webb, Walter Prescott, *The Great Plains.* New York: Grosset & Dunlap, 1931.

Weigley, Russell F. *The History of the United States Army.* New York: Macmillan Co., 1967.

Wellman, Paul I. *Death on the Prairie.* New York: Macmillan Co., 1934.

Weniger, Del. *The Explorers' Texas: The Lands and Waters.* Austin, Tex.: Eakin Press, 1985.

Wesley, Charles H., and Patricia W. Romero. *Negro Americans in the Civil War: From Slavery to Citizenship.* New York: Publishers Co., 1967.

Westrate, E. V. *Those Fatal Generals.* New York: Knight, 1936.

Wheeler, Joseph. *The Santiago Campaign.* Philadelphia: Drexel Briddle, 1899.

Williams, George W. *A History of the Negro Troops in the War of the Rebellion, 1861–1865.* New York: Harper & Bros., 1888.

Williams, T. Harry. *Americans at War: The Development of the American Military Systems.* Baton Rouge: Louisiana State University Press, 1960.

———. *The History of American Wars: From Colonial Times to World War I.* New York: Alfred A. Knopf, 1981.

Woodford, Frank B. *Father Abraham's Children: Michigan Episodes in the Civil War.* Detroit, Mich.: Wayne State University Press, 1961.

Woodman, Lyman L. *Cortina: The Rogue of the Rio Grande.* San Antonio, Tex.: Naylor Co., 1950.

JOURNALS AND MAGAZINES

Bonsal, Stephen. "The Fight for Santiago." *McClure's* 11 (October, 1898): 499–518.

Byrd, Cecil K., ed. "Journal of Israel Cogshall, 1862–1863." *Indiana Magazine of History* 42 (Spring, 1946): 69–87.

Carlson, Paul H. "Baseball's Abner Doubleday on the Texas Frontier." *Military History of Texas and the Southwest* 12, no. 4 (Spring, 1976): 235–44.

———. "The Discovery of Silver in West Texas." *West Texas Historical Association Yearbook* 54 (1978): 55–64.

Coffman, Edward M. "Army Life on the Frontier." *Military Affairs* 20 (Winter, 1956): 193–201.

Colby, L. W. "The Sioux Indian War of 1890–91." *Transactions and Reports of the Nebraska State Historical Society* 3 (1892): 180.

Conway, Walter C., ed. "Colonel Edmund Shriver's Inspector-General's Report on Military Posts in Texas, November, 1872–January, 1873." *Southwestern Historical Quarterly* 67 (April, 1964): 559–83.

Cornish, Dudley T. "The Union Army as a Training School for Negroes." *The Journal of Negro History* 37 (October, 1952): 368–82.

Crane, R. C. "Settlement of Indian Troubles in West Texas, 1874–1875." *West Texas Historical Association Yearbook* 1 (1925): 3–14.

Crimmins, M. L. "The Border Command at Fort Davis." *West Texas Historical and Scientific Society Bulletin* 1 (1926): 7–15.

———. "Camp Peña Colorado, Texas." *West Texas Historical and Scientific Society Publication* 5 (1935): 8–25.

———. "Fort McKavett, Texas." *Southwestern Historical Quarterly* 37 (July, 1934): 28–39.

———. "General Grierson in West Texas." *West Texas Historical and Scientific Society Publication* 7 (1937): 30–44.

———. "General Mackenzie and Fort Concho." *West Texas Historical Association Yearbook* 10 (1934): 16–31.

———. "Old Fort Duncan: A Frontier Post." *Frontier Times* 15 (June, 1938): 379–85.

Crimmins, M. L., ed. "An Indian Raid Near Laredo." *Frontier Times* 10 (August, 1938): 489–94.

———. "Shafter's Explorations in West Texas." *West Texas Historical Association Yearbook* 9 (October, 1933): 82–96.

"Dakota Military Posts." *South Dakota Historical Collections* 8 (1916): 77–99.

Daugherty, Capt. W. E. "The Recent Messiah Craze." *Journal of the Military Service Institute of the United States* 12 (1891): 577.

Dinges, Bruce J. "The Court-Martial of Lieutenant Henry O. Flipper: An Example of Black-White Relationships in the Army, 1881." *The American West* 9 (January, 1972): 12–17, 19, 21.

Fletcher, Marvin. "The Negro Volunteer in Reconstruction," *Military Affairs* 32 (December, 1968): 125–27.

"General Shafter at the Critical Moment." *Review of Reviews* 18 (October, 1898): 447–48.

Gordon, Douglas H., and George S. May, eds. "Michigan Journal, 1836, John M. Gordon." *Michigan History* 43 (March, 1959): 257–71, and (September, 1959): 257–93.

Graham, Roy Eugene. "Federal Fort Architecture in Texas during the Nineteenth Century." *Southwestern Historical Quarterly* 74 (October, 1970): 165–88.

Haley, J. Evetts. "Pastores del Palo Duro." *Southwest Review* 19 (April, 1934): 279–94.

Hunter, J. Marvin, Sr., ed. "General Shafter's Exploration of West Texas." *Frontier Times* 29 (December, 1951): 78–83.

Lewis, William Ray. "The Hayes Administration in Mexico." *Southwestern Historical Quarterly* 24 (October, 1920): 120–53.

Mattes, Merrill J. "Revival at Old Fort Randall." *Military Engineer* 44 (March–April, 1952): 88–93.

"Mexican Border Grievances." *The Nation* 27 (August 29, 1878): 125.

Nalty, Bernard C., and Truman R. Strobridge. "Captain Emmet Crawford, Commander of Apache Scouts, 1882–1886." *Arizona and the West* 6 (1964): 30–40.

Neighbors, Kenneth F. "Tonkawa Scouts and Guides." *West Texas Historical Association Yearbook* 49 (1973): 90–113.

Peck, Harry Thurston. "Twenty Years of the Republic, Part XIV—The War with Spain." *The Bookman* 22 (1905–06): 586–606.

Peters, Bernard C. "No Trees on the Prairie: Persistence of Error in Landscape Terminology." *Michigan History* 54, (Spring, 1970): 19–28.

Porter, Kenneth W. "The Seminole-Negro Scouts, 1870–1881." *Southwestern Historical Quarterly* 55 (January, 1952): 358–77.

Potter, William. "Address Delivered at the Dedication of the General Shafter Monument at Galesburg, August 22, 1919." *Michigan History Magazine* 4 (Spring, 1920): 485–91.

Reddick, L. D. "The Negro Policy of the United States Army, 1775–1945." *Journal of Negro History* 34 (January, 1949): 9–29.

Reeve, Frank D., ed. "Frederick E. Phelps: A Soldier's Memoirs." *New Mexico Historical Review* 25 (Summer, 1950): 187–221.

Remington, Frederick: "With the Fifth Corps." *Harper's Magazine* 97 (November, 1898): 962–75.

Rhodes, Charles D. "William Rufus Shafter." *Michigan History Magazine* 16 (Fall, 1932): 370–83.

Ringenberg, William C. "College Life in Frontier Michigan." *Michigan History* 54 (Summer, 1970): 19–32.

Rippy, J. P. "Some Precedents of the Pershing Expedition in Mexico." *Southwestern Historical Quarterly* 24 (April, 1921): 292–316.

Romero, José Ynocencio. "Spanish Sheepmen on the Canadian at Old Tascosa," ed. Ernest R. Archambeau. *Panhandle-Plains Historical Review* 19 (1946): 45–72.

Schellings, William J. "The Advent of the Spanish-American War in Florida, 1898." *Florida Historical Quarterly* 39 (April, 1961): 311–29.

Seymour, Charles G. "The Sioux Rebellion: The Final Review." *Harper's Weekly* 35 (February 7, 1891): 106.

Shafter, William R. "The Capture of Santiago de Cuba." *Century* 57 (February, 1899): 612–30.

———. "The Boers and the British." *Independent* 52 (April 5, 1900): 829.

"Shafter and Willington." *The Nation* 67 (December 29, 1898): 479–80.

"Shafter Lake: A Strange Body of Water." *Frontier Times* 9 (February, 1932): 240.

Sheffy, L. F., ed. "Letters and Reminiscences of General Theodore A. Baldwin: Scouting after Indians on the Plains of West Texas." *Panhandle-Plains Historical Review* 11 (1938): 7–30.

Slaughter, Linda W. "Fort Randall." *Collections of the State Historical Society of North Dakota* 1 (1906): 423–29.

Sullivan, Jerry, ed. "Lieutenant Colonel W. R. Shafter's Pecos River Expedition of 1870." *West Texas Historical Association Yearbook* 47 (1971): 146–52.

Taber, Morris C. "New England Influence in South Central Michigan." *Michigan History* 45 (December, 1961): 305–66.

Temple, Frank M. "Federal Military Defense of the Trans-Pecos Region, 1850–1880." *West Texas Historical Association Yearbook* 30 (1954): 40–60.

Thompson, Erwin N. "The Negro Soldier on the Frontier: A Fort Davis Case Study." *Journal of the West* 7 (April, 1968): 217–35.

Utley, Robert M. "'Pecos Bill' on the Texas Frontier." *American West* 6 (January, 1969): 4–13.

Walker, Jimmy. "A Town Returns to Dust." *Houston Chronicle Magazine,* November 22, 1959, 6–7.

Wallace, Edward S. "Border Warrior." *American Heritage* 9 (June, 1958): 22–25.

———. "General John Lapham Bullis, Thunderbolt of the Texas Frontier." *Southwestern Historical Quarterly* 55 (July, 1951): 77–85.

———. "General Ranald Slidel Mackenzie: Indian Fighting Cavalryman." *Southwestern Historical Quarterly* 56 (January, 1952): 378–96.

Wallace, Ernest, and Adrian S. Anderson. "R. S. Mackenzie and the Kickapoos: The Raid into Mexico in 1873." *Arizona and the West* 7 (Summer, 1965): 105–26.

Whitney, Casper. "The Santiago Campaign." *Harper's Magazine* 97 (October, 1898): 795–818.

Williams, Frederick D. "Michigan Soldiers in the Civil War." *Michigan History* 44 (March, 1936): 1–35.

Woodhull, Frost, ed. "The Seminole Indian Scouts on the Border." *Frontier Times* 15 (December, 1937): 118–27.

Index

216

"Pecos Bill" was composed into type on a Compugraphic digital photo-typesetter in nine and one-half point Trump Medieval with two and one-half points of spacing between the lines. Trump was also selected for display. The book was designed by Jim Billingsley, typeset by Metri-comp, Inc., printed offset by Thomson-Shore, Inc., and bound by John H. Dekker & Sons. The paper on which the book is printed is designed for an effective life of at least three hundred years.

TEXAS A&M UNIVERSITY PRESS : COLLEGE STATION